the Outdoor
Leader

JEANNETTE STAWSKi

the Outdoor Leader

RESILIENCE, INTEGRITY, AND ADVENTURE

ILLUSTRATIONS BY LATASHA DUNSTON GREENE

MOUNTAINEERS
BOOKS

MOUNTAINEERS BOOKS is dedicated to the exploration, preservation, and enjoyment of outdoor and wilderness areas.

1001 SW Klickitat Way, Suite 201, Seattle, WA 98134
800-553-4453, www.mountaineersbooks.org

Printed in Canada
Distributed in the United Kingdom by Cordee, www.cordee.co.uk
First edition, 2024

Illustrator: Latasha Dunston Greene
Design and layout: Heidi Smets and Kim Thwaits
Photos on pages 8, 92, 164, 190, and 195: Jeannette Stawski
Cover photograph: molchanovdmitry/iStock

"Four Choices of Leadership" illustration on page 17 © Humanenergy

Photo credits: p. 28: Alison Crabb; p. 43: Kerkez/iStock; p. 56: AscentXmedia/iStock; p. 69: gurendemir/iStock; p. 105: SolStock/iStock; p. 114: scotto72/iStock; p. 124: simonkr/iStock; p. 153: Nash Mas; p. 174: Chenmin Liu; p. 203: filadendron/iStock; p. 210: Cleardesign/iStock.

Library of Congress Control Number: 2023944853

Printed on FSC-certified materials and 100 percent recycled materials

ISBN (paperback): 978-1-68051-588-6
ISBN (ebook): 978-1-68051-589-3

An independent nonprofit publisher since 1960

Everything in nature invites us constantly to be what we are. We are often like rivers: careless and forceful, timid and dangerous, lucid and muddied, eddying and gleaming, still.

—Gretel Ehrlich, *The Solace of Open Spaces*

CONTENTS

INTRODUCTION: FINDING TRUE NORTH / 9

CHAPTER 1. CHOOSING TO LEAD / 12

CHAPTER 2. SELF-RESPONSIBILITY AND LIFELONG LEARNING / 30

CHAPTER 3. MANAGEMENT AND SYSTEMS / 45

CHAPTER 4. DIVERSITY, EQUITY, AND INCLUSION / 60

CHAPTER 5. RESILIENCE AND GRIT / 81

CHAPTER 6. INTEGRITY / 95

CHAPTER 7. TOLERANCE FOR ADVERSITY / 108

CHAPTER 8. ADVENTURE OR ORDEAL? / 120

CHAPTER 9. MAKING GOOD DECISIONS / 132

CHAPTER 10. LEADING CHANGE / 146

CHAPTER 11. AN AUDACIOUS AND COMPELLING VISION / 159

CHAPTER 12. MAKING MISTAKES / 169

CHAPTER 13. LISTENING / 180

CHAPTER 14. CONFIDENT, COMMITTED, AND COURAGEOUS
            COMMUNICATION / 192

ACKNOWLEDGMENTS / 208

APPENDIX / 211

SELECTED BIBLIOGRAPHY AND RESOURCES / 216

INDEX / 219

INTRODUCTION
FINDING TRUE NORTH

I grew up in Grand Rapids, Michigan, the only girl in a family of boys. My dad loved the outdoors, and while my mom liked looking at nature, she loathed camping. I spent my summers at Camp Manitou-Lin, first as a camper and then as a counselor. Camp—and the outdoors—has been a constant companion in my life. But a turning point for me came when I drove across US Highway 2 in a beat-up Suburban on the way to Glacier National Park, where I had secured a summer job as a rafting guide. . . *if* I could pass training. I had never rafted at that point, so it was with anticipation and fear that I jumped into unknown waters.

I cried the entire drive to Montana—and for the better part of my first month there. I had never been more scared, more alone, colder, or more afraid. I was scared I'd let down my family or not be able to keep up with everyone else or fare poorly so far from home. I was intent on being a rafting guide even though it was new to me and not something my family or friends had pursued. There was emotional tension as I stubbornly pursued this goal yet was simultaneously riddled with insecurity. I was miserable and full of self-doubt. But as I faced those fears, my view of myself transformed. As I spent that summer living in a tipi tucked between the Bob Marshall Wilderness Area and Glacier National Park, doing something I never thought myself capable of, I became alive. I discovered my true north.

Do you know how to read a map? I mean, not following Google Maps or Siri, but truly navigating? To read a map, you need to know how to adjust for declination—compensating for the angle between magnetic north and true north. A compass points toward magnetic north, but a map is based on Earth's rotational axis, or true north. As the earth spins and tilts, the angle between magnetic north and true north changes constantly, which means the direction you are headed on a map changes as well. Setting off in the direction of magnetic north would be a big mistake. Instead, you need to adjust your compass so you're headed for true north. You can apply this skill not only to your quadrangle map— the topographic location you inhabit—but also to your life. Adjusting for declination is critical. It requires you to have correct information—and know where you are at that point in time. That summer in Montana, I was compelled to adjust my perspective to find my true north, and it changed my life's trajectory toward a career in the outdoors.

Working in the outdoor profession is not for the meek or uncommitted. It is a career that compels you to take risks, to forge a new path, to get dirty, to be alone, and to be vulnerable.

READING YOUR OWN MAP

It turns out that the force that pulls you and your passion might not align with the trajectory your friends and family have envisioned for you or led you to believe is right for you. I came from a traditional family with very high expectations for grades, career, and social status, but my summers in Glacier National Park flew in the face of those expectations. I hope this book offers you the ability to find your own true north on the map of outdoor leadership.

I am passionate about outdoor recreation because nature and adventure can be transformative for individuals and for groups. Outdoor adventures are unique activities in unique environments, creating shared experiences that require interdependence between participants. While many adventure activities require technical competency, all outdoor leadership demands social competency—the ability to adapt to new and ever-changing people and environments. Nature, with its sometimes-immediate pressures and circumstances that cannot be controlled, can be an equalizing force that eliminates and strips down biases and pretenses. In the hills, everyone is a leader, and leadership starts with us—we, as leaders, are responsible for our choices.

LEADERSHIP AS AN ONGOING JOURNEY

I've been thinking a lot about what it means to be an outdoor leader who is also a woman—what that has meant in the past and could mean in the future. Maybe that is the story I have to share: years of chasing achievement and compiling an ever-growing outdoor checklist in order to be validated or considered equal by my peers, only to realize I've been seeking approval from the very people, in coveted leadership positions, who've been writing a narrative of exclusion. My leadership journey, which is an ongoing process, has moved beyond this—from what I thought I needed to be doing (to achieve or become) to considering what I can do to help lead others on their own journey. My expertise as a listener, facilitator, and convenor is key in this modern vision of outdoor leadership that emphasizes accessibility, diversity, and inclusion.

I am interested in a leadership style based on care and commitment: leadership as a choice. In this view, leadership starts with the individual, and anyone can be that individual. Leadership *is* choice, and strong leaders consistently make better choices. Building the capacity to lead is an opportunity for everyone. Anyone can develop the stamina, focus, and awareness needed to become a strong outdoor leader. Truly transforma- tive leaders have a high commitment to care for the greater good and a devotion to curiosity and continuous personal growth. Best of all, leadership skills are transferable—personally, professionally, and recreationally.

ABOUT THIS BOOK

Combining my own experiences and a few dozen anecdotes collected from a broad range of fellow outdoor enthusiasts, this book offers teachable moments and focuses on the attributes of excellent outdoor leadership: resilience and grit, integrity, tolerance for adversity, and highly developed listening and communication skills. In these pages, I'll explore the ways a transformational leader makes good decisions, creates and champions a vision, and leads change through a lens of diversity, equity, and inclusion.

This book is less about "hard skills" for outdoor adventure, such as knot-tying, and more about the core communication and foundational emotional skills of outdoor leadership. I want to show how we can apply what we gain and learn from outdoor leadership to our lives anywhere—not just in the backcountry or a wilderness setting. To this end, I have included stories from leaders in the outdoor industry whom I admire—people I've led with, worked with, volunteered with, and, most importantly, grown with. I have modified certain details relating to my own experiences—some names, places, and other elements—to protect some individuals' identities, as well as to highlight a learning outcome rather than present a simple historical re-creation of events as I experienced them.

Finally, this book is about you, the reader, and how you see yourself in the passages, connect with the "Takeaways," and respond to the "Thirsty for More" sections at the end of each chapter. My contribution is merely a recounting of my ongoing maturation as a leader. I am a leader in my family, in my community, on my team at work, and for my outdoor organization. I lead on a national stage and in my own life. These are the places I lead. May this book offer coaching and guidance as you step into your own leadership role and begin to lead others farther along their own paths.

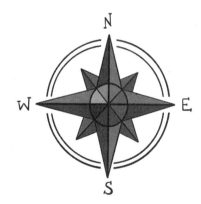

CHAPTER 1
CHOOSING TO LEAD

Though there are many leadership styles, they're most often categorized into one of the three core styles: authoritarian (autocratic), participative (democratic), and delegative (laissez-faire). However, I am interested in a (new-to-me) leadership style based on care and commitment: leadership as a choice. In this view, leadership starts with a single person who chooses to inhabit that role and who, as a result of their strong leadership, makes consistently better choices.

Leadership and building the capacity to lead are equally important in the field, the workplace, the boardroom, and personal interactions with friends, family, neighbors, and acquaintances. Given society's tendency to either elevate or demonize our leaders (by revering or passing judgment on their competency), the ability to lead yourself, others, or an organization toward a desired outcome or destination is at the core of the choice to lead.

This chapter introduces the notion of leadership choice using a matrix that juxtaposes a continuum of care for self and for the group with a continuum of commitment. Depending on where you land on these continuums, there are four possible leadership styles: compliant, productive, destructive, and transformative. We'll explore each of them, getting to the heart of what choosing to lead—and how you choose to lead—means for your and your team's desired outcomes.

HOW I LEAD

I strongly dislike being cold and wet—most of us do—including while on outdoor adventures. But the outdoors is filled with cold and wet, and if you choose to spend time recreating there, you'll need to accept these conditions as the price of admission. However, the big question becomes, will you view them as unwanted visitors or as welcome companions?

In addition to my disdain for being cold and wet, I am always scared and nervous when I start a hike. There is a feeling of unease as I lock the car or as the van that brought the group to the trailhead bounces away down a dirt road. I look at my pack, which either does or does not have all the things I will need for the trip. I look at the weather and ponder what it means for my physical comfort. I fear I may not be fit enough or that my gear is inadequate. This happens to me every time I set out—and has, ever since my very first outdoor adventure when I led an overnight trip as a camp counselor. On that trip, while our destination was only a handful of miles from the main camp, it felt like we were unreachable in the event of an emergency, and both the privilege and pressure of being accountable for those I led was palpable.

I often wonder why people see me as a leader. I'm a mom, an employee, a teammate. What are the qualities that make me a leader? It's hard to pin down one's own characteristics, so I asked some colleagues. They told me things like: "You are a person of influence." "You influence others to think differently, to try more, to do more." "You hope for more from yourself and everyone around you—to me, that is leadership; at its simplest, leadership is influence." "You lead because you cast a vision for a better tomorrow."

These things are true: I like to make things better, but I don't always know what that better actually is. Thus, it requires some investigation. I want everyone to feel like they are a part of something, that they belong, that they can do it, and that they should try something new or challenging. I like challenging situations, and I like to see what is going on, try to understand it in a cursory way, and then offer other ways to look at the issue, all while helping people keep their focus on the process—and not the outcome.

By employing this approach, I know I lead and aim for continuous improvement, and I am always pushing forward. For most of my career and, I must admit, in my growth as a leader, I have become aware that it is not necessarily the *type* of leadership that is important, but my ability as a leader to embody different leadership styles, depending on the situation or desired outcome. Not too long ago, I was approached by someone pursuing their PhD, whose assignment was to interview a leader in the outdoor industry, a role I'm flattered to have matured into. After some small talk during which I got a better understanding of the context for the call, the PhD student asked me, "What would you say is your leadership style?" It's a question I've been asked more than once before, and so have had a lot of time to come up with an answer.

Pause. What exactly *is* "leadership style"? Well, it's a leader's approach to providing direction, implementing plans, and motivating people—and, if done correctly, it will be flexible and fluid. So while I imagine my interviewers would prefer that I answer by citing a very specific leadership theory—something they've read about in a class—for me, the correct answer is that my preference has been and will always be an ongoing process to use all styles whenever and wherever necessary.

LEARNING FROM POOR LEADERSHIP

There are many poor leaders out there. Our society has done an amazing job of glorifying leadership and a horrible job of not expecting poor leaders to change or be held accountable. When I look back on the different leadership styles I've interacted with, I find it disappointing to realize I've been led by a lot of poor leaders. In the past, I took a lot of things personally and tried to work around difficult situations. But sometimes a terrible leader is the reason for a terrible experience or outcome, and I began to realize that any failures or missed goals often did not reflect my own incompetence but were instead the result of poor leadership. That is the hard thing about calling out poor leaders: They have often been in control for so long that they are comfortable, biased, and probably not open to feedback or to changing their ways. There is fear and trepidation for followers, and their path is usually one of endurance until the leader moves on.

Many outdoor leaders fall into this category: They are blinded by their own ego and personal desires. They are intent on achieving a summit rather than cultivating and maintaining a positive and fulfilling trip experience for all. Time and time again, we don't admonish but instead praise their inappropriate behavior, justifying the end—the fastest or longest hikes, the first ascents, the nomadic adventures across desolate landscape—rather than the means. In the process, we devalue adventures that elevate community-building, time away to reset, and being outdoors closer to home.

Still, there are many great outdoor leaders—some of them famous and some who have flown under the radar. Good leaders are everywhere, but they may be harder to see because their leadership strength is in cultivating an environment and community in which their position goes unnoticed. I have been fortunate because, while I've known some bad ones, I've also been inspired by many great leaders in my personal and professional life—in outdoor settings, in my various jobs, and in volunteer opportunities. Many of these great leaders are highlighted in this book, and they share their insights.

When I am turned around—lost—outdoors, I look for indicators for how I got there. Leadership is a lot like wayfinding: we can look back to see how we've built our understanding of where we are. And once we know where we want to go, we can make a series of informed decisions to move forward.

THE TRADITIONAL LEADERSHIP MATRIX

In 1939, the psychologist Kurt Lewin and a team of researchers determined the three basic leadership styles mentioned earlier: authoritarian (autocratic), participative (democratic), and delegative (laissez-faire). Researchers have since increased our collective understanding, defining many other styles of leadership that you may have heard about in books, blogs, podcasts, TED Talks, or magazine articles, and then studied or practiced yourself, including in outdoor settings.

The common understanding is that the best practice is to be flexible and adaptable in your leadership style, depending on the situation and needs of a group. For example, in an outdoor context, it would make the most sense for the leader of a group of novices working together to cross a river to use the autocratic leadership style. Group members in this situation need to be told what to do: how to physically move their bodies and gear, how to manage risks (above and below the crossing site), how to negotiate the time of day/weather and its effect on water levels (e.g., with a glacier-fed river or recent rainfall), and how to respond if someone gets hurt. The group would need to follow this autocratic leader until everyone traversed the river safely.

Let us imagine the same group, now safely across the river but realizing that camp is still some distance away and that some participants are safe but struggling. Here, a switch to a more democratic leadership style could build buy-in and give everyone a voice in deciding how far to push forward (until camp, until dusk, etc.). Alternatively, under a laissez-faire leadership style, the leader would be in the background, allowing the participants to work through things on the river—in this instance, not depending on the leader for the last word. The group might even decide not to cross the river, but instead to walk more miles to cross at a bridge. This hands-off method is designed to encourage participation and problem-solving among group members, and it centers on the process rather than the result.

These traditional styles of leadership were founded in research, but they are based on theories that are more than seventy-five years old and that were proposed by white men, the dominant culture at the time. Thus you'll hear certain adjectives ascribed to "strong leaders"—"unwavering," "formidable," "confident," and "empowering,"—that come directly from this tradition but fail to encompass a true feminine perspective, even with modern-day leaders such as Michelle Obama, Alexandria Ocasio-Cortez, Brené Brown, and Sonia Sotomayor. Instead, these amazing women's leadership styles are seen through the reductive lens of *how might they best lead by adopting characteristics of male leadership voices?* These women will often face a choice: either emulate male leadership attributes to be accepted (assimilation) or lead unabashedly as a full female leader and run into systemic barriers.

I've been thinking about a unique style of leadership—one that's different from autocratic, democratic, or laissez-faire but incorporates key aspects of each while also putting the emphasis on choice.

Caring for the Whole

COREY FERNANDEZ

When COVID-19 collided with the world in early 2020, my son was three and my daughter one. Like many families during the early years of the pandemic, we enjoyed countless days outdoors. I can close my eyes now and recall some of the first times I took my kids on local trails. These were places we could be safe together. Three days a week, I was their trail guide—an experience I will always treasure.

Under the transformational canopies of forests and nature preserves, there are countless discoveries, including learning how to be a better dad—the most important leadership role I'll ever have. When setting off to lead humans with tiny feet, developing muscles, outstretched hands, and super-sized blue eyes, I came to understand, with the gift of hindsight, that my own self-leadership was the difference-maker in our best of times and worst of times.

When my own ambitions and needs on the trail become a priority, I become less connected to my kids' needs and interests. What does my leadership look like in these moments? When our collective needs and interests as a group are prioritized, how does my leadership differ? Too much focus on myself triggers more control and rigidity, while a stronger orientation on the group unlocks the necessary care, flexibility, and creativity that make adventures extraordinary and challenging times even a little bit fun.

It's human nature for us to focus primarily on ourselves at the cost of others, but we're capable of rebounding and being better for our teams (and our little people) the very next go-round. This self-leadership helps us pause before, during, and after we take to the trails. It allows us to forgive ourselves and recommit to the whole, to the task in front of us. Caring for the whole is a result of our self-leadership. When we focus on the whole more often, it inspires the rest of the pack to care for each other as well.

Corey Fernandez (he/him) is a leadership coach for executives and teams that are growing into more complex roles and leading change. He loves outdoor work, play, and adventures with his family in Michigan.

THE NEW LEADERSHIP MATRIX

In 2018, I took part in Humanergy's high-performance leadership-development program called High Impact Leadership Training (HILT), which resonated greatly with my evolving ideas about leadership. I learned that leadership isn't about position or personality or power of experience; leadership is simply about choice. Every day, each of us has the power of choice in our personal and professional roles and responsibilities, and each of us can decide how we will lead. Founded in 2000 by John Barrett and David Wheatley, Humanergy was built on the premise that "the world needs a new kind of leader—people who are passionately committed to the greater good and who have the character, wisdom, and competence to make a difference." The work and training of Humanergy, which is focused on the individual, empowers those who choose to lead by offering a new construct based on care and commitment.

The Four Choices of Leadership matrix (see Figure 1.1) shows the relationship between care and commitment. Ranging from low to high, the matrix sets a continuum of care for self and for the group (greater good)

☼ HUMANERGY
FOUR CHOICES OF LEADERSHIP™

Productive — I'll help us succeed

Transformative — I'll ensure we're successful

Passive — I'll do what's easiest for me

Destructive — I'll get what I want even if it hurts others

Greater Good / Self — CARE

Comfort / Impact — COMMITMENT

© Humanergy 2021

against a continuum of commitment. Four leadership choices result: destructive, passive, productive, and transformative.

If leadership is a choice, then everyone can be considered a leader. This framework allows the possibility for each person to lead. The practice of leadership, as applied to leading others, is about two things:

- managing your actions, words, and choices in a situation that is not about you
- being centered on yourself but not being self-centered

To lead effectively, a leader must always be conscious of their influence on others—to recognize the outsized role they have on a group. For instance, on a group hike, if the original plan was to do an eight-mile hike, it might be challenging for a leader to reduce the mileage if it turns out that the group is not up for this. How a leader responds or whether they convey any personal disappointment has a tremendous impact on the group. Thus, it's paramount to being a transformational leader that they manifest the appropriate levels of care and commitment—ideally, as much as possible of both—for the needs of the situation and the group.

Care and Commitment

Leaders own who they are and what they do. They make choices, and their ability to make consistently better choices informed by reflection on their lived experiences makes them more effective leaders. With a thoughtful leader, every choice becomes an opportunity to balance care and commitment.

- CARE: Is the choice limited to oneself or made for the greater good? A person who makes a choice for the greater good considers the effects of their actions both on themself and others.
- COMMITMENT: A low-commitment choice is passive and disengaged, while a high-commitment choice reflects passion and intense focus.

DESTRUCTIVE LEADERSHIP

I'll get what I want, even if it hurts others.

- High intensity and passion (high commitment)
- Self-interest (low care)

When a leader's care is focused on themselves and their commitment is intensely focused on an outcome, leaders become destructive.

According to the Four Choices of Leadership matrix, a combination of high commitment and low care can lead to destructive leadership. In the outdoors, there are plenty of examples of destructive leadership; indeed, countless books have been written about destructive leadership, usually detailing how the expedition failed or how miserable (or tragic) the experience was, even if the goal was met. These tales share a commonality of relentless pursuit: achieving the summit, being the first to complete a climb, navigating the virgin rapids, exploring the deepest depths of a cave system.

Destructive leadership can play out on a smaller scale, too, as with adventures pursued near a trailhead or in more urban settings. It could be a meetup for a local day hike that goes south when the frustrated organizer either waits impatiently—or not at all—for slower members. Or perhaps the leader didn't give directions to their group to help them find a remote boat launch for a canoe trip. Or maybe disaster struck when the leader failed to secure the boats to the car or didn't properly fit a life jacket because of perceived time pressures.

Destructive leaders can be charming, incredibly charismatic, and draw followers through their sheer stature or through past accolades and success. Their destructive tendencies may not be immediately apparent, but a series of seemingly small poor choices—not ensuring a team member has the proper equipment, not slowing down to deal with a blister—can accrue to eventually culminate in injury, miscommunication, or loss of life or limb. Destructive leaders can cause group failure by fracturing the expedition into those who choose to follow the leader and those who will not follow any further. This splits the resources, erodes trust, and destroys the expedition—and, along with it, the ability to achieve the desired outcome.

Case Study: Destructive Leadership

The outdoor program I used to manage ran multiple weeklong trips for spring break. After one such break, I learned, through debriefing with the students, about the destructive leadership of one of my student leaders on a hiking trip to the Grand Canyon. This trip had been something everyone in our outing program was looking forward to, anticipating that the warm Arizona weather would be a welcome relief from the long, cold, snowy Michigan winter. Steve, one of the two student trip leaders, was universally admired in the program, providing a welcome addition to the trip leadership and bringing experience in the field which far exceeded that of the other trip staff. On this trip, other factors of note included the fact that it had been difficult to acquire National Park Service group permits for the early-March trip, and the distances between group campsites were a concern for the trip participants, who were all novice hikers.

After the descent into the canyon, which required the use of crampons because of icy conditions at the top, one participant, an older woman, twisted her ankle and began moving at a slower pace. When they arrived at Phantom Ranch at the bottom of the canyon on the first day of the program, Steve determined the group would not be able to travel each day's distance to the subsequent camp because of the slowed pace. Instead of modifying the route to accommodate the needs of the woman as part of the whole group, Steve, who was focused on spending a week in the canyon at all costs, convinced his co-leader to push forward with the original agenda with the rest of the group. The next day, Steve advocated for and then allowed the older woman to hike back up to the top of the canyon by herself so the trip could proceed. Fortunately, she made it out okay and was able to adjust her flight to travel home earlier.

The choice not to choose is still a choice, leaving the success or failure of the adventure to luck or happenstance.

PASSIVE LEADERSHIP

I'll do what is easiest for me.

- Path of least resistance (low commitment)
- Self-interest (low care)

When a leader's care is focused on themself and their commitment is low or passive, leaders become passive.

On the leadership matrix, a combination of low commitment and low care can lead to passive leadership. In this case, the leader may eat first, taking advantage of a leadership position for personal comfort, gain, or interest, but then fails to have hard conversations, make difficult decisions, or take decisive action. The choice not to choose is still a choice, leaving the success or failure of the adventure to luck or happenstance. If the outing succeeds, great. But if it fails, the leader blames it on external circumstances, such as weather, and then, because of a low level of commitment, refuses to take ownership for their actions or inaction. If it rains, for example, the leader might want to stay put and not get wet, and therefore, not move to the next campsite. Never mind that it might be a permitted campsite or that the group needs to return on time.

The passive leader can be easygoing and amiable, which may attract followers, but may find the idea of an actual adventure daunting. At first, group members might like that they have equal say in the decision-making process, but as soon as difficult decisions must be made, the attraction fades, and they become affected by the leader's lack of competence or willingness to direct the group. For example, getting an alpine start to see a beautiful sunrise remains only an idea if the passive leader is not willing to encourage others to become excited about it, perhaps themself preferring to stay in bed later or reasoning that the participants have already seen plenty of sunrises, so what's another one?

Moreover, passive leaders can often be recognized by their unwillingness to pursue or gather additional knowledge, certifications, and perspectives through books, podcasts, expanding networks, or professional development. This indicates an individual who may lead when it's easy, but who is not committed when the going gets difficult.

Case Study: Passive Leadership

I was asked to co-lead a month-long outdoor-leadership course in New Zealand, which provided me the bucket-list opportunity to co-lead hikes and to paddle with my good friend Nick. Nick was very much loved and adored by course participants and in our professional circles for his amiable and vibrant personality. The course was set up as a series of three- to five-day treks interspersed with a day of classes and other adventures. One of our first hikes was on the Kepler Track out of Te Anau. In the months preparing for this program, Nick and I had discussed and studied different leadership styles and had practiced backcountry skills with the students. In New Zealand, students took turns being "leader of the day," and they made decisions for that whole day.

When we set out from Te Anau on the Kepler Track, it was very overcast, and as we hiked from the lake to a higher elevation, the rain and wind kicked up. As the elevation, wind, and rain increased, the temperature dropped. Many students, including the leaders of the day, were not putting on their raincoats or covering their packs with rain covers, and I told Nick we should encourage them to do so. But Nick did not see the issue and insisted it was not our position to tell the designated leaders of the day what to do, but rather allow them to figure it out.

Interdependence

A canoe requires a partnership between the bow (front-of-boat) and stern (back-of-boat) paddlers to move the boat in a coordinated way, not only in the right direction but also straight, so that the boat doesn't turn with each stroke. In rock climbing, two climbers are connected by the belay system, and each relies on the other to communicate what's going on by using climbing terms like "slack" and "take." Likewise, a group of backpackers distributes the weight of communal gear among themselves, often separating components of the tent, the cook kit, and the food. After reaching camp, the backpackers will reassemble the gear to establish the kitchen and sleeping areas. These relationships all highlight our interdependence—or the ways that individuals come together.

Interdependence presents itself in both the productive- and transformative-leadership choice quadrants. In a team or group environment, there are vital connections that create success between people. These relationships, or interdependence, are what this book examines: how a leader can promote clear and open conversations, be candid in communication, and lead by example with care for the greater good.

From my perspective—as co-leader but also overall program leader ultimately responsible for the group—I was aware we had four days of hiking in higher elevations, and I was concerned about hypothermia. So it was hard for me to understand why Nick did not want to tell the others to put on their layers. Having the hard conversation with the leaders of the day was not something Nick was open to. In reflecting on Nick's passive leadership and the potential impact of his decision, I realized that I too had become passive by not addressing these issues with him. Many of the students were very cold and wet when we arrived at the first hut. The resulting wet clothes and equipment needed extra time to dry out before we could head out the next day. Fortunately, the delay and discomfort were the only repercussions, rather than a cold-weather emergency like hypothermia.

On the Four Choices of Leadership matrix, rising above the horizon line and leading for the greater good requires that we explore the integral concept of interdependence. In outdoor leadership and in professional settings, "going it alone" can be tempting for those looking to remove potential interpersonal challenges or complex group decision-making. Rudyard Kipling said this well in his poem "The Winners": "He travels fastest who travels alone."

Groups, however, require cultivation, care, and an investment of time, as well as creating space for relationships to form and be maintained. A leader who focuses on the greater good not only understands this but is consistently looking for ways to open communication and engage the entire group. This leads us to the next matrix quadrant: productive leadership.

PRODUCTIVE LEADERSHIP

I'll help us succeed.

- Will do the right thing, unless it's difficult (low commitment)
- Understands interdependence (high care)

When a leader focuses on the greater good, and their commitment is low, leaders become productive.

A combination of low commitment and high care can lead to productive leadership: *What can I do to help? What support do you need right now?* A productive leader focuses on the greater good and helps lead the group to achieve the set goals. Productive leaders are champions for consensus, and are at their best when the group is moving along with a positive critical mass of attitude and energy. People admire and like productive leaders. Followers feel cared for and, with little need to challenge the status quo, comfortable.

When a productive leader understands the role of interdependence in a group, they are also appreciating the need to cultivate relationships and awareness of group dynamics. To move to the outcomes desired by the group, the leader works with the group to ensure that conditions remain positive and conducive to productivity for all the group's members.

Productive leaders are champions for consensus, and are at their strongest when the group is moving along with a positive critical mass of attitude and energy.

But a productive leader's desire to deliver a positive outcome—achieving the team's stated objective, for example—may come at their or the team's expense, pushing everyone beyond their capacity. Trying to motivate participants during a challenging situation, such as continuing on to camp as darkness falls, or the leader taking on more weight to assist a struggling backpacker, are short-term solutions that can obscure bigger issues. So while the trip might, on paper, meet its objectives, this comes at the cost of disempowering individuals who perhaps do not benefit from the process.

Case Study: Productive Leadership

One of my summer jobs while I was in college was leading extended leadership adventures for high school students. Dave and I co-led a monthlong expedition for a group of high schoolers, which included paddling in Alaska's Prince William Sound and backpacking in the Talkeetna Mountains. We knew that all the route planning and decisions made by the company we were working for would have to become ours when real-time weather, group dynamics, and injuries came into play. The program was designed as an outdoor-leadership trip for these students, all of whom had previous outdoor experiences. The students were motivated and energetic, and they worked well with and through challenges, such as rising tides and unmoored boats, glacial-river crossings, and following bear precautions on the open tundra.

On the paddling portion of the trip, we were outfitted with single and tandem kayaks, and we were ferried out into Prince William Sound with the objective of paddling back to the mainland over a week's time. One participant, a larger boy who could comfortably fit only in the bigger tandem kayak, had a previous shoulder injury that made paddling the long distances increasingly more challenging, and the tandem boat did not track well compared to the single kayaks, slowing progress. Dave and I, along with the rest of the group, became aware of not only the physical challenges the boy was experiencing, but also the increased risk the rest of the group was exposed to as the tandem boat fell farther behind. Working together, and with input and modification from all participants, we were able to explore other options to modify the trip, boat-partner pairings, and weight distribution. We had open discussions about the challenges of perceived strength related to size and learned how, in this case, physically strong people did not need to carry or move the weight for the entire group.

Leading from Below

KENJI HAROUTUNIAN

Although I had skied the backcountry a dozen times, having the chance to ski a bucket-list adventure across the daunting and remote Sierra High Route was exciting—and slightly terrifying. This trans-Sierra route is nearly 40 miles across five major mountain passes over 13,000 feet, in as remote a place as one can get in the Lower 48. This adventure of a lifetime would certainly test my outdoor skills and leadership abilities.

I was invited on the trip as an alternate, so I only had eight weeks to come up to speed with gear, fitness, and mental prep for the seven-day self-supported ski tour. I was not planning to lead any section of the trip, so I was mostly concerned with just keeping up! My teammates were seasoned, extreme athletes and leaders. Two had recently participated in an all-women's expedition to Antarctica, completing a 600-plus-mile slog across the continent. I had served in lead roles many times before, but I was the rookie in this group.

As we embarked, I felt strong, but I also had the heaviest gear of the group. I wondered if I was going to pay a price for that. The trip began with more than 6,000 feet of vertical climb before getting through Shepherd Pass, at 12,500 feet. There, the route stays above 11,000 feet for 30 miles and five days of backcountry winter travel. As we moved along, I felt well prepared. Despite a fuel-bottle leak into our breakfast rations, I had my kit together. My heavier boots were now a blessing because of the variable conditions we encountered en route.

About three days into the journey, at Coppermine Pass, my preparedness met an opportunity. I was first through the pass after a very long traverse, heading into the setting sun. The snow was hardening, and the pass was becoming treacherous. The trip leader and I decided to split up, so he could belay the trailing teammates as they approached the pass while I took the "sharp end" and, by headlamp, dug out a campsite for the night in the unknown terrain ahead. From this point on in the tour, I was co-leading.

Timing is everything when it comes to supporting other leaders, taking the reins when needed and deftly sharing the load when a highly skilled group comes together. My prior experience as a climber had paid dividends, and maintaining a calm demeanor in the face of fear was key to working out creative solutions as challenges presented.

Kenji Haroutunian (he/him/his) is an outdoor-industry veteran, with thirty-five years of experience in specialty retailing, skills instruction, and guiding and event management, as well as in high-profile roles on the national outdoor-recreation scene, including Outdoor Retailer Show director and Access Fund board president. He lives in Culver City, California.

TRANSFORMATIVE LEADERSHIP

I'll ensure we're successful.

- High intensity and passion (high commitment)
- Focus is on interdependence (high care)

When a leader focuses on the greater good and their commitment is high, leaders become transformative.

Here's the real sweet spot: a combination of high commitment and high care, which can lead to truly transformational leadership. With stated intentions, consistent behavior, and acute perception, a transformative leader sees their success connected to the greater good. A transformative leader consistently models taking responsibility for their choices, which influences those who are actively following. In this manner, the leader knows they ultimately guide the group's outcome. Through inspiration, influence, and coaching, a transformative leader achieves lasting success.

A transformative leader consistently works on:

- building trust and credibility
- getting people to come and work together as a team
- focusing on what is important and essential
- helping others be their best
- doing what is best for the expedition or organization
- proactively reducing misunderstandings and working for mutual understanding
- reflecting upon and seeking ways to improve themself and others

Transformative leaders are highly aware of the role of interdependence, and they continually cultivate open communication, feedback, and active listening, ensuring every individual has their voice and input heard. The investment in relationships that deepen among group members allows everyone to be at their full, best self.

A weekend backpacking trip, navigating a river by canoe, climbing at a local crag, and mountain biking an epic trail are experiences in which a transformative leader, by design and intention, can lead others to experience success. By showing consistent care and commitment, a transformative leader can help participants fully appreciate an outdoor experience, managing and influencing them in a seemingly effortless manner.

Case Study: Cultivating Transformative Leadership

After twenty years of working, leading, guiding, and teaching in the outdoor industry, I had never led an all-female expedition. I had always had male co-leaders and participants, and so it was with some trepidation that I organized and facilitated an international expedition solely for women. The trip, to Costa Rica, was novel in many ways: I invited another national association to join and help plan, and the women were at different points in their careers in different aspects of the outdoor industry—some participants were outdoor educators, while others worked in upper administration.

The program was designed around various activities throughout the country—tackling rope swings into a stream, rafting the Sarapiquí River, hiking along the side of a volcano, learning about sustainable coffee production, hiking in national preserves, and kayaking down a jungle waterway. The evenings were filled with time for small-group reflections, incorporating the day's activities to catalyze conversations or connect to the assigned readings.

Our group was a mixture of women with varying outdoor experience, ranging from novices to instructors. We intentionally changed roommates at each new location; our living arrangements were always double occupancy and ranged from local hotels to bunkhouses. The program was designed to hold space for transformational leadership understanding by allowing the group to experience both low and high care and low and high commitment. Each night, we would debrief, reflect, and process the day's events in the hopes of applying new knowledge to our choices the next day. Over the course of the week, the leadership team watched participants transform from individuals experiencing new activities for the first time to a cohesive group watching out for each other's emotional and physical safety.

There were tears and triumphs that affected both the individuals and group throughout the week, but perhaps even more so after we returned to the States. This group of sixteen women still connects and communicates in various forms and places, including at conferences, virtual presentations, text groups, and on video calls. Each woman certainly has gained a greater sense of her own leadership potential as she moves forward with her life outside the expedition, but they all remain firmly connected to the experience in Costa Rica, which provided a basis for ongoing growth.

THE GREATER GOOD: SERVANT LEADERSHIP

Building the capacity to lead is an opportunity for everyone. Leadership skills are transferable—to your personal life, your professional world, and recreationally in the great outdoors. If you desire to be an impactful leader, you must learn and continually revisit how you lead. When guiding others toward agreed-upon outcomes, your success or failure will be determined by how you navigate your care for the greater good over self, your level of commitment, and the leadership decisions you make. A great leader is committed to lifelong learning and personal responsibility.

It has been my experience, through my work on and for myself, that when I can identify ingrained habits and behaviors that no longer suit me, I build the capacity to be more present, aware, and intentional. Some of these ingrained behaviors, such as those that make me feel valued and accepted, come from my upbringing and ways my family showed me love. It turns out that more is not always better, especially when it comes to quantifiable goals like good grades or accolades. I've learned instead that knowing myself and understanding my value is the best way for me to lead.

> With stated intentions, consistent behavior, and acute perception, a transformative leader sees their success connected to the greater good.

On a cold April evening a few years ago, I sat around a firepit with six other women. Our connection was sports, and we had met through a master's swim program. Some in the group had been friends for many decades before I was invited to join, with a shared foundation that included child rearing and social activities like church groups and dinner parties, while others were relatively new to the group. We gathered to celebrate one woman's most recent professional accomplishments—she had been promoted in university leadership. I really enjoyed the conversation that night and was excited about her choice to lead at a very prominent post. The group supported her opportunity, acknowledged her efforts, and shared her excitement for what was to come, as well as expressed support for the other group members who had recently changed jobs or returned from living overseas.

These leaders, even those not navigating change at the time, had many common attributes, but the one that stood out for me was their reflection on the greater good. It was even more impressive to learn about how the need for leadership presented itself and to hear each leader's choice—after considering how it would affect them, their families, their partners, and other people in their lives—to pursue it. I'm honored to be among leaders who do not seek leadership titles for the titles' sake, but instead consider the significance of what they're doing, how they can contribute to a situation, and how they can continue to improve their leadership skills and not get complacent or stagnate. I wondered if I had always been as honest and forthright as a leader. I realized their humility was the most important part of the conversation, and that on reflection, I too could work on my own humility and growth as a leader.

TAKEAWAYS

- Leadership guides outcomes: it determines success or failure.
- Leadership is a choice, and everyone can choose to build their capacity to lead.
- Strong leaders make better choices, consistently.

- Effective leaders grow and improve continuously.
- Leaders achieve agreed-upon outcomes.
- Building trust and credibility as a leader motivates others to work together toward a common goal.

THIRSTY FOR **MORE?**

What tools do you already use to assess your leadership style or effectiveness? What types of new tools would you be willing to incorporate?

Can you remember a time when you were a transformative leader? Upon reflection, what are one or two takeaways from that experience you could use moving forward?

Can you recall a time when you were a destructive leader? Can you identify one or two factors that you controlled that contributed to your choosing to behave this way?

Think of a time you chose not to lead. Can you identify the reasons for this decision?

Whom do you admire as a leader? What traits do they demonstrate that you seek to emulate?

How have you shown high levels of care and commitment in leadership?

How have you demonstrated low levels of care and commitment in leadership?

CHAPTER 2
SELF-RESPONSIBILITY AND LIFELONG LEARNING

In the previous chapter, we explored how care and commitment relate to leadership, and how these two themes support self-responsibility. But to have the privilege of leading others in any endeavor, we must also learn to lead ourselves. This "self-leadership" doesn't mean striving for perfection or expertise, but rather being fully present and aware of our actions and words, as well as prepared and in good shape physically and emotionally for the upcoming adventure. If these concepts feel like a lot, they are! Remember that leadership is like hiking down the trail: the journey builds on each step you have previously taken. You don't need to be perfect, complete, or at the summit to start!

This chapter explores the importance of lifelong learning. When we embrace feedback and continuously take ownership of our ideas, actions, and words, we avoid becoming complacent. Seeking opportunities to re-create, reinvent, or amplify ourselves and our options, as well as address accountability (for ourselves and others) establishes a critical foundation we can then build on.

IT ALL BEGINS WITH SELF-RESPONSIBILITY

Back when I operated a college outdoor program, it was my responsibility to ensure that my staff could facilitate day, weekend, and weeklong outdoor experiences around the Midwest. We thus created trainings to ensure the staff understood program policies and procedures, demonstrated competency, and knew what their resources were. These trainings gave me the opportunity to spend a week in the field assessing ten to fifteen potential staff of eighteen- to twenty-four-year-olds, observing how responsible they were so I could trust them to lead programs to the best of their abilities.

In my role, I began evaluating these would-be leaders' ability to take self-responsibility—to put their best selves forward—from the very beginning of the application process. What amazed me, year after year, were the many applicants who submitted incomplete applications, were late and/or had not prepared for the interview, and who were hard to contact or did not return my calls or emails. I needed to hire trip leaders whom I could trust to drive a twelve-passenger van seven to ten hours out of state or to northern Michigan with a group of people they had just met, and then lead a potentially risky activity in a remote environment. Could I trust them to do this work if they couldn't be bothered to put their best selves forward in the application and interview process? Ultimately, the applicants who demonstrated self-responsibility from the get-go were the ones I hired.

OWNING OUR LEADERSHIP MISTAKES

Most certainly, you, like I, have botched a leadership opportunity when you were in charge. Perhaps it was because you could not manage your energy or attitude, or you didn't have the appropriate skill for the task at hand, and so the experience failed miserably. These things happen. Over time, we learn that the leaders who came before us were also human. Once we gain a better understanding of the influences past leaders have had on others, we realize the positive effects we too can have in a leadership role when we fully manage ourselves.

So take responsibility for your actions and intentions. It is the most gratifying feeling when positive results emerge because of decisions you made or actions you took. At the same time, if you do make a mistake, taking responsibility for it can yield positive results as well, namely in the form of a learning experience. All leaders make mistakes. The best leaders are ones who acknowledge those mistakes and then learn from them with an intention of change.

CASE STUDY: LEARNING FROM MY MISTAKES IN ISLE ROYALE

Once trip leaders were hired for my university program, they had to undergo a series of meetings and training exercises that covered departmental and university policies. We built into the program a weeklong leadership trip for incoming and returning staff. One year, that trip headed to Isle Royale, the largest island in Lake Superior. As usual, the trip kicked off with a pre-trip meeting held about a week before the departure date, during which we focused on building community, covering trip expectations and logistics, agreeing on desired outcomes, discussing required gear, and submitting final paperwork, including waivers, releases, and health forms.

At this meeting, to help orient our newer leaders, we'd have experienced trip leaders come in with a backpack filled with personal gear, and then remove and discuss each item to help participants understand what they'd need to bring on the trip. In addition, we discussed things such as cell-phone use, drugs and alcohol, and how leaders' actions positively and negatively affect the trip participants.

Isle Royale is a very challenging place to travel to because it's accessible only by boat or seaplane and ferry service is quite limited. Thus, we would need to be prepared and focused with our goals. Our training trip used a "leader of the day" model in which each potential trip leader was to act as trip leader for one day and receive feedback from the other staff on strengths and areas for improvement.

On departure day we set out in two vans, using two-way radios to communicate between the vans and relying on multiple-page printouts from the internet for directions (this was in the era before smartphones). Things got tense by the first rest area. Both drivers had forgotten about the need to travel together; the lead van rushed through a couple yellow lights, and the following van did not want to speed to keep up. The trip leaders blamed each other, which, based on my years of overseeing this trip, wasn't unusual. Ultimately, this kind of non-issue gets resolved over time, but there can be lingering damage for the followers—doubting the competency of their leaders and seeing how they respond to stress.

There are two places to catch a ferry to Isle Royale from Michigan's Upper Peninsula (the UP): Houghton (a six-hour boat ride) or Copper Harbor (a three-hour ride). Copper Harbor is about a one-hour drive past Houghton to the tip of the Keweenaw Peninsula. Our tickets were from Copper Harbor, and after driving for more than ten hours, we pulled into camp and set up in a magnificent rainstorm. The next morning, we got on the ferry and made it an hour out into Lake Superior before the huge swells made it necessary for us to turn back.

The designated trip leaders for the day faced a challenging situation. Waiting for the storm to pass would mean catching a ferry a couple days later, and that would nullify our camping permits on Isle Royale. If we drove instead to Houghton, where the National Park Service office was located, we might be able to update our itinerary, though this wasn't certain. Having to decide, while being evaluated by a boss and peers, was stressful for the day's two leaders, who had to lead a group of leaders and discern the best course of action in an unfamiliar environment, all while being new to leadership positions. In the end, they had to get creative. The leaders devised a plan to let everyone suggest ideas about the ferry, the permits, the weather, and contingencies like visiting other sites in the UP where we knew we could potentially take a five-day hike. There was a sense of community, and the collective problem-solving revealed different options for the future of the trip.

As a result, after working with the park service in Houghton and adjusting the permits for different dates, the day's leaders formulated a plan for a shorter on-island trip. We traveled back to Copper Harbor after a full day spent adjusting plans. We had yet to set foot on the island, but the stress of the situation had affected everyone. That night, we held a debrief circle in which every participant offered thoughts about the things they felt the day's leaders did well or could improve on. One leader took the feedback well, but the other, Nancy, took it quite personally, feeling that her actions and things that challenged others were direct reflections of her as a person rather than her leadership style. She soon became distraught.

In hindsight, I realized this student had never received feedback that was anything less than positive. In her school, social, and other experiences, she had yet to navigate challenging or candid feedback on her individual role and how it affected others; she did not understand how to sit with this information or look for ways to incorporate change into her actions. When I checked in with her later that night, I learned she was devastated that she had not "measured up," and she felt a tremendous pressure and burden she simply did not know how to process.

We finally got to the island, two days later than planned. We shouldered our bags and started our hike, traversing the spine of the island. During the day, Nancy's behavior was changing—becoming odd and more distant. At one point, I worked to address it with her and found she was still upset about the feedback. She felt it was unfair and that her co-leader was more to blame for the challenges of the day. I decided to hold back with her and the young man who had been her co-leader to see if we could all talk it through. I sent my co-leader and the rest of the group ahead to the next camp.

The three of us sat at a picnic table and revisited the conversation from the mainland. Nancy was quite aggressive toward her co-leader and very defensive about any comments or conversation he or I offered. She was unsatisfied with the experience and would not let it go, could not see it as a learning opportunity, and wanted only to be cleared of any perceived deficiencies in her leadership. As evening fell and weather moved in, I insisted the three of us continue to camp so my co-leader would not worry. More time had passed than I had anticipated.

We started hiking, and Nancy mumbled and repeated phrases quietly under her breath. As we moved along the trail, she said increasingly vicious things to the young man, so I sent him just ahead and walked closer to her. She stopped and got off the trail, and then began chanting. I didn't really know what to make of it and was just as concerned about the approaching rainstorm as I was her odd behavior. With too many starts and stops, the three of us inched toward camp, and it was a relief to meet my co-leader, who had circled back to find us.

My co-leader and I talked, and I shared my observations of the student's behavior and my increased concern for her safety. We discussed the possibility that she might be on drugs, and we talked about what we could do to observe and protect her and the others. We really did not know what to think or the best course of action to take. It was now night, and we were at camp. It was raining. We continued to watch her. At dinnertime, she ate from a plastic bag—putting the served food into that instead of on her plate. I noticed her going in and out of her backpack repeatedly, as well as stepping away from camp. She also had two sticks in her tent alcove, and upon checking them out we realized they had been sharpened and could be used to hurt someone.

We hunkered down for the night. The rain and wind and dark were in full force coming off Lake Superior. Every time a tent unzipped, my co-leader and I peeked out. Next, we heard a commotion—Nancy had gotten out of her tent and was yelling at the group to come have a meetup, going tent to tent and asking the other campers to come out in the rain. Not sure what to do, but feeling she was at risk, I got out of my tent—being careful not to physically move her—and asked, then yelled, for her to get into my tent. This was very dramatic—I actually yelled multiple times and sometimes not very nicely, "GET IN THE TENT!" In time Nancy moved toward our tent, and we were able to get her inside for observation. She was visibly not herself, rocking back and forth. We started to fill out a SOAP—Subjective, Objective, Assessment, and Plan—note to document her behavior, and then spent the night observing her.

The next morning, we announced the group would be leaving because we needed to move Nancy off the island to get the help she needed. Working together, we broke down camp, distributed her gear among all of us, and coached her to walk with us along the trail back to the docks. After a quiet but arduous hike, we arrived at a ranger station, using the phone there to contact counseling and psychological services at our university to find out what our next steps should be. Taking her to a hospital was the goal—either by helicopter or boat—and we waited until the next ferry.

LEARNING AND GROWING IN A LEADERSHIP ROLE

We were able to get Nancy to definitive care, where she was stabilized and had medical observation resulting in mental health intervention and support. Leadership requires knowledge, but this knowledge is gained over time and from experiences. If we wait until we experience everything before we attempt to lead, we will never lead! When I reflect upon the Isle Royale trip, I look for ways I could have been a better leader. What are things I could have controlled and done better? Could I have prevented some of the issues by noticing behaviors earlier or have been more consistent in my feedback to and coaching of the participants? I could not control Nancy's mental health, but I was able to take responsibility for ensuring that she—and the other participants—remained safe on the trip, and that Nancy was evacuated to get help that was beyond my ability to provide.

Learning opportunities abound every day. See what you can, and search for what you can't see. Be aware and take note. So what are the lessons that can be drawn from the experience with Nancy? Some are simple and some are more complex. For example, if a leader isn't fully prepared and forgets something critical, like a rain jacket on the packing list, or fails to check the group's gear and discovers too late that the rainflies are missing, it can make a big difference in the group's perception of their leadership if they own up to their mistake. Time and time again, I have observed leaders who admit to a mistake but then fail to state clearly that it was their decision or oversight—to fully own it—and move on with a solution. That's a fairly straightforward lesson. Others involve learning and growing as a leader in longer-term ways.

Fail Better!

LAUREL HARKNESS

I am that person who can't remember song lyrics, plotlines of popular books and movies, or names of rapids, peaks, and trails. Trust me—I should be your last pick for your karaoke or trivia team. Somehow, long ago, I became attached to a line written by the playwright Samuel Beckett: "Ever tried. Ever failed. No matter. Try again. Fail again. Fail better."

I could not tell you where I first came across this line—maybe on a tea bag or the back of a cereal box or the vision board at the local yarn shop. Who knows. However, that notion of having the opportunity to fail, learn, grow, fail better, and then rinse and repeat has provided a compass for me. Here are a couple of my notable "fails" and "fail betters":

Almost three decades ago, I learned to row on the Colorado River through the Grand Canyon (I do not recommend this as a starter river). I flipped a raft on day one of an eighteen-day trip and lost the entire kitchen to the deep-brown water. The only thing saved was a chicken-shaped potholder, floating along amidst the chaos. I returned this summer to row that same 226 miles of river. Fail better.

I'm not even sure how I graduated from college given how much time I spent chasing outdoor and other pursuits, but somehow I managed to earn a degree in viticulture—with minors in whitewater kayaking, mountain biking, live music, and world river exploration. Twenty-five years later, I am back in school, working with self-determination toward a master's degree in public policy. Try again. Fail again. Fail better.

If you are like me, maybe you have trouble centering yourself. So here's a pro tip: center others—the ones you love, your community, other species, the planet—instead. Continued curiosity and investment in learning positively impacts decision-making, not only for you but for all who are upstream and downstream of you. This way, the learning is a gift to yourself in the form of enlightenment and the opportunity for deepened relationships—a kinship.

Setting the intention to learn is self-determination, which is really the essence of what many of us love about outdoor adventure. Picking a line and committing—it is the foundation of democracy. In the outdoors, life, learning, and democracy, there are fails and fail betters. My favorite T-shirt has a ridiculously silly and giant line drawing of a rabbit. I like it for two reasons: (1) when I wear it, children near me giggle and light up with curiosity, and (2) it reminds me that I have the privilege to learn and follow my curiosity down all sorts of rabbit holes, seeking understanding, cultivating kinship, and learning to lead.

Since her first mountain-bike ride, in 1987, **Laurel Harkness** *(she/her) has dedicated her life to rural community development and outdoor recreation. She serves as the coalition director for the Rural Voices for Conservation Coalition while pursuing a graduate degree in rural policy at Oregon State University.*

Invest in Yourself

Investing in yourself is the best investment you can make. A major point of education is learning how to learn. Self-responsibility begins when we start to see any gaps in our learning, and then act to address them. We don't act because of a deadline or a to-do list someone else gave us, but because we're directed by our own desire or ability to take ownership of ourselves and our actions.

Staff training for an outdoor program and staff training at a new job have more similarities than differences. In both cases, you may not be able to competently demonstrate all your skills while also showing your ability to contribute and lead. Neither the participants on the Isle Royale trip nor I had ever been to that location, but we had transferrable skills we used. We knew how to plan and pack appropriate gear and food, as well as how to set up and manage our camp. Even though we did not know each other before the trip, we committed to building a successful living community with clear expectations and communication. Though the trip's outcome was not what I'd desired, I was able to work with the students to ultimately coordinate and execute a successful evacuation.

On a personal level, recognizing I still had a long way to go was a blow to my ego. It was difficult for me to discover and admit that learning does not stop after completing school or a certification program and that most of life's learning happens outside the classroom. My maturation process unveiled how little I really knew, yet it also revealed to me that there is continuous room for improvement.

If you're waiting for permission to invest in yourself or to pursue that which you find interesting, consider your wish granted! There are many ways and places to learn, and the paths you start down may not be the ones you finish on. Even if you feel limited by time, finances, or worries about acceptance, you will find a way—if you think it adds value (and to you, it will!). So don't let boundaries set by others limit your growth. For example, many industries require certification and ongoing licensing. Upon getting a new job in one of those industries, an employee may be told by their employer that they'll receive a certain amount of time and financial support for professional development. However, having to do so within a time limit set by the employer can taint the learning process. A better approach might be, even within these constraints, to cultivate an attitude of continued curiosity, which will serve to expand your perspective and positively impact your decision-making.

Be Coachable

After I'd become a bit more removed from the Isle Royale trip, I realized how, as young people develop, they are motivated and encouraged to do great things and to see their accomplishments celebrated with accolades. I've had this same experience myself—I was raised to pursue top grades in academics, varsity teams in athletics, first chair in music, and the lead role in volunteering. What we as a society are not honest about is that in the pursuit of being our best, we will most certainly face a journey laden with setbacks, adversity, unknowns, and the realization that we may not get what we want when we want it. Not a lot of coaching and attention are dedicated to learning how to navigate through the hard times, being open to feedback and change, and seeing the opportunity to learn when we don't get what we want or expect. Becoming coachable is a major step in overcoming these setbacks—the ability to learn is an invitation for opportunity and change.

I can't remember where I first heard the phrase "feedback is love," but I thought it was stupid. In fact, it really irked me. Feedback isn't love; feedback is accountability. Most people don't like to hold themselves or others accountable because it is uncomfortable. Accountability means saying we will do something a certain way by a certain time—we will make decisions. And because we are human and want to be regarded in the best light by others, we fear not knowing how to do a task or not completing it on time, or we simply fear being ultimately responsible. We might avoid these situations to avoid the discomfort of scrutiny or disappointment.

Feedback can be solicited, which can be easier to hear, or unsolicited, which can be more difficult to hear, but in my experience the hardest type of feedback for me to accept has been that I am no longer relevant. I'm then forced to realize that maybe I avoided *growing*—developing a new skill set, technique, or relationship—because I was lulled by complacency or was fearful of being defensive. But I've learned that not being able to contribute is the greater discomfort for me. To counter this, I try new things, ask for feedback, and remain open to being coached. This approach has opened new opportunities for me to learn. Investing in myself, no matter the course, topic, or skill, allows me to get excited about learning something new, and it lets me better hear and incorporate feedback.

Leaning into Feedback

KATHERINE HOLLIS

I started my career as an outdoor educator. I was so passionate about the work that I wanted to be as good of an educator as possible as quickly as possible. In my first two seasons, I observed co-instructors and modeled my leadership in their styles. I designed lesson plan after lesson plan, cribbed off the lead instructors' work.

This was sometimes successful, but it often fell flat. Why couldn't I make the magic happen? Why couldn't I create those *aha!* moments like other outdoor educators? Did I just not understand things well enough? I'd refocus on building lesson plans in my time off, observing and asking others how they taught things. And I'd try to replicate. And things kept not sticking.

I asked myself why I wasn't improving, why wasn't my instruction where I wanted it to be in terms of both effectiveness and inspiration. I couldn't come up with any answers except to work harder, so I asked others for feedback. I learned that being true to my personality was the best way to shape my leadership style.

Feedback can feel uncomfortable, both to give and receive, and this was especially true for me when I was starting out. Constructive feedback initially felt like I had failed. However, by leaning into feedback from others and asking follow-up questions, I found many of the answers I was seeking about my instruction. I also discovered that in pushing myself to provide feedback to others, especially to folks with more experience than me, I learned how to identify areas for improvement in how I collaborate, as well as how to better understand my own leadership style.

While I might have learned the integral importance of feedback in the context of outdoor education, seeking feedback from others has supported me in every career transition since. It is the most effective way for me to discover my own leadership style, helping me construct an understanding of how to mesh my passion for outdoor education and effective instruction and leadership. Feedback has also helped me understand where I did things well naturally, and it's helped me focus on leading from those strengths—not just work on my weaknesses.

I learned I didn't need to change who I am by teaching in someone else's style, but rather that I needed understand my personality well enough to develop my own teaching style. In practical terms, this meant stepping back from a specific lesson plan to identify what about the content interested me, and then building my own lesson plan from that. Or it meant approaching conflict between students not based solely on how I'd seen others navigate similar situations, but by taking the time to identify what about the situation was important to me and working to address it from there. Learning how to use feedback for self-understanding helped me define my own leadership strengths. I learned to teach and lead from who I am.

Katherine Hollis (she/her) considers herself one of the lucky ones— her parents had her adventuring in nature before she could walk. This connection to the outdoors has continued through more than twenty years of work, catalyzing authentic connections to create sustainable, impactful solutions for people and the natural world.

CONSISTENCY IS NOT COMPLACENCY

Things I know about myself: I loathe complacency. I appreciate consistency. I am relentless in my pursuit of what I believe is best for the things I take on. I think there is always a better way, and I am willing to put my time and energy toward exploring it. I don't work well with those who don't work. I don't know if my behaviors stem from a competitive mindset fostered in sports (as I'll share later, open-water swimming is a passion of mine, and I took competitive rowing very seriously in college) or from my insecurities—feeling like my efforts are not enough. It's most likely a combination of the two.

As I see and interact with the world, it is through my lens—like all of us, I'm just a person trying to be accepted and navigate through life in a way that works for me. And I've never been satisfied with complacency or the status quo; in fact, it irks me to think that good enough is just that—good enough. I think I can always learn more and be better, and I think being the best I can be means I can have a more positive influence on those I lead.

The adventures you seek and the journeys you envision can become epic to you too if you consistently act in ways that support learning and self-betterment. Focusing on your own goals, not those imposed on you or on boundaries society might set for you, is part of being consistent. For example, you might not perceive that you fit into the outdoor experience. Perhaps you've seen social media and publications showcasing epic adventures with beautiful people using expensive gear, and it makes you feel like not everyone belongs in the outdoors. But there are mountains to climb and rivers to run—for everyone. If you know what you want and stay true to that, you'll succeed in your own experience—and that's a true quality of leadership.

As a leader, I work best when I am complemented by a co-leader who is consistent as well. Consistency in action and words builds trust; consistency is stability. While I may find or choose a leadership role, the position and title are afforded to me only if there is a team that follows. Consistency in action is the solid base from which people and ideas can move forward. Complacency is apathetic; complacency is the antithesis of self-responsibility. It removes any ownership and investment in improvement.

The Role of Active Follower

When we think about leaders, two storylines frequently emerge: The first is that it is often desirable to be the leader—the captain, the president, the boss. Not only are books and stories built around past and present leaders (or how to become a future leader), but they're often framed such that only one person gets to claim that title. The second storyline is that we too should aspire to be like or become this leader—in outdoor narratives, perhaps it's a top climber, biker, hiker, or adventurer. When we are a leader but are not *the* leader at that moment/in that situation, it is important to choose and participate as an **active follower**. As an active follower, you engage and support the leader—respecting their leadership, even if you would lead differently.

However, for us to have the privilege of leading others in any endeavor, we must first be able to lead ourselves. This doesn't mean being perfect or being an expert; it means we can be fully present and aware of our actions and words, be prepared, and be in good shape physically and emotionally for the upcoming adventure. A leadership journey is an ongoing endeavor, and I invite you to try to lead your next adventure in ways that are both comfortable and not. You can move with intention between being an active follower and a leader in many group settings—state your intention and try!

SEEKING GROWTH AS A JILL OF ALL TRADES

I am a Jill of all trades and a master of none. I hike, bike, paddle, swim, rock climb, and engage in myriad outdoor adventures. I'm not the strongest climber, and while I can ski, I don't expect a sponsorship deal. What I know is what I know and, more importantly, I know what I don't know—and so I can choose to let others take the lead on specific skills where I am not as competent.

There are skill-development courses, classes, certifications, and training for almost every outdoor endeavor. If you have an interest in a specific activity, look for people or programs that can help you enhance your competency. Don't be fooled, however, into thinking that a weekend or semester program will make you an expert. There are many people with driver's licenses who are not good drivers—it's always a long journey to true expertise. In addition to activity-specific training, I often look to better understand both my strengths and my weaknesses. These can include areas like communication, self-care, fitness, and conflict resolution. Seek growth to enhance areas you're strong in or to mitigate your challenges—either way, you will be better able to lead others once you can better manage yourself.

However, expect some bumps along the road. In a cruel twist of fate during my own ongoing maturation process, I was devastated to discover I was responsible for myself. What a bummer! Once you've finally attained the autonomy that you sought as a child—no longer being confined or defined by parents, teachers, whomever—one of adulthood's great disappointments is surely the realization that you, and you alone, are responsible for your actions and inactions. Ugh. Self-responsibility can feel like the wet blanket of no fun—and no one packs a wet blanket for outdoor adventures. Still, through the course of life events both large and small, we learn to take responsibility for our own actions. And, as we do so, we become better at making decisions.

As a parent of two kids, I am amazed by how incredibly challenging self-responsibility can be. Parenting is like having front-row tickets to a show in which you are hoping for a great ending all while watching the characters' story arcs oscillate between success and difficulty and between good and bad decisions. My daughter, Gretel, and my son, Thor, struggle with the fact that the autonomy they crave comes with many uncomfortable responsibilities and realities, such as accountability for their actions or inactions, limited finances, and learning to ration the precious commodity of time. It's maddening for me to watch my teenagers insist on having freedoms and want to make their own decisions while they continue to avoid most responsibilities and not take ownership of their actions. And yet, there are glimmers of hope: I see my kids start to practice self-responsibility when they take care of a family task without being asked, such as unloading the dishwasher or taking out the trash. I also see how they check the weather before going outside, so they can bring the right clothes to be dry and warm. Ultimately, raising them has been a good show filled with major plot twists. I enjoy watching my kids' maturation, and I am confident they will continue to grow and shine.

Just like my teenagers might be considered novices at life, every expert climber, biker, and skier starts as an understudy as well. In my own growth as an outdoor enthusiast, knowing a little bit about many different outdoor pursuits, rather than specializing in one area or one sport, has suited my attention and abilities. And I accept the strengths and weaknesses of my approach. I know when I'm not an expert, I take responsibility for what I don't know, and I also take responsibility for always finding ways to expand my learning. I approach outdoor activities with one main skill set: a willingness to learn and to try.

There is no better investment you can ever make than in yourself. The wonderful thing is that there is no singular professional development or learning opportunity to pursue—anything meaningful to your growth will be worthwhile.

For example, if you want to improve your health, then prioritize working out, resting, and eating well. If you want to expand your network, join an association to meet people who have similar interests, more experience, and greater perspectives or connections. If you want to become more accomplished in a skill, join a group, attend a class, or complete that training. This self-initiated learning gives back to you and what you are trying to do or become in so many ways. Sometimes it isn't the content, but how it is delivered. Maybe the weeklong course you put aside money and time for reveals that the industry isn't where you want to be after all. That's the gift of lifelong learning—new ideas, people, and opinions will challenge your assumptions and views, helping you home in on the trajectory that's best for you.

When I am being belayed, I take great comfort knowing that my belayer is ready, that the belay device is set up properly, that the carabiner is locked, and that both the rope and my climbing harness are secured properly. I think nothing of telling my partner or being told by them to double-check the system. This feedback is to ensure our safety. Same goes for life jackets being on and buckled correctly, helmet chin straps clipped, or ankle leashes affixed to standup paddleboards (SUPs). In an outdoor context, feedback needs to be more directive—with a leader taking owner-ship of the activity and setting the participants up for success. With a good leader, we feel reassured, looked after, confident in our gear, and ready to participate.

Why don't we seek feedback like this in our personal and professional lives? Why do we prefer not to expose ourselves or avoid seeking feedback that might help us realize our full potential? On my own journey, filled with insecurity as a woman in a predominantly male, egocentric industry, I have spent plenty of time trying to be someone I am not—pretending to have knowledge I don't actually have, for example—or sheepishly avoiding new things for fear of failure.

Upon reflection, it took me too long to lead in my role as executive director. This was especially true in governance, which is how a nonprofit works to fulfill its mission. I had the knowledge, but not yet the lived experience, and I was scared to lead. I prioritized being accepted—by not making the cultural changes that needed to be made—over making

tough decisions and leading. After some time, I finally took up the mantle of leadership by clarifying roles between the board of directors and the staff, as well as creating and maintaining boundaries in the work. Once I did these two things, many members and colleagues who now follow and support me shared their observation of how uncomfortable it had been to watch me give away the power that I had and how heartened they were when I fully accepted my position as leader.

TAKEAWAYS
- If you can't lead yourself, you can't effectively lead others.
- Leading yourself means taking responsibility for your actions, intentions, and influence.
- Continued curiosity both expands perspective and leads to better decision-making.
- Investing in yourself is the best investment you can make.
- Being coachable—being willing to learn and change—expands your opportunities.
- Learning opportunities abound every day. Be aware and take note.
- Consistency is not complacency. Understand the difference and make a choice.

THIRSTY FOR **MORE**?

Seeking feedback, rather than playing it safe and keeping quiet, can help you achieve your full potential. Do you seek feedback in your personal and work life? If so, how?

What leadership traits do you demonstrate consistently? Where are you complacent? What factors contribute to both your consistency and your complacency?

Often individuals focus on the cost—time and money—rather than on the return on investment in themselves. This return may come as a job opportunity, expanded competence, a connection made, or increased knowledge that could advance you personally or in your career. How are you exploring lifelong learning?

How are you expanding your outdoor recreation or professional network? Can you identify at least three different outdoor communities you currently engage with or will volunteer with in the future?

CHAPTER 3
MANAGEMENT AND SYSTEMS

I am a terrible manager—the absolute worst. The problem with my management style is it works in direct opposition to all my strongest skill sets. I have a hard time slowing down and reviewing past notes and work, and it's challenging for me to not become bored doing the same task. For some people, repetition brings comfort, but for me it brings crazy thinking. Management, however, is all about consistent, repetitive, disciplined actions; it's about details and analytics, accountability, and control. On the other hand, leadership is about encouraging change and about vision, influence, and inspiration. Just like stuff sacks and sleeping bags, management and leadership should have a working relationship.

Establishing and maintaining well-organized systems, in combination with time and resource management, is crucial for outdoor leadership. Systems create simplicity, allowing a leader to focus on the more complicated issues at hand in the outdoors. This chapter will help you demystify the process of management and systems. We'll address systems thinking, with tips on organization and time management, and how it relates to preparing to lead. We'll cover the fitness required to lead, including physical and mental training and how to make training a priority. We'll consider gear selection, acquisition, care, and maintenance. And finally, we'll look at how to establish and maintain systems and processes as you step into a leadership role.

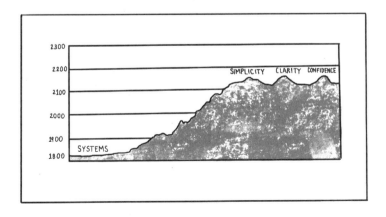

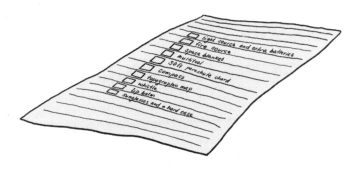

SYSTEMS THINKING

Systems thinking for outdoor leaders means creating standardized procedures so you don't have to reinvent the wheel every time you need something, pack for a specific type of outdoor experience, or teach a skill, for example. This requires first establishing those systems, followed by developing a process for maintaining those systems. Doing so creates confidence and helps a leader anticipate and address special concerns, as well as prepare for the unexpected.

One way to do this is to create and follow checklists, which allow participants to have what they need to perform their best, leading to optimal outcomes. Some examples of checklists include a packing list of recommended or required gear, including the ten essentials (more on those in the gear section); a training list; a documents list; and a food list for individual or shared meals. For more information, see the Appendix.

> The first decisions to make are what you intend to do, where, and with whom. Once you figure out those details, it's time to plan the work—and work the plan.

PREPARING TO LEAD

The first decisions to make are what you intend to do, where, and with whom. Once you figure out those details, it's time to plan the work—and work the plan. An exciting thing about outdoor leadership is plans can, and do, change. But having the appropriate gear and knowing how to use it, and having the right knowledge and being able to apply it, make the experience better for you and those you lead. People overlook crucial things like checking the number of tent stakes (do it each time!) or having paper maps (as a backup to Google). These are systems. Systems add to happiness. Systems *make* you happy because they help you to avoid drama! Issues don't even come up because you've prevented them!

TIME MANAGEMENT COMPLEMENTS LEADERSHIP

My kids allow tasks to expand to the time allotted, regardless of how much time is actually required to complete them. A family rule is that when we specify when we'll be leaving to go somewhere, that is when we expect everyone to be ready and out the door. We don't give reminders once the time is set or identify what needs to get completed. My husband, Justin, and I have thought that from a young age our kids should be able to figure out what needs to get done and allocate enough time to do it, such as getting out of bed, showering, dressing, eating breakfast, and packing for the day. Time is a funny thing to manage because, once you're running behind, a series of other poorly made decisions end up having a big, cumulative, and usually negative effect. There's not only the running-late-in-the-morning-because-you-overslept fiasco; there's also the staying-up-too-late-the-night-before debacle or the train wreck of not getting yesterday's work done, waking up late, and thinking there would be more time to do those leftover tasks plus the things you need to do this morning. Hence, I'm sitting in the car waiting . . .

We hope that when our kids are old enough to move out and live on their own, they'll be able to lead themselves by making good decisions. This means deciding the direction in which they'll steer their lives, and pursuing that with gusto. For them to achieve the "big" things—financial independence, a career they are passionate about, fulfilling relationships with friends and family—they must do things when they are younger that will bring them opportunities later. Managing their time is critically important at this stage in their lives. If they can't have the discipline to do the little things now, they won't have the time, capacity, or resources to achieve the big things later.

TRAINING: PHYSICAL FITNESS

I am not an expert in any single pursuit, but because I train, both physically and mentally, I know I will at least be competent. What I do have expertise in is managing my body temperature, food intake, energy, and attitude—which makes me not only able to enjoy these outdoor activities myself but also to lead others successfully. If you choose to lead others, you don't have to be the fittest in the group, but you must have the stamina and wherewithal to make sure your fitness does not impede your followers.

Training comprises a series of small decisions and actions that are put into practice, repeatedly. Just as you would not consider running a marathon without first following a training plan, so too does it go with outdoor pursuits. Simple is better: Everyone on an outing should be physically able to get outside and be honest about their fitness and the level of difficulty/exertion they can withstand. Think about what you might need to show up ready for the adventure (for your desired comfort and safety levels), and then think about how that might be different if you were leading.

Time Management: A Slippery Beast

I'll use a common scenario of coordinating many vehicles for a group outing with the outdoor program as an example of how multiple parties might manage their time as they work toward a common goal. I recall climbing trips to the Red River Gorge, Kentucky, which is roughly a six-hour drive from Ann Arbor. My trip leaders and I were always the drivers, with each vehicle equipped with maps and directions and various numbers of participants. We always planned to reach our destination when there was still light to set up camp, so we would leave town midmorning. It was hard to caravan on account of the flow of traffic, lights, and each vehicle's speed, so we would plan to meet at the destination. While we'd all leave town at the same time, one of the vehicles would inevitably show up after dark—easily an hour and a half behind using the same roads! This experience played out almost like clockwork, year after year, as the newer trip staff hadn't yet developed their time-management skills and also failed to properly account for the variability of human behavior.

Here are some things I did differently than the tardy vehicle to make it to camp in daylight. Before leaving the center, I asked everyone to use the bathroom and fill water bottles, indicating our first stop would most likely be at least two hours into the trip. When stopping for food and bathroom breaks at rest areas, I announced the current time, how long we would be stopping for, and where and when we would be meeting to leave. I did this because a stated twenty-minute break can easily turn into forty-five minutes if someone takes a call, orders food last minute, or wanders off through the rest area. To maximize the break, I'd also gas up the vehicle while the group was inside ordering their food.

Given each of our peculiarities and how each of us perceives and manages our time as individuals, it's critical that we maintain respect and communication in a group, looking out for our individual interest but also our common space. This is as true in caravanning as it is on an outdoor expedition—in a group, time management is rarely, if ever, a solo proposition.

On a side note, body shape and size should not be used as milestones for fitness. Linking them to a person's ability to take on a human-powered outdoor activity or asking someone to change their size to participate will undoubtedly backfire—it's enough that they understand and are prepared for the level of exertion they'll face. As a leader, you'll want to be mindful of your word choices. To create an inclusive program, you must be very intentional, clear, and candid with your expectations and word choice. If you indicate it is a "beginner" trip, and the mileage suggests otherwise, or an event is promoted as "novice" but requires technical know-how, the misrepresentation can lead to barriers and negative experiences for participants.

Finally, rest and snack breaks should always be part of an outing. Not only is it important for participants to refuel, but it's an opportunity for the leader to check in on how others are doing—preventing hot spots on feet that could lead to blisters, or adjusting equipment that's begun to chafe.

TRAINING: MENTAL FITNESS

Leadership can be intimidating, whether it is your first time as an outdoor leader or your hundredth. Preparing mentally includes making sure you have clearly communicated and continue to communicate to those you lead, and in turn getting assurances that they're prepared to participate. Make sure you take care of your own mental wellness. This means getting rest, attending to any mental or emotional needs that have come up lately, and reducing stress wherever possible.

An idea was shared with me about how to open a conversation. It goes like this: Before starting a meeting or conversation or trip, you say, "If you really know me, you know . . ." Then list three behaviors and your feelings at that time. For example, I might start by saying, "If you really know me, you know I am anxious about writing this book, incredibly proud of Gretel and Thor, and worried about my aging parents." When we share our mental condition with others, we can ground and prepare followers as well as ourselves. Everyone is given an opportunity to recognize the dynamics of being human and how that affects those around us.

GEAR

There's no denying that you need adequate gear to flourish in the outdoors.

Buy the Best You Can Afford and Cry Once

I have a friend who really likes gear—new gear in particular—and spends a lot of time and money researching, buying at pro-deal pricing because he works in the industry, and later selling so he can buy the next thing. He likes fancy things, or things people consider fancy, such as carbon-fiber bicycles, waxless Nordic skis, and rooftop tents for overlanding. But you don't need the newest or highest-end gear to spend time outside. You need the gear that works for you and for your adventure.

You may opt to buy gear that will last so you can use it for many years to come, repairing it as needed or using it until it wears out. This is my husband's and my approach, and it's fun to look at photos from twenty years ago and see us wearing the same fleece and using the same cook kit we use today. Yes, we spent a little more to buy these top-quality items way back when, but the fact that they're still going strong is testament to the "buy the best you can afford and cry once" philosophy.

My 2 Percent

I don't know who originally called these things "2 percent," but I always store these items in the top of my pack in a trusty, and now threadbare, blue sack. My 2 percent is the gear I carry with me on *every* adventure and use 98 percent of the time—they bring me comfort and security on any outdoor adventure. I touch these things the most:

1. light source and extra batteries
2. fire source, such as matches or a lighter
3. space blanket
4. multitool
5. fifty feet of parachute cord
6. compass
7. topographic map
8. whistle
9. lip balm
10. sunglasses and a sturdy sunglass case

While there is some overlap, the 2 percent is not the same as the "ten essentials," the classic list for traveling in the outdoors that you can find in so many how-to books and guidebooks—and that appears in the Appendix of this book as well. What sets my 2 percent apart from the ten essentials is having easy access to these items—I keep them at the top of my pack, and I always know exactly where they are. I also make sure they're always in good working condition.

Of course, I also bring stuff beyond my 2 percent and the ten essentials on most adventures, including:

- **An 8-by-10-foot nylon tarp.** I use this tarp in many ways, and I carry it in addition to any other shelter—like a tent or camping tarp—I may be using. This tarp allows me to place my gear at camp on a dry surface, keep items organized, and have a place to change my shoes and keep my feet and socks dry and protected from the elements. At night, I use the tarp to wrap up everything outside my shelter so it will be dry in the morning. In other situations, this tarp can be used for an emergency shelter, a hypothermia wrap, or as a stretcher or other way to evacuate a patient.
- **Hat and gloves.** I'm always cold, and I don't thermoregulate very well. So, I always bring a hat and a pair of gloves regardless of the outside temperature.
- **Extra wool socks.** When I'm camping, I *always* hide an extra pair of wool socks in the bottom of my sleeping bag. I use them only for sleeping, so I can have warm, dry feet every night.

Keep It Simple

Getting outdoors for yourself and leading others does not have to be complicated. Certainly, there are many decisions to be made, as well as gear to prepare, but safety and enjoyment can come with minimal costs in time and with maximum enjoyment. So while there will always be a new piece of gear, a new resource to read, a new app to download, or someone who has an interesting upcoming outdoor adventure to follow, once you make peace with the continuous churn of equipment, resources, and opinions designed to lure you, the quicker you can get outside with the gear that makes the most sense to *you*.

I like bags and then more bags. I feel more confident when I have a handful of things, especially "just in case" items: food, batteries, a headlamp. Knowing I have these things in my pack makes me rest easier. I don't eat the extra granola bar, even when I'm hungry. I save it for another day. It's like keeping a big bill in my wallet "just in case," even though I really hate having to use it.

I once led a trip with colleagues who were about the same age as me. As we recounted our personal journeys, each of us fondly recalled *Campmor* magazine, a paper catalog of outdoor equipment, with its soft pages and quaint, handmade drawings of equipment. I coveted an external-frame Kelty backpack, an MSR stove and cook kit, and, for whatever reason, a Sawyer extractor kit. Those drawings of equipment with the little descriptive paragraphs helped me budget for and acquire the things I would need for many trips to come. Each of us remembered wanting to upgrade our external-frame backpack to an internal-frame backpack, desiring the magic of an MSR WhisperLite stove, and the promising comfort of a self-inflating sleeping pad.

Gear will always change—new fabrics and lighter designs, new technologies. You don't need to be fancy, but you do need to be mindful of what you ask of your followers, given the variety of budgets and price points on gear. So, what is the appropriate piece of gear for the task at hand, and how can you and your followers balance the need for quality and reliability against the price?

Women's-Specific Gear

As a 6-foot-2-inch woman with a size 12 women's shoe, I still haven't found a women's line of hiking boots that are big enough or pants that are long enough. Instead, I buy men's boots and then modify them with extra tape on my heels at the start of hikes to fill in space in the heel box. And, for pants, I will continue to buy men's raingear that is long enough to cover my legs and fit over my hips, which have borne children. Wherever you shop, select clothes and footwear that are appropriate for the activity and that keep you warm and dry. These should be your main criteria.

Imagine if quality women's-specific gear were the norm: hip belts that accommodated a woman's frame, zippers that were built to be used, pockets in (1) pants and dresses that were (2) in the right place. The outdoor clothing and gear industry has a long way to go in terms of accommodating body diversity. But what if outdoor clothing was readily available beyond the so-called "straight sizes" (typically those found in retail stores, up to size 14 for women)—for those who are tall, or petite, or who need clothing that accommodates various disabilities and medical needs?

Tents

Finally, let's talk tents. Always check all the parts before you go—stakes, rainfly, the tent body, the ground cloth. They must also be stored properly to ensure their longevity: when you return from a trip, set up the tent again to dry it out, recount the stakes, and inventory all the other elements before packing everything away. Once, some student trip leaders in my outdoor program did not follow this procedure, got to camp (hours away), and realized they didn't have any rainflies. This resulted in a damp night and cold participants, even with their ingenuity of using trash bags to try to keep moisture at bay. Appropriate shelter is critical on an outing, and having a good intact system is paramount. Defective clothes, shoes, or gear, or not packing all the necessary parts can be a harsh teacher.

Managing Resources

You'll need to actively manage as resources the items you bring on a trip. One perfect example is the ubiquitous first-aid kit. A well-stocked and -maintained first-aid kit is mandatory, but if it becomes wet from being left out overnight or dropped into water, then the bandages and dressings will be useless. And if the iodine bottle you are carrying to clean wounds is left open after use, the bottle might be knocked over and spilled, so you lose that resource. Having tweezers or scissors go missing limits your ability to remove a splinter or cut moleskin

Leaders thus need to manage group gear like first-aid kits, setting clear expectations of how communal items are to be accessed, treated, and returned. Managing the first-aid kit starts in the front country! I use a system in which first-aid kits, when properly stocked—with Band-Aids, medicine, antibiotic ointment, rubber gloves, etc.—have a piece of tape around them. I then have the confidence that a kit with unbroken tape is ready for any adventure, so that I never find myself in the field trying to treat an injury without the right items.

Don't Overcomplicate It
(and Take Care of Your Feet)

MEGAN A. SMITH

Those in the outdoor industry, particularly its consumer branch, like to focus on the newest gadget, piece of equipment, or electronic this-or-that. However, when it comes down to the basic premise of spending time outdoors, whether solo, with friends, or leading a group, simple systems and good habits are key. When simple systems become good habits, they either keep you out of trouble or help you decide the best course of action to escape less-than-desirable situations.

In my late twenties, I solo-hiked the Long Trail (LT), a 270-plus-mile trail that runs along the spine of Vermont's Green Mountains. The southernmost portion of the LT coincides with the Appalachian Trail (AT). At the time, I was leading a college outdoor program and, quite frankly, needed a break. To date this story, this was before cell phones.

I had attended a one-night informational session prior to embarking on my hike, but otherwise hadn't done much to prepare. I had confidence in my backpacking abilities and systems, and I was going for a walk—what more was there to it? I also had the advantage of being able to stop in at home and reassess at the midpoint of my hike. That and mailing a box of food to a friend so he could bring it to me at a road crossing were pretty much the extent of my planning. The hike was lovely. I was successful, and I achieved the much-needed break from life that had motivated me to hit the LT in the first place.

The following spring, I found myself back at that informational session, but this time I was on the panel rather than in the audience. As the discussion went on and on about how ounces add up to pounds (a very important lesson when hiking long distances or merely trying to extend the longevity of your knees and back) and the ideal food choices for nourishing your body (all important topics), I began to tire of the conversation.

To me, the beauty of the trail was in the pure simplicity of the activity, being in the woods, the people you meet, and challenging oneself. The informational session missed this whole aspect. When the facilitator prompted me to summarize my LT experience, I knew what I wanted to emphasize. The beauty of this activity is that you have the privilege to spend a month or so enjoying the natural world around you. The basics of your day are the same. Get up, eat, take care of your feet, walk for a bit, eat some more, check on your feet, take a quick nap (if you're me), walk some more, arrive at your destination, eat again, take care of your feet, sleep, and repeat. If you do that for twenty-plus days, you'll get to the end of the trail. That's it. Enjoy yourself, don't carry more than you need, eat, hike, sleep, and take care of your feet. Without sustenance and healthy feet, you're going nowhere.

*Formerly Middlebury College's director of outdoor programs, **Megan A. Smith** (she/her) now spends her time running EcoConnect Consulting (ecoconnectjh.com) and Deliberate Dollars (deliberatedollars.com). Based in Jackson Hole, Wyoming, she can be found enjoying the outdoors by ski, bike, paddle, foot, or through binoculars.*

ESTABLISHING AND MAINTAINING SYSTEMS AND PROCESSES

If you want to successfully lead people, you will need to rely on a variety of systems and processes before, during, and after a trip. In chronological order, these systems include the initial decision to go outdoors with others, planning your gear, food, and training, a risk-management assessment, communication preparation, the actual time spent recreating, and then bringing closure to the experience. Leading a trip means managing the trip.

Leading a trip means managing the trip.

There are many moving pieces in an outdoor experience, and thinking things through—or using a checklist, system, or process each time—ensures you can be present and *lead* and handle whatever is coming your way! What works for you *and* what works for those whom you lead? It's a good question to ask because, whether you are heading out on a personal or professional trip, you will either create or work within a system meant to facilitate planning and communication. Consider making lists for every aspect: trip communication, pre-trip meetups, packing lists, menus, and so on. Do you already have waivers and releases prepared? What about participants' medical-history forms? Is there a policy manual?

If you are leading others for a program, there may already be established protocols—it's your job as a leader to be trained on and understand these so you can relay information to those under your lead. Insurance may also dictate the way you lead, and you must understand your obligations and scope of practice. When you lead others, over time you will develop what works for you, and as a result, you can create your own systems.

Systems Create Confidence

Systems help leaders anticipate the unexpected, but also avoid future headaches. Take coolers, for example. Sure, they might be somewhat of a luxury item in the outdoors, but they can also enhance the experience by keeping your food, drink, and even medicine cool. And when you maintain ice and proper storage protocols in your cooler, you can feel confident that these key items will be kept safe from spoilage in the field. As I write this, I am looking at two coolers that are both empty, clean, and drying after a trip this past weekend. I was taught to always clean and stow any equipment when I am done with it, which ensures that the next time I use that equipment it will be (1) in working order, and (2) where I can find it. I don't put away gear if it is not ready to be stored. Focusing on this process, even though it may be challenging after a long trip when I'm tired, means I always have confidence that my equipment is ready. If my gear is ready, then I am also ready, and there is nothing better than feeling ready to go into the wilderness.

Systems Cultivate Clarity

Outdoor recreation is a lesson in simplification. It's fulfilled by practicing mastery of simple things, like setting up camp properly to give you shelter from the elements and making sure you have access to a water source you can purify for drinking and cooking, which requires a basic stove or campfire. Meanwhile, your footwear, clothing, and technical equipment need to be appropriate and sized correctly for the activity and environment, and you need to dispose of waste—both human and trash waste—properly.

Every area listed above requires leaders to research what's appropriate and what's required—to develop systems that bring clarity to meeting these basic needs. Being disciplined in managing gear and other items on your pre-trip to-do list—such as collecting medical forms and shopping for food—gives you clarity. That way, as the leader, you can be confident you are prepared and not leaving anything to the last minute. Additionally, as a leader you'll need to research current and anticipated weather; be aware of trail, river, or snow conditions; and know the group's abilities and experiences. All these will help you determine what you need bring and which systems to put in place.

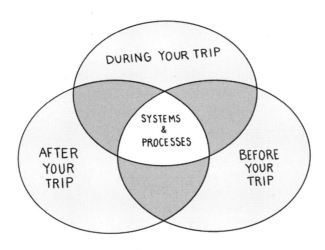

Systems Create Breathing Room to Resolve Complications

When traveling and living outdoors with a group of people, complicated issues do arise—things like challenging group dynamics, an injury or accident, unanticipated bad weather, or trails that are unmarked or overgrown. Following systems when preparing for an outing opens mental space to deal with the issues at hand, knowing that the group has the appropriate clothing and footwear, the food is adequate and accounted for, and the gear is in working condition for establishing camp.

Let's look at one of the main complications you'll encounter: weather. Inclement weather can impede forward progress in many ways, including by creating terrible trail conditions and making it difficult for participants to stay warm and dry. Breaking camp in the rain is not uncommon. Wet tents, wet bags, and wet participants can result in a slower day, decreased morale, and potentially hypothermia. However, there are solutions: Following a clear system for camp breakdown and pack-up ensures the equipment is accounted for. Requiring participants to have a rainfly for their tent and a waterproof sack for their sleeping bag helps reduce water exposure. And setting up camp to ideally have things dry out and people warm up immediately helps a leader attend to the personal and group dynamic needed after a hard day.

For information on where to find examples of systems to emulate, see the Appendix.

Know What You Know and Know What You Don't Know

There are some things you cannot know or predict, such as when the rain will stop or what the rapids will look like after the spring runoff. There are things you should know how to do but may need a refresher on, like reading topographic maps, fixing a tent pole, cleaning a clogged stove, or accounting for declination. And there are things you may not know, including how to make a Z-drag to free a pinned raft or how to build a reliable top anchor for climbing. However, when recreating, you may have to try something you are rusty on or have never done before to quickly resolve a tense situation, ideally with the knowledge and input of your co-leader and your group to help you.

There are nonnegotiables, too—risks that jeopardize your health and safety or that of the group. It is hard to even present a checklist of these things because each situation is different. If you are unfamiliar with the terrain and your group is lost, it's probably not appropriate to continue. Hold tight. If you are not prepared for the adventure you are about to lead, for whatever reason, you should cancel or modify the plan. It is not worth the potential loss of life or limb to be a hero—especially when it's more likely you'll end up a zero.

Establish and Hold Expectations

Finally, it's important to establish trip expectations early on. This is true not only for trip logistics but also for participants and their equipment. Packing lists are crucial, but what's more important is making sure your participants understand those lists. For example, it might seem obvious to you that "two shirts for layering" means packing a base layer that wicks moisture away from your skin as well as a mid-layer that retains your body heat. But other participants might think cotton would work for both layers. Or there's the possibility that "hiking shoes" would be interpreted as Crocs, which are not suitable for most outdoor terrain.

As the trip leader, you need to have confidence that people will bring the things they need to protect themselves from the elements, as well as the right safety gear to participate in the activity, and that they can fully participate (this includes being sober) if the activity requires judgment and decision-making. All this may require creating policies and agreements leaders need to ensure the group's safety, not to mention to cover themselves legally.

Everyone should have the chance to recreate, but if a person's clothing isn't correct, their safety gear isn't adequate, or their judgment is impaired, you should not allow them on your outing. There will always be another opportunity.

The Shower System

Shower preparation in a campground is a good example of how systems create confidence, cultivate clarity, and create breathing room to resolve complications.

Shower prep should not be underestimated. Start with the basic elements: quarters to pay for the shower (thinking ahead and having a stash in the car is a critical best practice), flip-flops, a towel (or two if you use one for hair—though you can use a clean(ish) T-shirt for your hair), shampoo, conditioner, soap, and a waterproof watch with a timer or a second hand. A Dopp kit—or toiletry bag—may have a loop on it so you can hang it in the stall, but if it doesn't, just go into the shower space with things that can get wet, leaving other things like a comb and deodorant where they will stay dry. You are entering two battlefronts here: wet versus dry (keeping your clothes and personal items dry in a very wet landscape) and hot versus cold (there is never as much hot water as you would like). Let's do this!

When you enter the stall, look for signs of water—and mud, from where the last person didn't clean up after themself. Keep as much as you can high and dry by using the hooks farthest from the showerhead, or drape things over the door. Place your shampoo and conditioner in the stall, and put your clean clothes on the hook or over the door. What you will put on last should be at the bottom of the pile. Undergarments should be at the top of the pile. Drape the dry towel on top of your clothes as a barrier against errant spray.

Getting undressed is a game. The winner keeps their clothes out of the water-mud combination by balancing on their shoes or flip-flops. Think of the shower floor as hot lava. It's best to remove one pant leg at a time and go slow. Odds are you will drop something and throw a few swear words around. After all, you're vulnerable and practically naked. Next, if you need to pay, see how much time you get for each quarter, and assume you will have less time than shown. The idea is to take the fastest shower you can before the hot water or your quarters run out. You need to get in there and wash your hair quickly: just get it done so you are not left without hot water or covered in suds because the timer ended. When you wash your body, do each appendage by itself—wash and rinse, so if all goes dry, you are not left covered in soap.

Having a well-considered plan, even for something as basic as showering, can make the difference between a successful outing and a miserable one.

TAKEAWAYS

- Management complements leadership. This means managing time and decision-making.
- You do not have to be the fastest or strongest to lead, but you need to be able to take care of yourself and not affect or impede others.
- Buy the best gear you can afford.
- Embrace systems planning: establish and maintain systems and processes—systems create simplicity. Building and updating systems creates confidence and helps anticipate and address special concerns or the unexpected.
- Know what you know and what you don't know.
- Establish and hold expectations and requirements for participants and their equipment.

THIRSTY FOR **MORE?**

Whether you're heading out on a personal or professional trip, you will either create or be involved in an in situ system that must work for your planning and communication. Which systems work for you? And which work for those whom you lead?

Consider everything needed to make your trip successful, and make lists for everything. As you lead more and reflect on which items are or are not working for you, commit to updating these lists after every outdoor experience.

Collect, review, and distribute any needed waivers and releases, medical-history forms, and similar documents that trip participants need to complete. Do you have the information you need to help support your group?

Review the policy manual as part of pre-trip training for staff. If you don't have a policy manual, create one. The exercise of processing how you would expect yourself or your staff to make decisions in the field can help serve as a baseline for decision-making.

Which systems do you need to create? Which do you already have in place? Which need to be updated? And, with systems that are clearly defined, what is your plan to address current or future gaps?

How does your mindset complement and enhance your checklists?

CHAPTER 4
DIVERSITY, EQUITY, AND INCLUSION

I am a white woman in a leadership role in the outdoor-recreation industry, and the inherent privilege this status gives me may not be (and in many instances, has not been) afforded to others. I have been reluctant to change, but I am learning, and I am unlearning. I am eager to learn what others are willing to share with me. My goal is to do more than just hear; I want to understand, which is necessary for my evolution as a leader.

I have a compelling vision for change in the outdoors that supports diversity, equity, and inclusion (DEI) for all, names and reduces biases, and improves diversity in hiring, leading, and working in outdoor spaces. I hope this book is inclusive, from cover to cover—that the stories shared, and the examples of success and struggle are all-encompassing. Those who have historically held leadership positions in outdoor spaces (white men and to some extent white women) must recognize their privilege and share their power with those who historically have held little to none.

This chapter addresses, names, and discusses diversity issues through our messaging, clarifies the roles that individuals can play in learning, and provides examples that introduce concepts and barriers both to those who are new to them and to those who are already inclusive in practice. If you are just beginning a personal and leadership DEI journey, you'll want to build a team of internal and external partners to support you.

BARRIERS IN THE OUTDOOR INDUSTRY

From my perspective, the outdoor industry has accelerated and matured dramatically in terms of DEI since the early 2000s. From other perspectives, however, this same work has been too little too late—and it's too slow. I am not an expert on DEI. The more I see, the more I listen, and the more I experience, the more I realize how unaware I've been of the challenges others have faced in overcoming systemic barriers.

To counter this, it's been helpful for me to understand that our industry was built by and for individuals who are predominantly non-disabled and who have disposable income and time. At first, I thought the challenge was to provide outdoor experiences and access in a way that I can now label as assimilation—that is, telling someone how to recreate or inviting them to conform to previous standards. But then I realized that, to build more inclusive outdoor spaces, I needed to co-create *new* ways of experiencing the outdoors, opening up opportunities for any individual or group to choose where and how to participate. That's the goal as a leader: focus on the process, and then let the learning and leading move that process along.

Tireless leaders and advocates have been working to elevate these conversations for decades, and thanks to their efforts, individuals and organizations now see the power and wisdom of leveraging social media for change or calls to action. Still, it has not always been a smooth ride, and countless individuals working in businesses, for brands, and for nongovernmental organizations (NGOs) have endured racist behaviors, been subjected to oppressive systems, and been overlooked for opportunities, financial support, and mentorship for years. While positive change is happening, it is long overdue, and it is most likely not enough to make up for the missteps of the past.

A PLACE FOR EVERYONE

Many outdoor organizations, associations, guiding companies, businesses, and nonprofits are now making the necessary changes. Meanwhile, new nonprofits are using mission-driven work to address DEI issues, providing communities and networks for individuals to get outside with others they identify with. Although where and with whom and how to get outside is changing for the better, there continue to be systemic barriers that reduce opportunities for all.

I have the privilege to work with and volunteer with many extraordinary people. Karel Hilversum is the type of charismatic person who leaves you wanting more—more of his contagious energy and optimism, more of his insightful reflections, more of learning what he is reading and studying and cultivating. Karel has a unique perspective on the DEI issue. He is a Boricua, born and raised in the US territory of Puerto Rico to a Puerto Rican mother with close ancestry to the Taino culture and Spanish heritage, and to a father born in colonized Dutch Guyana (current day Suriname). He speaks Spanish, English, and Portuguese. This is all to say Karel has a multicultural, multiracial, and post-imperialist sociopolitical worldview and lived experience.

Karel has been working in the outdoor industry since 1990. For twenty years, he owned and operated a successful outdoor-education business, whose work spanned throughout South, Central, and North America as well as the Caribbean. Since 2016, he has been working at Cornell University's outdoor-education program (Cornell Outdoor Education or COE) and currently serves as co-director. He is the first person of color to lead COE in its fifty years of existence. COE is the largest and most comprehensive university-based outdoor-education program in the United States, and probably the world. There, Karel has spearedheaded the program's DEI initiatives.

"When I got there, DEI was an addendum to the strategic plan," Karel told me. "Today, it is one of the four strategic pillars of the organization and the strategic imperative that will ensure COE's relevancy for the next fifty years." Under his tenure and with the support of his team, COE has increased collaborations across the various DEI stakeholders on the Cornell campus, led the drafting of COE's DEI statement and vision, established and fundraised a $5 million targeted endowment for program access for any student in financial aid, expanded the participation of Black and Indigenous people of color (BIPOC) students in COE programming by creating student-of-color-specific affinity-group courses, and set up an overall model for what a new outdoor education organization can be. He also happens to be an organizational psychologist, and his doctorate research has landed at the intersection of DEI and organizational leadership. I share Karel's journey not to impress you, but to impress upon you that his personal and professional intersectionalities and his hands-on work of diversifying his own outdoor organization are highly relevant to our conversation about DEI in the outdoors.

After deep thought about how to tackle such a massive challenge of diversifying the outdoors, Karel remembered that the outdoor industry had successfully solved similar large-scale problems before. As with the DEI challenge, the outdoor industry had been haunted by environmental-ethics problems for decades. Years of overuse and poorly planned and led outdoor ventures left scars on the fragile natural spaces we all loved. So the outdoor industry stepped up and addressed the problem head-on, combining bottom-up strategies presented by guides and practitioners from the field with larger-scale public-private collaborations that charted the path forward. Out of these efforts came the "Seven Principles of Leave No Trace," and today, LNT is a core component of all outdoor recreation and education programs, one that would be unimaginable not to apply in our field.

At the center of LNT's success is the accessibility component—it's a collection of simple ideas that when combined create a practical roadmap anyone and any organization can adopt. Experts provided ideas, but it was the practitioners at the National Outdoor Leadership School (NOLS), Outward Bound, the US Forest Service, the National Park Service, and others that made it happen—it was the *individuals* in these organizations who championed the initial efforts. The program was not intended for scientists or experts in environmental science. It was intended for everyday users of outdoor spaces: outdoor guides, youth leaders, and family members. This open access and democratized use of knowledge is, in Karel's view, a key component of LNT's success. He often says, "Imagine if the environmental ethics work of LNT had been implemented from a top-down approach and done exclusively by the biologist, resource manager, or field scientist. I doubt it would be what it is today." There is an ownership aspect of the problem—by democratizing the solutions, individuals own the problems and thus take part in solving them.

Karel sees parallels between the DEI and environmental-ethics challenges. So far, most of the outdoor industry's DEI efforts have been left to the "experts." By experts, he means those individuals who have a professional or academic relationship to the topic of DEI, or BIPOC folks in our industry who, after much stress and immense personal burden, have stepped up to engage in these difficult conversations. These individuals deserve to be acknowledged as incredible groundbreakers! Yet, as with environmental ethics, a top-down approach led by experts will have only a limited impact.

Karel developed the "Seven Principles of DEI for the Outdoor Professional" to be used much like the "Seven Principles of Leave No Trace" (see chapter 6). This means anyone who interacts with the scheme can reach the same general understanding of the DEI challenge, gain a base-level knowledge, and take steps that lead to meaningful change in their practice. Anyone can teach it forward. His aspiration is to democratize the role of DEI educators and changemakers in the outdoors.

The Seven Principles of DEI in the Outdoors

The Seven Principles "scheme" is intended to serve as a baseline curriculum for outdoor instructors on the topic of DEI. Hopefully, it will be used in a similar way as the Seven Principles of Leave no Trace. This means anyone can reach the same general understanding of the DEI challenge, gain a base level of knowledge, and take steps that lead to meaningful change in their practice. Even more, anyone can teach it forward. The goal is to democratize the role of DEI educator and change maker in the outdoors.

1. Acknowledge the differences.
2. Explore your identity.
3. Expand your knowledge.
4. Uncover assumptions and biases.
5. Connect with others on a similar journey.
6. Invite, include, and involve those who are not present.
7. Transform your practice and commit to change.
8. BONUS: Celebrate your success!

The basic belief behind this scheme is that you do not need to be a DEI expert to be a DEI change agent and a supportive outdoor leader. In other words, all of us can help lead DEI initiatives, and all of us are responsible for building a more inclusive outdoor industry. These seven principles are the start of a larger, lifelong conversation. We might modify them along the way as we keep on learning, but we need to start somewhere. So here we go.

PRINCIPLE #1: ACKNOWLEDGE THE DIFFERENCES

Although we all experience life and the outdoors in different ways, this fact is not consistently portrayed or understood. The pictures in magazines, books, movies, and on social media reflect a predominantly white, able-bodied, fit, young, epic, and affluent point of view. Yet this is not the full story of everyone who recreates in and enjoys the outdoors, and it is a disservice to exclude marginalized and underrepresented outdoor enthusiasts. For someone to choose to learn more or experience something they've not yet tried, it is important for them to see themselves as able and included. They need role models. Many people literally don't see others like them outside. Why take a chance on the unknown when there is such a long legacy of painful, divisive, and horrific experiences for nonwhite individuals in wild places?

I went to camp as a child and was fortunate to experience the awe and wonder of both nature and wildness. In college, I discovered NOLS, and thought that if I wanted to become an outdoor educator, going to NOLS was the only path. After being rejected by the NOLS instructor course many times, I finally got in. The NOLS experience, while foundational, certainly made it difficult for me to be open to other approaches to outdoor education. I perceived there was just one way to do it—the NOLS way.

I camped as a child, I had access to wild places, and I was outdoors a lot. My memories teem with images of far-off national parks, buffalo plaid flannel, huge bonfires, and beautiful sunsets. But what if that is not how other people were introduced to being outside? Maybe their experiences are of family celebrations or spiritual events. And what if time "away" in remote places sparks more unease than peace? Why would people pay to experience a lack of electricity, running water, or toilets—all seemingly uncivilized—when some of these things are not consistently accessible at home?

If we can't imagine that there are different, equally valid ways to experience the outdoors, then we will very likely judge others and constantly force them to assimilate to our way of recreation, rather than embrace, welcome, accept, and amplify the way they recreate. This perpetuates the divide of who is, and who is not, invited into the outdoors.

Understanding that there are many ways to experience the outdoors frees us from our own frameworks and assumptions. It opens many possibilities. It also makes us more empathetic to situations that,

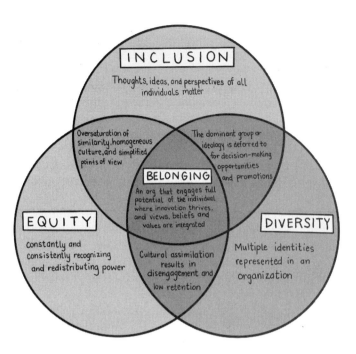

INCLUSION

Thoughts, ideas, and perspectives of all individuals matter

Oversaturation of similarity, homogeneous culture, and simplified points of view

The dominant group or ideology is deferred to for decision-making opportunities and promotions

BELONGING

An org that engages full potential of the individual where innovation thrives, and views, beliefs and values are integrated

EQUITY

constantly and consistently recognizing and redistributing power

Cultural assimilation results in disengagement and low retention

DIVERSITY

Multiple identities represented in an organization

though seemingly "fine" for me, are very wrong for others, such as what an Indigenous hiker might experience when visiting a national park, or the lived experience of a Latinx climber walking into a Cinco de Mayo "celebration" at a climbing gym where people are eating chips and salsa and white folks are wearing big sombreros. "Acknowledge the Differences" means making a genuine effort to understand the world you and others share.

There are many resources available to discover and appreciate other stories, perspectives, experiences, and opinions. Refer to the list of suggestions in the Appendix.

PRINCIPLE #2: EXPLORE YOUR IDENTITY

Consider how you appear to the world—your personal history, visibility, intersections with others, status, power, and privilege. I am white and female-identifying, and I have a dry sense of humor. I have some (but not all) of the answers. I am tall, intense, relentless when I want something, hardcore, and scared of the dark. I am a vegetarian who hates peppers and cucumbers. I am an athlete, a wife, a mom, and a daughter with three brothers. I use she/her/hers pronouns. My mom was born in Riga, Latvia, to my Russian grandparents. My mom was six when she immigrated to the United States on a boat. My dad's family is Scottish and Polish. I grew up in Grand Rapids, Michigan, and attended a public high school, which was primarily white and middle class.

Most expectations for me—my own and others'—have centered on achievement. High school was the springboard to college; I also had academic success and athletic scholarships that opened doors and set expectations for my behavior and became the lens I view life through. Without the burden of college loans and the pressure to make significant amounts of money each summer, I spent my summers out west as a rafting guide, a low-key, low-paying job. These formative experiences set me on a course of exploration into adventure leadership, but I can now see, in retrospect, that they were afforded to me only because I could afford them.

During my tenure as an outdoor professional, I have gained more understanding about the outdoor industry. When struggling through aspects of my career path and finding my voice as a female outdoor educator and executive director, I have navigated misogyny and other significant challenges in a male-dominated, "bro"-cultured space. I've often had to adopt masculine tendencies like competitiveness, the expressing of brazen opinions, and sarcasm to gain clout and acceptance. In essence, I have had to assimilate.

Based on my upbringing and often (mis)guided by my identity—not recognizing my many unconscious biases—I truly thought the way to have a more diverse outdoor industry was to offer more experiences like my own to more people. So, I looked to reduce barriers such as finances for programs or equipment. It took me more time and learning to see that the systemic structures, the same ones I benefit from, are the root cause for a past and ongoing lack of diversity in the outdoor industry—and to understand that people experience the outdoors in myriad ways that are unique and relevant and perfect to them, their culture, and their community.

I've tried to apply this learning in both my professional and personal work. One example is the Association of Outdoor Recreation and Education's (AORE) Virtual Inclusive Summit. AORE's membership demographic is primarily white and able-bodied, and I—like much of the membership—hold positions of privilege and power. We created the summit for our membership to become more aware *and* provide tools and resources to help members make their programs more inclusive. I'm not only proud of the content—two days that focus on outdoor pursuits such as wilderness medicine and climbing and a third day centered on human resources—delivered by industry leaders who share their perspective, expertise, and research, but also the format, which holds space for reflection and individual and group processing of the content. Additionally, we've worked to better understand the challenges of recruiting, supporting, compensating, and elevating our speakers by going beyond general calls for presentations (which restrict the content to a limited sphere), providing clear expectations and candid discussion about compensation, and asking presenters how we can best help them convey their lived experiences and perspectives. We have worked hard to encourage, and have almost implored, members to work on themselves, because the dominant narrative and structures have allowed me—and, in my opinion, many members—to bypass owning this learning and growing ourselves in ways that facilitate more equitable, diverse outdoor programs.

Exploring your own identity is an invitation to truly know yourself. To pause and reflect on what makes you you. What circumstances, labels, crucible moments, or transformative experiences inform your worldviews? It is also an invitation to realize that there is no one else exactly like you. Beware, though: exploring yourself also includes owning all those "ugly" things you and the different groups you belong to represent—power imbalances, privilege (or lack thereof), et cetera. The aim of this exploration is to come out of the process as a more unified and integrated self, one who can start making informed choices moving forward.

Lastly, a word about privilege. The concept of privilege has received a very bad rap, but this is largely due to misunderstanding it. In his work, Karel defines privilege as *the opportunity to act* (Hilversum, 2022). Privilege is value neutral; it is neither good nor bad. It is what we do with it that defines us. If after your exploration you identify parts of your identity that grant you some type of privilege, ask yourself this fundamental question: What am I doing with this privilege? The answer will inform your next steps.

PRINCIPLE #3: EXPAND YOUR KNOWLEDGE

Karel often says, "Those in the minority are not here to teach you anything." They are not responsible for helping you understand; you are responsible for your own growth. It is an intense experience to simultaneously be the recipient of discrimination, the advocate, and the teacher. Those burdens are too heavy to be carried by one person all at once. So expand your knowledge about the specific group you are trying to engage with, before you engage. In today's hyper-information age, there is no excuse not to come prepared with some baseline knowledge of how others experience life.

Learning diversity, equity, and inclusion is an ongoing process: to begin or continue your education of inclusivity, you'll need to learn the vocabulary, concepts, history, and ideas. These include studying DEI, JEDI (justice, equity, diversity, inclusion), and LGBTQIA+ identities (lesbian, gay, bisexual, transgender, queer, intersex, and asexual). Familiarize yourself with issues concerning disability and access. I've learned how, as a person with privilege and power (a white cis woman with no mobility limitations), I can easily continue to do damage to underrepresented and overlooked individuals, even as I attempt to make the outdoors more inclusive.

A good example of this was a misfire of mine at a conference social event when I asked a young person about the "they/them" pronouns on their name tag. At that point in my life, it was out of curiosity, and I am sure I said, "I want to learn," and then asked them to explain to me who "they/

them" referred to. Still, even after an explanation, I stumbled over their pronouns in our conversation and misgendered them at another point. I also recall saying something terrible like, "I am not used to this," though I did apologize—which, unfortunately, put this young person in a place to have to console *me*, rather than me just thanking them and noting I had much to learn.

Champions for Change

In my work as a nonprofit executive director in metro Detroit, I had the chance to attend what was then called Allies Academy, as part of the Nonprofit Enterprise at Work (NEW) Center's Champions for Change program. At that point, my understanding of the ongoing impacts of systemic racism was incredibly limited. Per their website, the tagline for the program is "Champions for Change inspires and cultivates leaders as we all work toward a co-liberated future. Together, we can find new ways to disrupt the many forms of racism. Here, Leaders of Color are nurtured and supported as they grow their social change work. White Leaders learn ways to wholeheartedly leverage their power and privilege for justice." For more than six months, I met with other white leaders and followed a curriculum of readings, conversations, and local events.

There was and is so much to learn from this program. What I can most easily share is the late awareness I gained that even my nonprofit had been structured and continued to operate in a way that relied on biased, racist, and inequitable systems and structures. The seemingly positive DEI changes that the board and I were making were just treating symptoms, not addressing the core issues. AORE, as an association, as well as the volunteer and paid individuals who guide the association, has since stepped back to evaluate and reconcile our role(s) in perpetuating and dismantling the systems of oppression within our association and industry. We have been working toward greater diversity, equity, and inclusion both internally, as an organization, and externally—in how our members can facilitate change in their own programs and practices. Inside AORE, we have worked to promote involvement, innovation, and expanded access to leadership opportunities that maximize engagement across identity groups and levels of professional experience. Outside our association, we are advocating on diversity-related public-policy issues that affect AORE member programs' operations. We provide tools and resources to cultivate a culture of inclusiveness, collaborative practice, and innovation in the fields of outdoor recreation and education.

It has been some time since this incident, and I have come to realize, with additional learning and work, that understanding gender, for me and for anyone, is a continuous process. I will continue to meet individuals who are on a continuum on their evolution—some who confidently express their full selves, and others who are newer to that process. Regardless, I too need to continually work on my understanding and work alongside anyone I meet and interact with to see them as they are. I have attended many professional-development training courses on bias and have encouraged my board of directors to work with DEI consultants. While these have all been positive learning experiences, they have also, upon reflection, been siloed—like learning how to tie knots in a class, where you can easily master the figure eight or bowline or trucker's hitch when tying it around your leg with P-cord, but when it comes time to use that knot to set up your tent's guyline in the rain, you find out you're rusty and incompetent.

PRINCIPLE #4: UNCOVER ASSUMPTIONS AND BIASES

While I was having a conversation with Karel at an AORE conference on the topic of personal bias, he told me, "Remember, you are not responsible for your first thought. Those are too deep for you to have control over. You are, however, responsible for your second thought and for your first action." The idea behind this, he said, is that biases are mental shortcuts we have developed over time so we can quickly assess a situation and come to a fast decision. Some of these shortcuts have served us well in the past, thus we find some usefulness to them. But, at times, the automatic response does not conform with the experience. These are the biases. Freeing yourself from the guilt of that first thought is liberating. He makes the point that we can give ourselves some grace when these biases arise. The critical question is what to do once you identify a bias. As an example, he shared the following story.

A few years ago, Karel's organization was working with a group of 150 BIPOC college students on a multi-activity day that included hiking, climbing, challenge courses, and canoeing. As the students approached the instructor team at the beginning of the day, he heard one of his senior instructors say, "These people don't care for the outdoors." The comment struck him as disturbing, especially right before the instructor was about to take a group of twelve of these students on a day hike. He turned to the instructor and said, "Really? Well maybe they need a great outdoor educator to make them fall in love with the outdoors. Are you that educator?" The instructor immediately realized the depth of his bias. To say that he felt horrible is an understatement. That day, the instructor decided to replace his biased thought with a more empowering one; acting on it, he facilitated a wonderful hike with the group, introducing his students to the outdoors.

Uncovering assumptions and biases is a lifelong process and one that requires reinforcement over time. We all see the world through our own lenses and hold our own worldviews, values, and norms—we read books, listen to podcasts, and donate to causes and nonprofits that confirm our beliefs. We all need to check the mental shortcuts we're taking that might conflict with the experiences we're involved with. In this way, we open new possibilities for a more meaningful life.

At a board retreat, we did an exercise in which we stood in a circle as a facilitator read off questions, things like: What was your highest level of school? Are your parents divorced or separated? Do you have a car? There were also questions about food scarcity, disabilities, homelessness, and sexual orientation.

"Thank You"

"Thank you." These two words can take a very long time to say when it's brought to your attention that you have offended someone or been prejudiced or discriminatory in your actions or words. *Thank you.* It is hard not to be defensive, to try to explain, or to ask for forgiveness—no matter how you identify. Of course, you did not intend to harm someone, but the effects of your words or actions can last. Change begins when you take ownership of your impact, and it all begins with these two simple words.

Then the facilitator would read off answers, and any individuals who identified with an answer were asked, if they so choose, to step into the center of the circle. We would then reset the circle for a new question. Colleagues participated who had volunteered together for years, but as people moved in and out of the circle, it became clear that we did not all come from the same place and perspective, even though we might have assumed otherwise.

These assumptions and inherent biases are pervasive in how leaders speak and how they address and lead themselves and others. Things once seen can't be unseen: who are we to assume the abilities of our participants and what they can or can't do based on visible or assumed disabilities? Are we really making preventative safety or risk deci-sions when we choose easier hiking routes on which to take kids, older people, or heavyset participants? Or have we been biased and judgmental of their capabilities? When we share examples of gear we own and places we've adventured to—or hope to visit—are we understanding of those who can't afford these things or have not been exposed to them, perhaps because they lack the disposable time or access to read about new gear and travel? If we are to lead well, we need to constantly be asking ourselves questions like these, to uncover our hidden biases.

PRINCIPLE #5: CONNECT WITH OTHERS ON A SIMILAR JOURNEY

DEI is a collective and longitudinal endeavor, one that requires tireless awareness and perpetual advocacy. It is not a list of things to do or a statement to recite, but an ongoing journey that everyone must travel for themselves as well as with others. In the outdoor industry, various organizations, both new and established, are tackling DEI head-on and range widely in their focus, from meeting the needs of identi-fied communities or issues, to supporting specific adventure sports, to addressing environmental concerns.

Affinity Spaces

Affinity spaces are places (whether physical or virtual) where people of similar identities come together to connect and build community, share resources, and discuss ideas. Many of these transformative spaces have been established in the outdoor industry, as well as inside organizations and businesses. Moreover, anyone can join or create an affinity space.

Why would you want to join or create an affinity space?

- It's a chance to meet other people with whom you identify—who have a similar background, experience, or understanding.
- You'll have a role in a bigger community. Engaging with others outside your current work or volunteer sphere will allow you to contribute to and participate in something greater than your immediate world.
- It's a collection of resources and tools—information sharing gives you access to materials or assets that can help support the full individual.
- You'll help bring forward amplifying voices and perspectives that may otherwise not be heard.
- The ability to acknowledge and name challenges together validates and supports our growth, making us feel seen and valued.

Creating a space for individuals to meet can sometimes feel like a threat to leaders, in the form of slowed momentum or a challenge to the current operations and hierarchies. Affinity work can also take incredible capacity—of both finances and time.

There may also be pushback. Many individuals have been and continue to be hurt, overworked, objectified, overlooked, underpaid, and undervalued, and as a result they may have limited trust for others, specifically the dominant culture (white) that's attempting to support them. Therefore, it is important for would-be changemakers to recruit others for this journey. Check out the Appendix for a list of some existing affinity spaces.

In addition to supporting these organizations and businesses financially, there are other ways to become involved:

Follow and interact with organizations on social media. Seeing and participating with brands and entities on social media platforms allows you to develop a greater understanding of the variety, interest, and capacity of others doing DEI work.

Volunteer, assist, and support in person. Look for events or other offerings to give your time and talent to annually or episodically. There are a lot of national and regional events—both in person and virtual—that need volunteer support.

Donate gear and supplies. Volunteer outdoor organizations always need new or replacement gear; not having to sink all of their budget into it frees up money they can spend advancing the work. So donate usable gear and supplies—or your time and expertise to maintaining and repairing this gear.

Donate funds. Support causes, groups, and activities financially to further the resources—and therefore reach—of their work.

Spread the word and share the mission. You can have a meaningful influence by bringing sincere attention to the causes and work that align with your values—this ambassadorship can be a crucial way to support those doing DEI work.

PRINCIPLE #6: INVITE, INCLUDE, AND INVOLVE THOSE WHO ARE NOT PRESENT

The Invite, Include, Involve principle builds on the work done by Deborah J. Chavez (2000) and others at the US Forest Service. It is often called the "I" triad because each component—invite, include, and involve—builds on and informs the others.

To *invite* means to reach out and open up to others—to consciously expand participation by communities that have traditionally not been present in your programs, or at the very least to ensure that the way you present yourself isn't discouraging their participation. It requires self-reflection and organizational assessment. Action items may include revising marketing materials or images, literature, language, and messages. However, many organizations will invest substantial time and resources only to see no significant changes in participation. We all know them: they look the part, they rebrand, but at the core they are still the same. This is often because inviting is just the start—you often need to go further.

Include dives deeper. It requires you to seek feedback and solicit ideas and perspectives; it allows you to be influenced by others. It also requires you to listen more than you speak. To include means to add a community to your stakeholder groups, to share your annual program for review and comments, and to celebrate and observe community events. People feel included when they can see a reflection of who they are in your organization.

The last triad point is to *involve*. Very few organizations or groups have reached this point because it requires sharing power with others, transcending the merely superficial, rhetorical, or symbolic. An organization that involves will do things like add community members to roles that have decision-making power, such as serving on a board of directors or an action committee or hiring for managerial roles. That same organization will also properly support and allow these perspectives to be implemented. It is a transformational moment when, for example, you hire a person of color to lead your outdoor organization. Involving often comes with tension and struggle. Let's not be naive—most people don't like giving up their power, privilege, and control, and will at times resist letting others get involved.

Lastly, most people will see the "I" triad as a sequential progression of first invite, then include, and finally involve. However, you can start at any point of the triad and build from where you are. Some would argue that real change is only achieved if you start by involving first, since it is easier to enact the other points of the triad if you control power and leverage. Whatever way you do it, one thing is clear: to truly transform your organization, you need to take massive action at each triad point.

When we think about the history of the outdoors—recreation, education, wild spaces, adventure—the stories have been about exclusion rather than inclusion, exploitation rather than involvement. Yet as social beings, we all desire connection and community—we often feel at our best when working with others, together, both in celebration and struggle. That's why it's so important to reach out and invite others to participate, particularly those individuals who may not yet have had the chance to experience the outdoors, or even those who have recreated but not regularly.

Individuals rarely try something new without being exposed to it first by someone they trust, or unless they see themselves represented in the activity. And they certainly won't become involved if they don't see themselves represented in outdoor brands and organizations. That's why it's critical that the messaging on websites and social media be inviting to everyone, regardless of their race, gender identity, age, or mobility.

Once an adventure is agreed on, there are many facets to inclusion, none of which should be be left to chance. Including others means deliberately asking for, being open to hearing, and acting upon input, folding these considerations into your systems regarding packing lists, meal planning, sleeping arrangements, et cetera. What are other opinions on the activity, the gear and food, the location, and the duration of the trip? Is there a need to consider specific dietary preferences, provide single-gender tents, and allow for daily prayer or observance of religious holidays? A leader may have expertise within a certain skill set (such as climbing or hiking) but will still need to make accommodations that encourage others to participate.

Involving others means finding ways to foster DEI, specifically including these voices on boards and committees, as trip leaders, and in training and management programs, and then hearing and acting on what they have to say. This stands in stark contrast to assimilation, which is the act of inviting others to participate but then requiring they look and act like the dominant group. Assimilation is not an effective way to build a more inclusive outdoor industry; moreover, leaning on the familiar and on current systemic structures at the expense of considering new, more engaging ways to lead that spring from other perspectives does us all a disservice.

PRINCIPLE #7: TRANSFORM YOUR PRACTICE AND COMMIT TO CHANGE

To work successfully on DEI, we need to be open, forgiving, tolerant of mistakes, gracious, patient, and growth minded. We need to commit to changing as much as needed. There will be lessons and deepening understandings and feelings of pride and guilt. There will be missed opportunities, conflicts, and candid and maybe uncomfortable conversations. Success will not be arrived at by achieving a certain number of participants, sales goals, or social media followers but in overcoming bias, to the extent possible, to have greater diversity, equity, and inclusion so anybody (and everybody) can be outside, if they so choose.

Strategy, Connection, and Grace

ELYSE RYLANDER

My journey began on a warm summer morning in early July 1990. My folks loaded up their cedar-strip canoe and shoved off the sandy banks of the southern Wisconsin River with four-week-old me "secured" in an infant life jacket while my mom held me. This scene was to be repeated over and over again in the following years, and while I grew (and our family added one more), that change ran parallel with the ever-evolving landscape along the river and in my own life.

The profound luck I've had being born into a family that placed such value on time spent outside has never escaped me. When I was a child, the trails on my parents' property, the public lands and creeks that surrounded it, the rivers and warm lakes of the North Woods, and the runs down the local ski hill etched lines on the maps and in my life. On those trails, I learned life's most important lessons. I learned how to follow rules and how to break them; how to trust in myself and trust in others; how to take care and time for myself and the world around me; how to build and sustain community; and maybe, most importantly, that sometimes it takes two little girls and a full cooler to properly weight down the bow of a canoe in the face of strong headwinds.

Those experiences propelled me into the outdoor industry at age sixteen. Working first as a "junior leader" and then youth and adult instructor, I honed my canoeing and kayak skills, learned how to work with people, and for the first time in my life met a handful of other Queer women.

Growing up in a conservative town, I hadn't experienced a culture that supported diversity in thought, way of life, or identity. Keeping my Queer identity hidden seemed paramount in order to avoid social ostracization. So, when I found myself leading paddling classes alongside strong and confident Queer women while more fully coming to terms with my own identity, it all started to come together for me. The confidence and support I was able to build leading those paddling classes aided in my decision to step out of the closet and into the sun, as an openly Queer woman, when I was eighteen.

Later, after I'd spent a handful of years wearing the hats of outdoor educator, instructor, and rental tech, it became difficult to ignore the ways in which my journey, both outside and in, looked so different from those of others in my Queer community. This intersection inspired me to found OUT There Adventures (OTA), one of the first outdoor-education nonprofits created to work specifically with LGBTQ teens and young adults. This work also paved the way for the LGBTQ Outdoor Summit, a now-annual event that gathers LGBTQ folks and allies to further the conversation about how we can continue to [re]create more equitable and just experiences OUTside.

While I could review the data points of this work, what has been most important to me is hearing the stories of the teens who get OUT there with us every summer. I love nothing more than watching participants find their path in the industry, or receiving post-course emails from parents accrediting our trips with their child's newfound confidence and happiness.

As Queer folks, we exist in a world that bombards us daily with implicit and explicit messages that we are "unnatural." In truth, you could substitute "Queer" for any number of other communities who have been systematically disinvested in for hundreds if not thousands of years. Looking forward, it is imperative for those of us living in these margins and at the intersections thereof to keep this common thread top of mind, as the times require us to continuously evolve our movement for inclusion at every level of society (including outdoor spaces) with ever more strategy, connection, and grace. It is critical that we continue to ground ourselves and our movements for social change in our connection to not only each other but also with the natural world, which, no matter who you are, is one of the greatest healers of all.

Elyse Rylander (she/her) has spent her career wearing many hats in the Outdoor Recreation Economy. She is guided by her dedication to creating full and dignified experiences for all individuals and care for our external and internal landscapes. She never tires of seeing sunsets over mountains reflected on the water.

ACTIONABLE WAYS TO FURTHER LEADERSHIP

You may already incorporate inclusive practices into your leadership style, and some of those practices have probably evolved since you first began leading. Now is a good time to review those practices you already use and learn about those you don't.

An invitation to share. At the start of any group activity, expedition or training, invite the participants to share anything that feels relevant for the group to know and that will allow them to be seen authentically. This could include things like pronouns, acknowledgment of physical or emotional states, and recognition of minority status in the group (e.g. only woman, only Black person, etc.).

Integrate land acknowledgments. Land acknowledgments help you ensure that Indigenous people are not thought of only historically, but also as thriving in the here and now. So research whose land you are recreating on, and consider how you are supporting, advocating for, and understanding native populations in the present day. Words are nice, but actions create change. Ways you can act include supporting Indigenous organizations with your time and money, compensating individuals for their emotional labor, supporting grassroots campaigns, and committing to returning land.

Create a DEI strategic plan. Similar to a budget, program strategy, or marketing plan, it's critical that your organization possesses an understanding of the specific actions you are taking to evolve your DEI work. The most effective of these plans run for more than one but less than five years, span every facet of the organization, and make clear the specific role *every* person plays in bringing it to life.

Review organizational processes for creating opportunities. Applications, recruiting, interviewing, hiring, bylaws, compensation, position descriptions, training, succession planning, and advancement are just a few areas and practices that a diverse group of people should review and assess. This group needs to examine and explore barriers (and solutions) and engagement (invitation and inclusion), amplifying any issues that need to be addressed.

BUILDING A MORE INCLUSIVE OUTDOOR INDUSTRY

Outdoor recreation is an economic powerhouse in the United States. The US Department of Commerce's Bureau of Economic Analysis (BEA) has released economic data for 2021, detailing outdoor recreation's powerful and positive economic impact on the country's economy. Per the BEA's data, outdoor recreation generates $862 billion in economic output and accounts for 4.5 million jobs. This means outdoor recreation contributes more to the US economy than oil, gas, and mining combined. The report includes national- and state-level data.

The 2021 "Outdoor Participation Trends Report," which is commissioned by the Outdoor Foundation (OF), found that 53 percent of Americans over age six participated in outdoor recreation at least once in

Outdoor Organizations Advancing Access

Many outdoor organizations, including AORE, are evolving their DEI understanding and practices. Meanwhile, new nonprofits (and for-profits) are emerging throughout the country to address this important work. These organizations may be sport specific, mobility and ability specific, affinity group–based, or issue specific. The following list is not exhaustive, but it offers a starting point:

- Access 2 Parks Project
- American Alpine Club
- Association of Outdoor Recreation and Education
- Brown Girls Climb
- CAMBER
- Child an Nature Network
- Conservation Alliance
- Green Muslims
- Greening Youth Foundation
- Indigenous Women Hike
- Latino Outdoors
- National Park Service (for US residents with disabilities, the America the Beautiful and National Parks & Federal Recreational Lands passes)
- Native Women's Wilderness
- Natives Outdoors
- OUT There Adventures
- Outdoor Afro
- Outdoor Alliance for Kids
- Outdoor Asian
- Outdoors for All (adaptive and therapeutic recreation for children and adults with disabilities)
- Paradox Sports
- Pride Outside
- SheJumps
- Society of Outdoor Recreation Professionals
- Together Outdoors
- Veteran Outdoor Alliance
- YMCA Bold & Gold

2020—the highest participation rate on record. These activities included hunting, hiking, camping, fishing, and canoeing. Remarkably, 7.1 million more Americans participated in outdoor recreation in 2020 than in 2019. Unfortunately, the report highlights an alarming trend: that just under half the US population does not participate in outdoor recreation at all. The OF's 2022 "Outdoor Participation Trends Report" shows that "despite slight increases in diversity across outdoor recreation, the current participant base is less diverse than the overall population and significantly less diverse across younger age groups." And that "Currently 72% of outdoor recreation participants are white. If the outdoor participant base does not become more diverse over the next thirty years, the percentage of outdoor recreation participants in the population could slip from 54% today to under 40% by 2060." These numbers indicate there is opportunity for more people—and especially more diverse people—to engage in outdoor pursuits.

It's essential that outdoor spaces are inclusive and that every American can feel a sense of belonging when they venture outside. This has not been, and currently is not, the case, so it is important that we outdoor leaders continue to understand the barriers, systemic biases, racism, and cultural as well as historical discrimination that have permeated outdoor spaces. You do not need to be a DEI expert to be a DEI change agent and supportive outdoor leader. Leaders choose to lead, and anyone can lead DEI initiatives. All leaders in this space are responsible for building a more inclusive outdoor industry, no matter how or at what pace they choose to do so. It takes courage to do this work, and there will be mistakes and mishandling. That does not mean the work should stop, but that as a leader, you must find people and resources that give you the strength and space to learn and go on. (On a related note, overcoming financial barriers, while an important component of creating a diverse outdoor industry, is not the only obstacle; in fact, claiming that funding is *the* barrier to change removes our roles as change agents and allows us to deflect our leadership.)

Making the outdoors more inclusive is not an all-or-nothing activity. Just like the many steps it takes to hike a path or the strokes necessary to push away from shore, we need to take an ongoing approach to make sure everyone can access trails and float the waters.

TAKEAWAYS

- Acknowledge the differences. We all experience life and the outdoors in different ways.
- Explore your identity, including becoming aware of visibility, intersections, status, power, and privilege.
- Take responsibility for expanding your knowledge. Be curious and learn new-to-you vocabulary, terms, concepts, history, and ideas.

- Uncover your assumptions and biases. Assess your lenses, world-views, values, and norms.
- Connect with others who are on a similar journey. After all, DEI is a collective endeavor.
- Foster belonging and inclusion by inviting, including, and involving those who have not to date been present.
- Transform your practice. Commit to change, and then change as much as you can.

THIRSTY FOR **MORE?**

At the start of any group activity, expedition, or training, tell your pronouns and invite others to share theirs. It's a tremendous way to learn how others prefer to be included and referenced.

How does the presence or absence of privilege show up in the way you lead?

Land acknowledgment is an important practice that respects Indigenous people and the lands they steward. Research whose land you are recreating on. Take it one step further and communicate this with your staff and trip participants.

If you lead an organization, become familiar with its DEI statement and actively support its work in your practice. If your organization does not yet have a DEI statement, champion for its development and implementation. You can find resources through many nonprofit outdoor associations listed in the Appendix.

Review organizational processes and procedures for creating opportunities, with an eye toward implementing better DEI practices, including in areas like applications, recruiting, interviewing, hiring, bylaws, compensation, position descriptions, training, succession planning, and advancement.

Create and maintain an advisory group or leadership team that continuously examines and explores barriers (and solutions) and engagement (invitation and inclusion) where you lead.

Think about who you do not include when you lead. Whom are you alienating with your choices? According to the CDC, one in four adults in the United States has some type of disability. Do your leadership practices welcome people of all abilities?

CHAPTER 5
RESILIENCE AND GRIT

Fortitude, perseverance, and commitment require resilience and grit, and great leaders embody these qualities in spades. A great leader will gracefully handle the unforeseen situations, elements, and interpersonal issues that inevitably arise in the outdoors. A key understanding in these scenarios is differentiating an approach of "being tough" or "outlasting" challenging situations and people from establishing boundaries and cultivating tolerance and reflection. This chapter explores the many ways leaders can hone grit to build capacity and resilience.

THE EVER-PRESENT POTENTIAL FOR FAILURE

A close friend once told me that they'd observed my preoccupation with doing big things and challenging the status quo. I am not always aware of the potential to "fail big" when I take on challenging initiatives—things like a new way of connecting people, opening conversations between insulated service providers, or insisting on payment rather than product for sponsorship. Indeed, as a visionary person, I don't usually get mired in the details. Instead, I focus on the possibilities.

In pursuing bigger things in my work, I receive a lot of "no" and pushback. This takes a heavy toll on me personally because I think if I could have just been better, worked harder, or known more, I would have achieved the desired outcome. Fortunately, I have a strong support group that helps me pick myself up, and who help protect and care for me so I can take on these big things. In fact, that same friend commented that every time I am knocked down, set back, or told no, I consistently get back up—and for this I can thank my support network.

Leading a national nonprofit through the pandemic has provided a lot of time to navigate "no." Ironically, when the world stopped, people went outdoors. However, with health and safety precautions enacted nationwide, colleges and universities went remote, outdoor programs were unable to transport participants in vehicles, and many programs were furloughed. Professional development and trade-show budgets were reduced or removed. Anticipating significant reduction in our conference revenue (which comprises 80 percent of our association's annual revenue), we modified our forecasts accordingly. We looked to reduce expenses where we could but were unable to extricate ourselves from our hotel and venue contracts. The result was the biggest failure that I've experienced recently; the conference financially tanked, despite our trying new programming and even pricing packages, and we did not meet our budget.

Fortunately, my board and I had a fiscal contingency in place and were able to weather this setback. We have also tried to learn from this experience and use it to inform future event planning, in order to be relevant, accessible, and add enough value for attendees to participate. As a result, we are trying a new co-location model that places my association with a complementary industry, to offer both expanded education content and efficiency at scale.

Control What You Can and Release the Rest

I really don't like falling into the river when whitewater rafting; I take absolutely no joy in it. I can't stand it when the guide takes a wrong line on purpose to flip a raft, or thinks it is a good idea to try tricks like a highside—when everyone in the raft rushes to the higher part of the raft so it won't wrap around a rock or flip—for fun and not out of necessity. I'm a strong swimmer, I have been a raft guide, and I spend a lot of my time in and around water. But I hate being *in* the river when I'm not supposed to be there.

I've long wondered why I feel this way. Perhaps it's my fear of not being able to get back in the boat, or because I feel awkward about my height and body size and lack of upper-body strength. Or perhaps it's knowing how difficult it is to fight the water, a fear amplified by such terrifying nomenclature for river hazards as "strainers" and "washing machine" rapids. But mostly I think it's because I hate giving up control, and on rivers, the standard advice when you're dumped out of the boat is to not fight the forces and hydraulics but rather relax and let the water take you and release you downstream.

I like doing things outside because I feel free and alive, and I marvel at nature. On the one hand, I like how everything is seemingly in order, in its own way, but on the other I also realize just how random, uncaring, and chaotic nature can be. Thus as an outdoor leader and participant, it falls on me to balance my own need for control with the realization that I will never be able to control everything—like on a raging river. So how do *you* balance your own need for control with the reality of nature when recreating in the outdoors? How do *you* find that sweet spot where you're prepared for every eventuality but, when you need to, you "relax, let the water pull you under, and let it spit you out downstream"?

OVERCOMING A CRUSHING BLOW TO SELF-CONFIDENCE

One of my most challenging outdoor-leadership experiences occurred when I led a high school trail crew for the Student Conservation Association (SCA), living and working in the backcountry of Great Smoky Mountains National Park for five weeks with someone I unfortunately did not get along with. The experience was crushing to my self-confidence, and not being able to find common ground with my co-leader and knowing that he did not like me affected my ability to lead.

I was initially excited (and nervous) about leading six high schoolers on this project. It was my first time doing conservation trail work. Following a training on conservation-work skills in New Hampshire, during which we covered policies and procedures, I was proficient in handling a Pulaski (a special wildfire-fighting tool with an axe and an adze on one head), had broken in my Red Wing boots, and had a rudimentary understanding of trail construction, including tread and drainage. After the training, the leaders-in-training were assigned their co-leaders and their conservation project, and then we all had a couple months to coordinate our outings. There were many things to organize: working with the national park, selecting and communicating with the crew applicants, and managing the gear, food, and logistics. It was our responsibility to communicate with our agency partner, do a pre-site visit, and organize a weeklong recreation adventure at the end of our service.

The premise of the program was, as the SCA motto states, "changing lives through service to nature." By doing some of the backlogged work in forests and parks, the program both helped the partner agency and offered a chance for leadership development for the participants—and leaders.

For a month, my group lived near the Walnut Bottoms area, a five-mile hike from the trailhead. Our task was to build dips to help drain water off a stretch of the Swallow Fork Trail. This is both horse and hiker area, and has heavy annual rainfall. As a group of eight living in the backcountry for five weeks, we didn't want to attract bears, so we used a bear chandelier— an impressive device used to hoist our food, with a pulley system. Horses packed in our food, and we stored our rations in fifteen-gallon buckets attached by a carabiner to the chandelier. Together, we'd hoist and lower the food. It was team-building at its finest.

When the Sh*t Hits the Fan

I don't recall when my co-leader—Shane—and I stopped getting along. I may have caused the rift just as he could have created it, but regardless, our amiability toward each other was strained. Living and working in such a remote location, we were responsible for the participants, and a lot of care was required to support the physical and emotional needs of this work. So we kept our professional front solid for the students, even as trivial things like managing the cooking and cleanup became games of avoidance. Our duty was to build and live as a community, do physically grueling work, and be in service to the park. We quickly settled into our patterns and backcountry lives—working and taking our breaks, reading about the local area, and sharing our personal stories and journeys. It was a hard, but good, month. However, our animosity toward each other came to a head when we wrapped up the program: it is hard to work with someone you simply can't tolerate.

Having finished our work and the recreational leg of the trip, we drove two NPS vehicles to the airport to drop off the students. At the airport, Shane accidentally locked his keys in his vehicle, and the other set was back at the ranger station—two hours away. We had a lot of work to do in the coming days, so time seemed tight, but I verbally objected to Shane's solution of breaking a window to get the keys—which he did— rather than making the drive back to the ranger station for the spare set. Shane also wanted to hike back into our site to remove the bear chandelier that the park service had constructed for our extended stay. Still, Shane prevailed, and we drove back to the trailhead and hiked back to the campsite to remove anything we had built, including the bear chandelier. I walked behind Shane the five miles in, and we arrived at the camp later than I would have liked. I didn't have any experience gaffing up trees, removing taut cables, or deconstructing a pulley system thirty feet above the ground. Shane had never done these things either, but when we arrived at the site, he whipped out the tree-climbing spurs—gaffs—and started climbing. *What an idiot,* I thought. I stood there watching as he moved up the first tree. About three feet up, a strap broke. In a way, it was a relief—at least I wouldn't have to administer first aid after a longer fall. Realizing that he would not be able to ascend to the chandelier in order to take it apart, Shane hastily packed up. We took the items we could easily remove and carry, and then hiked the five miles back out, not speaking the whole way. After we completed and turned in our course paperwork, our experience—and our relationship— was finished.

Being in a hostile environment with no ability—only my attitude—to change the circumstances was one of the hardest things I've experienced.

I don't like tension, and I don't like feeling that I've failed. Being in a hostile environment with no ability—only my attitude—to change the circumstances was one of the hardest things I've experienced. My focus was on the students and on the project for the agency—and, I'm sure, on not letting my broken dynamic with Shane affect my responsibility to the students or their experience on the trip. I can't even say if I succeeded at the latter; perhaps the students saw through the veneer and made peace with our quiet drama. In any case, I'm certain that it was my grit—my inherent stubbornness—that got me through those five weeks, especially as things started to unravel at the end.

Discovering Strength

HANNAH MALVIN

The outdoors can be a great place to discover strength you didn't know you had. Leading canoe trips in Canada, I found new gears as my campers and I pushed ourselves paddling and portaging our way through the elements, hurling ourselves forward through roaring winds, blaring sun, piercing rain, and dogged mosquitos, then waking up the next day and somehow doing it again. We'd maneuver through complex terrain from deadfalls, trudge through mud pits, and then tackle whatever was around the next corner. This is where I started to learn to suspend doubts, to trust my body, my creativity, and my willpower.

The strength I uncovered on these trips was then available to me back in my life in the city. I took stock of this strength and recalibrated what was possible, and I carried it forward in athletics and activism.

The interesting part I'm still figuring out is when and where to apply that strength. I've learned that just because you have the strength to take on a challenge or obstacle, doesn't mean you have to. For example, I was asked to take on a demanding leadership role at a time when I had limited bandwidth. It was important for me to recognize that just because it was an exciting challenge didn't mean I had to do it. As you discover the far reaches of your strength, you get to determine where and when to apply it.

Hannah Malvin is a coach and consultant building workplace culture rooted in equity and well-being. She manages The Bridge Program, an equitable hiring pathway for the environmental sector focused on people of color and underrepresented communities. In 2016, she founded Pride Outside to boost representation and inclusion for the LGBTQ community outdoors.

"OUTLASTING" VERSUS "TOUGHING IT OUT"

When we face challenges, we tend to rely on our gumption and confidence to get us through. And while many of these issues will resolve quickly, in other cases they may seem intractable and not worth the work. Regardless, I like to take an approach of "outlasting" the problem, in which I take everyone's needs into account and then craft a sustainable, long-term solution that relies on resilience. A perfect example would be hiking in the rain.

Toughness Versus Resilience

In my mind, *toughness* has connotations of physically enduring some challenge. I am not the one to say who is or isn't tough—summiting a peak or hiking to camp in record time is not always the right goal. As leaders, we want to open people's minds to choose something they otherwise may not have tried before, but not to an extent that it would harm themselves, others, or the environment.

Toughness can be a destructive word if it sets a precedent an individual or the group feels obligated to follow during an outdoor experience. "Tough" might be someone who hiked with blistered feet or someone who bivouacked without a shelter. I'm not impressed by being "tough" like that because these situations are 100 percent preventable with proper planning, for example having broken-in boots and socks that eliminate friction and stopping to attend to hot spots with a first-aid kid; or bringing shelter and the right layers, and not getting separated from the group (not making it to the campsite).

Resilience, on the other hand, is a word I use to describe someone who has endured, or can endure, a challenging situation without putting others, themselves, or the environment at risk. Applying the lessons learned from a challenging situation to future situations is what resilience is all about. It is the capacity to grow from and learn from your experiences. Think about all the things you have worked on, or worked through, to improve yourself or create more opportunities for those around you. And think about the times you've worked passionately to help, most likely giving yourself fully, exhausting your stamina and resources all while being tempted to walk away.

You, and those you lead, are more mentally and emotionally resilient than you may first realize in a stressful situation. When we are near technology and creature comforts, we can spend more time avoiding issues than addressing them, but out in the field we find we have deeper reservoirs than we ever imagined. Understanding the gravity of the situation and what will be required to move through it can help pace and give you perspective as you, or those you lead, tap into their resilience.

Look, it is not ideal, and wet feet can become uncomfortable. However, if you have the right socks and shoes, and the ability to dry your feet and take good foot care that night and create a shelter for sleep, you can continue, one soggy step at a time. To me, this is a much better approach than merely "toughing it out"—suffering with inadequate socks and footwear, hoping the problem will somehow magically go away.

You are stronger than you think you are. This sounds like an inspirational refrigerator magnet or meme, but in times of trial—bad weather, personality clashes, dealing with a tired body—I've found that it's true. As I think about resilience and grit, it's hard to separate what is both ingrained in my behavior and idolized in most outdoor writings and media. That's the exact reason we should explore this concept further: What do resilience and grit mean to you? How do these concepts change over time? How do they fit in with your own leadership style?

You are stronger than you think you are.

In chapter 1, I talked about the continuum of care and commitment. Destructive leadership is the quadrant of high commitment and low self-care. In this vein, when people are pitted against the outdoors, the storylines often teem with buzzwords that sound like the superlatives in a muscle-enlarging commercial—#winning, #bigger, #conquest. These near-miss exploits sell the message of toughness— along with the continuing swill of ego. But is this real strength that's being celebrated here, with all this "toughing it out," or is it something less desirable?

WORKING THROUGH CHALLENGES

In life, there will be challenges, whether you're in your work/home environment or in the outdoors. One of the most incredible things about going outside is that, while you can plan and prepare to the best of your abilities, you can't always foresee everything that will arise. Despite every intentional review and addition to your packing list, items will be left off or lost; planning meetups or pre-trip meetings that review expectations and roles can't eliminate interpersonal dynamics. The goal for an outing is to have an *experience*, not a re-creatable event. There are sunrises and sunsets to see and perfect camping spots to find, but the way back to camp from a sunset vista, having forgotten your headlamp, may lead to a sprained ankle, or a campsite with a view might not have great places to stake out the rainfly.

There are different magnitudes of challenges—and leading through these will require different types of capacity, stamina, and fortitude. I'd like to focus on mental fortitude because everyone can strengthen their mind, whereas bodies tend to have more limitations. The following anecdote from Joe Stone shows how we can all go about building greater mental resilience.

Opening My Mind and Heart

JOE STONE

It was go time. I jumped out of the plane at 14,000 feet and had to spin a 360 in freefall. I was attempting to get my A license in skydiving, and it was my seventh skydive. I lost control at 120 miles per hour. At those speeds, life gets chaotic very quickly. I tightened my muscles to force my body to stop spinning. However, this only made me spin faster. I remember split-second views of my instructor telling me what to do as he entered one side of my vision and exited the other. I was scared out of my mind and no longer thinking straight.

Eventually, with the help of my instructor, I got my body under control, deployed my canopy, and landed safely. He told me that this experience would be both a skydiving lesson and a life lesson. When life gets out of control, he said, we instinctively close up and protect what's most important—but that never helps. In fact, it only makes the situation worse. The proper reaction is to open your arms and relax in order to allow the energy to flow smoothly over your body. If we can stay relaxed amid the chaos, everything will eventually calm down.

Five years later, I was lying in a hospital bed after sustaining a C7 spinal-cord injury from a speed-flying crash. Terrified of living with paralysis, I was facing the reality of being a wheelchair user for the rest of my life. Out of nowhere, the lesson my skydiving instructor had imparted after that failed jump popped into my head.

I decided to open my mind and heart to my spinal-cord injury. I opened my life to people whom I might have shut out otherwise. The result was positive energy flowing smoothly over my body. Since then, my life has progressed in a positive direction. I have experienced some of the most mind-blowing outdoor adventures, and I have been lucky enough to share these experiences with amazing humans. My smile is big, and my wheelchair is the tool that allows my life to be awesome.

This doesn't mean I never have bad days. It just means that when life gets chaotic, I open up so I can see what is really going on. Eventually, I find the right people and solutions to get life back on track. If only my instructor knew how the tools he gave me that day would shape the rest of my life. Life is good at throwing us challenges. Life is also great at providing us the necessary tools to deal with those challenges.

*On August 13, 2010, **Joe Stone** had a speed-flying accident in Montana, rendering him a C7 quadriplegic. Through his perseverance, he is now a public speaker, filmmaker, outdoor adventurer, and the executive director at Teton Adaptive. His goal is to help people push beyond the boundaries of perceived limitations.*

UNDERSTANDING YOUR RESPONSE TO CHALLENGES

How do you respond to challenges? Knowing this is empowering. What have you done that you thought you could never do? Reflect on a challenge that you navigated. What or who do you recall having assisted you? Understanding how you respond to, as well as work through, hurdles will give you a road map you can apply time and time again.

Choice is paramount to forward momentum. Look for the choices that you *do* have, rather than dwelling on the past or fretting about the future. You can control your current situation, making sure it is as stable as possible: Are you protected from the elements? Warm and dry as you can be? Are you hydrated, and have you eaten recently? Are you rested? Making sure these basic needs are covered gives you the time and space to reset and assess the situation, and then come up with action items for your group.

> **Choice is paramount to forward momentum. Look for the choices that you *do* have, rather than dwelling on the past or fretting about the future.**

After calming the stressors or limiting the addition of more challenges—like not continuing to hike if you are lost—it is time for a candid assessment of the situation. If the issue is interpersonal, it may be time to decide if you can address it in the field or if you'll accommodate new expectations as you venture out. If it is an equipment issue, you might be able to improvise or consolidate gear. If it is a weather situation, you can use what you have—maps, radios, or your contingency plan—to decide whether to press on or to stay put.

NAVIGATING DIFFICULT (BUT NOT IMPOSSIBLE) SCENARIOS

No doubt you have prepared and understood which challenges you might encounter on an adventure. You may have become certified in wilderness medicine or a technical discipline, such as climbing or paddle sports. You may have attended a course on fishing or snow travel. If you are leading others, you've done the research, know your limits, and have developed a contingency plan.

But things happen. I love to say Mother Nature always wins because it is the one consistent thing that holds true. Water is an endlessly powerful force that will move mountains, literally, by wearing them down. Trees and grasses will grow in the seams of rock. Tides and rivers rise and fall. Snowpacks build and glaciers crawl, continuously carving the landscape. While it is hard to get our head around time horizons and geologic scale, the message remains that, truly, nothing remains.

Fatigue might be the number-one difficult situation I've encountered when leading trips, and it often goes hand-in-hand with exposure to the elements. No matter how fit you and your participants are when you leave the trailhead, everyone will most likely get tired at some point. Most of us don't carry backpacks daily or move through nature for great lengths of time or navigate changes in weather and temperature without shelter and a controlled climate. Walking or rolling along a trail at a high elevation and on uneven ground is difficult, and hiking at night to make it to a campsite isn't ideal when you have a tired body and low morale. However, our fatigue can be navigated—it's not impossible to deal with.

After a leader recognizes the toll the trip is taking, they can encourage participants to make sure everyone is adequately fed and hydrated, set incremental goals, ask one-on-one questions, and tell stories to keep the mood light. For example, when leading young kids, I might set a goal of reaching a certain tree or rock up ahead before stopping for a break. And when leading a trip whose participants have a wide array of fitness levels, *before* we start hiking I'll set the expectation that we'll be hiking in increments punctuated by breaks—say forty-five minutes of hiking followed by a ten-minute rest—to regulate the enthusiasm of the faster hikers and motivate those who move at a slower pace.

The Most Challenging Adversary Is You

If you choose to lead, you are choosing to be vulnerable. You have never been perfect, and you can't make everything right for those who follow you. You may have insecurities as a traveling companion, facing doubt about yourself and your capacity to participate and to lead.

Perhaps you are coming to the outdoors later in life. Maybe your body type does not fit into fancy outdoor clothing, or you feel awkward using certain equipment. Perhaps you have not had welcoming experiences outdoors in the past, and you have feared for your safety—both individually and in a group. There are no words I can share to remove past and present barriers, but I believe you belong in the outdoors, and the decisions you make that end well and those you make that end miserably are yours to experience and learn and grow from.

It is so much easier not to start something new and not subject yourself to being a novice. It may be the first time you've gone car camping or the first time you've gone on a remote expedition. In these scenarios, we can all easily doubt our abilities, whether as leaders or participants. No one wants to be the last one to camp or to the top of the peak or off the boat. But the truth is someone *has* to be last—and the person who hikes the slowest may, in fact, surprise everyone and be the one who can go the longest. We are who we tell ourselves we can be.

GETTING COMFORTABLE BEING UNCOMFORTABLE

I don't particularly enjoy being physically uncomfortable in any situation I could prevent, and I have found in my time outdoors that there are things I will gladly carry, despite the added weight in my backpack, to increase my comfort level. As someone who always gets cold, I'm talking about extra layers, a personal means/way to rapidly boil water, or a full-length sleeping pad. At the same time, I know there will be plenty of things I won't be able to control, from the wind and precipitation to the water temperature at river crossings to the thin air at elevation when I'm not acclimated. We don't go outside to re-create what we enjoy in our daily lives; we go outside to embrace whatever Mother Nature has to offer.

If you choose to lead, you are choosing to be vulnerable.

As I've shared, I'm most uncomfortable when I start out from the trail-head, as I first lose connection with and access to the creature comforts of home. That's when I fear not having what I may want and feel nervous about my safety. But every time, as the miles pass beneath my feet, my confidence and comfort increase. It's a different type of comfort; I can be warm and dry and fed outdoors. I can be comfortable being uncomfortable; I know I am aware, present, and able to do anything.

COMFORTABLY UNCOMFORTABLE IN COSTA RICA

AORE works with individuals in Costa Rica to establish a similar association for Costa Rican outdoor facilitators. I recently returned from a site visit with others in the country, where I may host a future event. We presented the work AORE is doing, and after our presentation and meetings with local outdoor-recreation providers—and a handful of days doing the potential activities like rafting, hiking, and SUPing—we did a homestay in a local village. This community had a partnership with our Costa Rican partner (our host), and to showcase the town's history and community values, the locals showed us travelers around for an afternoon, taking us to homes to meet the residents and learn how to make corn tortillas, fudge, and sweetbreads. It was an experiential immersion—a chance for us to see and learn how these things were done and to bring some economic gains to the local people and exposure for the village youth.

As we packed up our things in the modern VRBO where we'd been staying and prepared to take a bus to the village, I found myself feeling super anxious. We had had significant rains the entire trip, and I knew we'd be taking a rudimentary dirt road deep into the jungle. The roads and drivers are impressive in Costa Rica—the roads hug cliffs and are often rutted, with neither turnarounds nor guardrails. This dirt track was no different, and four rough hours after leaving, we stopped at a clearing in the jungle far from modern civilization.

I was incredibly uncomfortable—weepy, almost—as fear and doubt filled me as we slipped down the steep incline to the village. The rain pounded down on the jungle canopy. We came to the first home and wiped our feet at the door. Inside, warmed by a wood-fired stove, the matriarch of the home and the community greeted us, introducing us to her family.

As we quickly learned, the matriarch's deceased husband, who was the community leader's (our host's) father, had likewise been a revered community leader. And so the son began by leading everyone in memory of his father. Then, our host showed us how to soak corn, run it through the press, and turn it into a dough. Using banana leaves as plates, we followed the lead of the matriarch, a woman who had made countless tortillas—

ours in no way resembled her perfect forms. We placed our creations on a skillet and made enough for the meal we were about to enjoy, sitting down to savor our feast. As we ate, we were told, through the translator, that the woman had given birth sixteen times (fourteen of the children had survived), and we learned more about her husband and the things that were important to their family.

Next, we met with two other households, making coconut and carrot fudge, and then sweet empanadas. Finally, we headed to the village center—a covered recreation area with an adjoining kitchen. There, the community put on local dances, and we played games and joined in a ceremony with the kids. Following the ceremony, we were each assigned to our families—I met up with Maria and her parents, and we ate dinner together under the cover of the recreation center. Maria and I were both vegetarians, and neither of us spoke the other's language. Using Google Translate, we made small talk. Because I didn't know Spanish, I felt insecure, like I was missing out.

FINDING CONFIDENCE THROUGH COMMUNICATION

As night fell, we headed to our assigned homes. Maria's dad carried my bag while the family used flashlights to light the steep path through the town to their home. It was super uncomfortable—and slippery in the rain!—for me to be disconnected from my traveling partners, especially given the language barrier. When we arrived at their home, they showed me my room. Then, I came out to sit with the family and meet their other daughter. As we struggled to communicate, my discomfort morphed into confidence. I tried to share about my family and where I lived; I asked about their school and their work. We laughed at our language difficulties and relied on hand gestures and Google Translate. I could see the family's love for each other, as well as their curiosity and generosity.

I've never regretted the perspective doing something uncomfortable has offered.

I woke up the next morning to the smell of coffee and the aroma of plantains and eggs cooking. I asked if I could help with breakfast, but a feast was spread quickly before me. The two sisters joined us, and we had a most wonderful time, over beans and rice and eggs and plantains, talking about daughters and parenting, hopes for future travels, and invitations to stay connected. Later that morning, I met up with my friends. We all described our homestays in a similar vein: we'd initially experienced apprehension about intruding and not knowing what to expect or how to communicate, but then found our homestays to be a highlight of the site visit. I don't always know where my fears and emotions come from in new situations, but I've never regretted the perspective doing something uncomfortable has offered.

TAKEAWAYS

- Failure can be an opportunity.
- Self-confidence is built through experience.
- There is a difference between being tough and being resilient.
- Work through what is difficult; it's not impossible.
- The most challenging adversary you face is yourself.
- Get comfortable being uncomfortable.

THIRSTY FOR **MORE?**

Understanding what helps you move through challenges is empowering. How do you respond to challenges?

What is a situation in which you have shown grit? Capture the ways you demonstrated grit in that situation. Identify ways you can develop this more in your leadership.

Identify a strength that you possess—something you are proud of—and consider how it helps you navigate life. To build on this strength, ask someone you trust if they've noticed instances in which you demonstrated this strength. Can they help you find a way to better apply this moving forward?

As a leader, in what ways do you support your group when they are navigating something difficult such as the terrain, the activity, or an interpersonal challenge?

CHAPTER 6
INTEGRITY

Integrity comes from the Latin words *integer* or *integra*, and it means "whole" or "sound." The broad definition of integrity is wholeness, honesty, uprightness, soundness (e.g., a solid building has structural integrity), the state of being complete or undivided, and adherence to strong ethical principles. In the context of outdoor leadership, integrity comes from trusting ourselves as leaders and being trusted by others in a contract that is built and maintained over time. This chapter focuses on understanding the cumulative currency that integrity keeps in account, especially in situations where following the leader is critical to everyone's safety.

Integrity is one of those non-sexy leadership terms. I'm a big fan of those home-renovation shows—the ones with young couples who have esoteric jobs like "stamp collector" and "magnet designer," are just out of school, and have inexplicably astronomical budgets. The story arc includes looking at three houses, picking the cheapest, most dilapidated one, and then renovating it until it looks like a showcase home in *Dwell* magazine. But the part that always trips them up is the time, cost, and trouble it takes to get things like plumbing, wiring, and the foundation corrected— all those invisible, but crucial, components of a house. Just like integrity, these things are not flashy, but they are essential.

The great thing about integrity is it is on display every day. The challenging thing about integrity is it is on display every day. Integrity shows itself in our repeated actions. As an athlete, and as a mom to teenagers, I can attest that what you do over and over is the best indicator of what you will do in the future. This is not to say you can't change in the future, but if you have not demonstrated integrity in the past, it's not looking good down the road.

DEMONSTRATING INTEGRITY: THE ATTEMPT TO DO RIGHT

We hope leaders will show integrity in their leadership, and this is no less true for outdoor leaders, who take on responsibility for participants trying new or different activities in remote locations. Outdoor leaders can't acquire a certification in integrity, but they can demonstrate it by practicing sound risk management, being candid and forthright with expectations, maintaining proper equipment, acquiring permits, and knowing the rules and regulations. Integrity does not imply perfection. I am not perfect (just ask my kids!); nobody is. But we can all still manifest integrity by doing things the right way and avoiding shortcuts both in life and in the outdoors.

We can all still manifest integrity by doing things the right way and avoiding shortcuts both in life and in the outdoors.

The Center for Outdoor Ethics developed the "Seven Principles of Leave No Trace" to offer a framework for those who recreate outdoors to lessen the negative effects of overuse and promote land and resource protection. The best thing is, we can *all* put these principles into play, whether as individuals or outdoor leaders, *and* they tie directly into our integrity. Choosing to stay on a wet, muddy trail instead of walking along the edges, which widens the trail, requires integrity—you're doing what may be difficult but right. So does packing out all the waste, food scraps, wrappers, and even toilet paper and menstruation products, instead of burying or burning them. And so does choosing to camp on a more durable surface rather than opting for the "perfect" campsite that's either on fragile or softer ground or too close to a water source.

BUILD INTEGRITY BY ALIGNING WORDS AND ACTIONS

By design, nature is wild, not prescriptive. When we're out in the field, we're often working with limited or no safety nets, which is why, in crucial moments, I prefer not to doubt the leadership. This means I can trust my co-leader to do what they say they're going to do, which is backed by past examples of them doing exactly that—say, taking on the onerous and messy task of washing the pots and pans when they say they are going to, without fail. A person with integrity follows rules and agreed-upon policies and procedures; ultimately, I know I can depend on them to do the right thing, even when the situation is challenging.

Imagine being on a trip during which the group gets separated. Now, as one of the leaders, you are responsible for the smaller pod, and you are working to reconnect back with the whole group. You know the other group is ahead of you—and, unfortunately, they have the map and other navigation resources. As you hike to catch up, you come to a junction and must decide which way to go. This decision is based on what you know about the other leader and group, the circumstances, and what you need to do for your group. In cases like this, someone's past behavior is a good indicator for the future.

If you know your other leader can be careless (say, to the point of not noticing the group has separated, and not knowing who has the maps), you can anticipate they will most likely push to the next campsite—without regard for the smaller group. However, if you know the co-leader doesn't veer from what they say they'll do—that they have *integrity*—you can guess that there must be a reason for the separation. Perhaps there's been an incident or an injury or some other event that prevented them from behaving the way they usually do, and they're likely along the trail somewhere attending to this unforeseen occurrence and waiting for you to catch up.

Seven Principles of Leave No Trace

1. Plan and prepare
2. Travel and camp on durable surfaces
3. Dispose of waste properly
4. Leave what you find
5. Minimize campfire impacts
6. Respect wildlife
7. Be considerate of other visitors

It takes integrity to follow the Leave No Trace principles, and while each of the seven points is important, the three that most stand out to me and that complement the message of integrity in outdoor leadership are: traveling and camping on durable surfaces, disposing of waste properly, and leaving what you find.

In the first case, when a hiker comes across a puddle or muddy spot, the best action is to go right on through and not try to go around in order to keep their boots dry. Sure, going around seems benign enough, but if one hundred people following that hiker make the same decision, the trail will widen over time, which makes for poor drainage and lasting water erosion. The second and third cases should be more obvious: we should never leave trash or waste in the backcountry, and we should always leave things as we found them, not picking flowers or taking artifacts, so that other users who come after us can enjoy them too.

This exact scenario happened once on a backpacking trip I co-led to Pictured Rocks, during which the group got separated. I was responsible for the smaller pod trying to reconnect with the whole group. Max, a student trip leader, was ahead of me with more than half the students— and, unfortunately, he had the map and other navigation resources. As I hiked with the slower hikers, we came to a turnoff to a small campsite area. Given that it was now dark, I decided to lead my fatigued and slow-paced group toward this campsite (which was not our planned destination) instead of continuing onward. I made my decision based on what I knew about Max and the circumstances: I knew he knew I was behind him, and I knew he would realize I was coming and would likely stop so we could reunite the group. Max has always been a very analytical and pragmatic person, and had demonstrated good risk-management skills when he worked as a climbing-wall manager. And lo and behold, Max put those very attributes to work that night—we found him at this smaller campsite, waiting for us!

In hiring student trip leaders for the outdoor program at the university where I worked, I was always cautious about those who were super excited about rock climbing and had a lot of personal climbing experience. While many of these students were very competent, experienced, and able to climb difficult routes, they weren't always the best climbing leaders. I made this mistake a couple of times, attracted to their climbing résumés and the impressive locations where they'd climbed. But these students' focus on their own climbing time often resulted in shortcuts: sloppy knots and anchor placements, and backups that were modified for speed. These impatient trip leaders would consistently ignore the program's institutional policies and procedures; they lacked the integrity to serve as student leaders and move at a more controlled speed on a certainly more limited scope of routes over a climbing weekend.

Leaning into Purpose, Vision, and Values

JACKIE OSTFELD

My purpose revealed itself during a field trip, in high school, to Hawk Mountain Sanctuary on the ancestral lands of the Lenni Lenape Unami tribe in rural Pennsylvania. This was my first mountain hike. The relief I felt after reaching the top, where I could rest my shaky legs, transformed into awe as I caught my breath and quieted my mind. Standing atop the Kittatinny Ridge, I looked out over forests and farmland, a bucolic painting come to life, punctuated by the soaring shadows of hawks flying overhead. Indigenous wisdom explains the presence of hawks as messengers from the universe, calling us to see the bigger picture and clarify our vision. It turned out I was beginning to develop my own *vision* for a healthier Earth and was coming into my *purpose* to protect this awe-inspiring planet and live according to my new *values*.

Over the years of listening, learning, teaching, campaigning, and coalition building, what's kept me grounded on my path is a commitment to continuously refine my personal purpose, vision, and values. When I first set out to protect the planet, I was blinded by my privilege and oblivious to environmental injustices. In all my college coursework on the environment, I hadn't learned about the history of racism and exclusion on our public lands—the Indigenous communities forced off their lands to make way for national parks, the Black and brown communities redlined into polluted neighborhoods with little access to clean air, clean water, and nature. As I continue to deepen my awareness and build relationships across lived experience and identities, my purpose, vision, and values will continue to evolve.

Today, my *purpose* is to disrupt the systems of oppression harming people and the planet. I strive to learn lessons from nature, such as humility, resilience, and mutualism, to support a shared *vision* for a just, equitable, and inclusive movement that ensures all people benefit from a healthy and thriving planet, strong and vibrant communities, and access to nature. My *values* guide me to listen to and follow the wisdom, teachings, and traditions of the BIPOC communities on the frontlines of our climate crisis.

Getting clarity of purpose, vision, and values is a first step, but living them is where integrity comes in. In the nonprofit space, there is pressure to make your work stand out in the necessary pursuit of scarce grant dollars. In Washington, DC, there are expectations to move quickly on policy matters. I have made mistakes over my many years in this space, including seeking out as much grant funding as possible without realizing it may have been at the expense of BIPOC-led organizations that could have better utilized the funding, and failing to ensure there was a diversity of lived experiences in the room when making important policy decisions.

As I become the leader I hope to be, I increasingly trust myself to lean into my purpose, vision, and values, and to hold myself accountable to the communities I am here to learn from. Like the hawk interrupting the stillness of the rural Pennsylvania landscape, I must co-conspire to interrupt systems of oppression, slow down, and move at the speed of trust.

Jackie Ostfeld (she/her) leads the Sierra Club's Outdoors for All campaign to ensure all people can exercise their human right to access nature. She founded the Outdoors Alliance for Kids, advises the Blue Sky Funders Forum, leads national outdoor-equity campaigns, and lives with her partner and two children in Washington, DC.

BE CONSISTENT (EVEN WHEN NO ONE IS LOOKING)

Integrity means consistently being honest with words and actions, even when there is no one to praise or penalize them. One time, I was raking the yard and pushing down my frustration that my kids were not helping me. Another thought in my head was about doing a job well. I would be last in line to be praised for my attention to detail, but I think I edge to the front when it comes to doing what I say I am going to do. As I loaded the leaves into a bag, I thought about shortcuts—maybe I could skip the leaves on the common swath of land between my neighbor's house and my own for the neighbors to rake up, or I could blow the final debris into the road for someone else to clean up.

Doing the right thing—including difficult actions like staying on the trail and hiking through that puddle even though there's no one around, or keeping your dog on leash in a remote but leash-required area—are ways to act with integrity. That got me thinking about how we often lean on other people picking up the slack, or the fact that no one is observing us, to rationalize our own poor behavior. You've seen it and you've likely done it. Me too: "I'll leave this bag of dog poo here and grab it on the way back" or "Someone else gets *paid* to remove the trash, so I'll leave it for them" or "I'm tired, and I don't really need to check the gear before I return it—the thing I broke [zipper pull, drain plug] will be found, and they can just charge me." Ways to demonstrate integrity include following LNT practices for disposing of waste properly and admitting to breaking the equipment and then taking action to repair it for subsequent users.

In thinking about lapses in my own integrity, I can see how it has changed as I have matured. Some of my past choices, like not packing out menstrual products, started with my not knowing better. Still, as I've learned more and realized the impact I have on natural places and the people I'm introducing to outdoor recreation, I can choose to be better. That intention of failing, admitting, and learning helps us grow and demonstrate integrity. Better leaders make better choices consistently, and a reputation for integrity follows suit.

ADVOCATE FOR DOING THE RIGHT THING—AND ADMIT MISTAKES

Ego. It was the original stimulant long before Red Bull or 5-hour Energy drinks became popular. Ego outdoors is like over-applied cologne: it is everywhere, and it stinks.

I want to be known as someone who can be trusted to do the right thing and who doesn't let my ego keep me from admitting, owning, and learning from my mistakes. I also want to make sure my ego's desire to reach the summit or to follow the bigger wave train does not blind my ability to see what the group needs or to properly evaluate risk. That doesn't mean I will get it right all the time, but I will try my best, use the available tools, and work to move something forward. I hope, when realizing there's been a miscommunication or misperception, that people will know they can approach me to work through the issue. I want to be the person people can depend on.

Those Who Follow You, Follow You

Many times when my dad and I are out walking, he bends down and picks up a piece of trash and carries it with him to dispose of it properly. He's done this my whole life, and he does it to this day. As a result, I emulate him: when I walk by a piece of trash, I pick it up and take it with me, too. My own children, Gretel and Thor, see me do this as well, often voicing their disgust as I pocket a candy wrapper or carry a plastic dog-poo bag to the dumpster at the trailhead, but I like to think they too will remember my actions and that soon enough they will do the same.

Look, I've pooped a lot in the woods, and I have been on my period countless times in the backcountry. I can remember a pile of poo I left in Nordhouse Dunes Wilderness Area when camping with my dad because, even though I knew better, I decided not to dig a cat hole and pack out my TP. I've left my share of tampons out there as well, when I did not know any better, and even when I did know better but couldn't be bothered to dispose of them properly (there was a time when I wasn't aware of the brilliance of a menstrual cup!). Sure, it's rarely convenient to properly dispose of or pack out your trash and waste in the backcountry, but failing to do so will negatively impact the experience of those who come after you.

Here's another example of applying integrity to leaving the outdoors as intact as possible. When leading a trip of high school students in Yellowstone National Park, my co-leader and I came across an arrowhead. We were excited with the discovery and shared our find with the students. We were camping nearby, and while I could tell them we should not and would not take the arrowhead, I worried that one of the students might still be tempted.

I decided to move the arrowhead from where I'd found it, placing it under the base of another tree adjacent to the original discovery. I don't know if it was the right thing to do, as it disturbed the artifact from its original resting place. But it did mean it would be there to discover for others later. Removing an artifact, a beautiful rock from a river, a piece of petrified tree, or something neat found on the trail means that the party behind you doesn't get to enjoy the experience of seeing it themselves.

One of the best things about watching my kids play sports is seeing the roles they play on their teams. My son, Thor, is a very accomplished lacrosse goalie, his talents known and recognized by other players, parents, and coaches across our state. It would not be a stretch to say he is one of the best in the state for his age division. Yet more impressive than his play are his lack of ego and his team-first actions. One time, Thor was asked to step in as goalie for another lacrosse team, which he gladly did; then, at the end of practice, he helped put away the goal and the loose balls, as well as made sure the younger kids got their rides home, even though it wasn't his team's turn to do these things. All of this warmed my heart more than any goals that he stopped that day—the fact that he did the work without being asked and stayed until the job was done.

Things evolve on a trip and may require modifying plans and adjusting the trip length or activities. The weather changes, and interpersonal dynamics are unpredictable—these things happen. However, one thing that you, as a leader, simply can't take shortcuts on is safety. Risks you may take on a personal trip have no place when you're leading others. Our ego often implores outdoor leaders to push on when situations are dangerous, and yet we have to do the right thing—which is minimize risk in an environment we don't control.

Life jackets come to mind as an often-cited inconvenient burden. It's been my experience that water can be one of the most dangerous things on a trip, including getting to the water (going down a ravine), crossing it (river crossing or trying to scamper across a tree, a mossy bridge, or a rock hop), swimming in it (diving in or jumping from a height, sustaining foot lacerations that will require evacuation or that can become infected), and boating on it. I get that life jackets are bulky and give us weird tan lines, but skimping on them, courting injury or death, is not an option when recreating on water.

That's the challenge in a group setting: helping your participants understand the context for seemingly "pointless" rules.

We venture to wild places because they are just that: wild! I've shared that we can't control things like water or lightning storms; however, we can take precautions like wearing life jackets and assuming the lightning position when necessary. As a further example, when I ran an outdoor program, I enforced three policies for trip leaders while cooking:

1. Wear closed-toe shoes.
2. Do not sit with your legs under a lit stove on a table.
3. Use pot grips, not stretched-out sleeves, to remove pots from the stove (remember, fleece is made from plastic).

I did not invent these rules. I was taught these tenets over many years at various places where I worked. I can see these policies from both sides: as a participant, they can feel prescriptive and annoying, but as a trip leader, you know that they can prevent avoidable accidents. That's the challenge in a group setting: helping your participants understand the context for seemingly "pointless" rules, things like taking an agreed-upon but longer route to avoid a hazard like a river crossing, or always wearing a helmet at the base of a climb to mitigate against dropped climbing gear or rockfall, or not allowing food in the tent to avoid attracting wildlife. Clear communication of expectations—to prevent incidents and manage risks—can help provide context for those who may not agree with these rules but who ultimately respect your leadership.

Accountability and Consistency

SARAH HARPER BURKE

"Don't speak to me like that," I barked in a defiant tone that landed like a punch to the throat. I had finally worked up the courage to confront my co-worker, and came at them because, in my mind, I was going to be a person of integrity who stood up for myself. This co-worker had continually demeaned me, taking great effort to undermine my leadership and creating a toxic atmosphere that had me wrestling with how to handle the situation. This confrontation had been long coming, and I was sure to approach it with a sense of righteousness because I was going to fight for what was right!

And, man, did that backfire! My bold move, standing up for myself on a pedestal of integrity, was a misguided effort that missed the mark in understanding how to strive for and maintain true integrity as a leader. While I have always aimed to lead with integrity, I was missing some key elements of emotional intelligence in my own journey. I wasn't self-reflecting honestly on how I'd contributed to this contentious relationship. I was reacting to the moment instead of responding to real conflict. I wasn't being accountable and active in creating solutions. Instead, I was taking things personally and choosing to be offended. I was being judgmental, not curious (thank you, Brené Brown via *Ted Lasso*!).

The integrity I purported to have had gone missing because I was choosing when to turn it on, instead of living it each and every day, in building relationships and being honest with myself and those around me. That work relationship never improved. We've all moved on in our careers and taken our leadership lessons on new journeys. But how I choose to show up as a leader today includes daily reflection to ensure I am demonstrating my ideals with a clearer sense of accountability and consistency.

Sarah Harper Burke (she/her) is a marketing leader in the outdoor industry. Starting in whitewater paddle sports, she has navigated a career building high-performing marketing teams and inspiring people to get outside with top outdoor brands. Burke has an MBA from Colorado State University and an MS in sports management from the University of Tennessee.

NAVIGATING POLITICAL LANDSCAPES
WITH INTEGRITY

It is hard to be a leader *and* be in a work environment with other leaders. Staff training, negotiating trip assignments, and picking the participants who will be in your boat, for example, can become political minefields. Working with someone as a co-leader can be tricky, especially if you don't appear to work well together. Because we are wired to avoid conflict, and we are predisposed to make ourselves feel better, we are often tempted to go along with an uncomfortable situation or play the victim rather than put in the hard work of confronting the situation head-on.

If you know about it, you are responsible for it, especially when you're the leader. So what role did *you* play?

If you know about it, you are responsible for it, especially when you're the leader. So what role did *you* play? When it's hard to keep up or to fit in, you might be easily tempted to take a shortcut, forward an email or text of ill will, and use phrases like "Someone said . . . or "I heard . . ." However, I'm reminded of this quote: "Don't tell me what they said; tell me why they were comfortable telling you." When people talk about other people—passing judgment or gossiping—you have an opportunity to lead. It is harder, of course, to be the voice in the communication chain that stops and checks the facts rather than act on hearsay, but doing so lets you lead with integrity.

As I have matured, gained self-confidence, and learned to better manage my insecurities, I have found less need to be bothered by gossip, group-think, and hearsay. I remember a distinctly difficult time during my tenure as an executive director when I transitioned from doing work that was heavily influenced by a small group of members to doing work more representative of the entire membership. In essence, I was finding my footing in fulfilling my position. As I asked and listened to more members, and identified issues that impacted their work, my decisions became different than the ones the association had been making. I took a path not followed by others in a leadership role. There was backlash, but I wanted to take the path for the greater good, and I wanted those working with me to respect and appreciate my choices.

Many didn't. I spent far too much time trying to convince a small but vocal group that I was right, rather than let them focus on the good work I was doing. However, over time, as I grew into my role, two things happened: (1) my previous insatiable need for this group's validation diminished, and (2) I realized how I, too, had perpetuated a toxic, gatekeeping culture—namely by seeking the approval of this small group instead of creating space for the wider array of members, who in fact started to contribute, participate, and lead when they saw I valued their and others' perspectives. I had made missteps and mistakes, but along the path to becoming

more aligned with how I led and the work I needed to focus on, I emotionally released the need to seek approval.

THE CUMULATIVE CURRENCY OF INTEGRITY

I have found that great leaders cumulate the currency of integrity over their lifetimes, holding it in an account of sorts. While some may marvel at an extensive outdoor résumé, I now see that *how* a person leads is more important than what they have done. We all have the capacity to grow our personal-integrity accounts.

I have come to understand that some people have advanced into leadership positions in work and volunteer environments—who is selected to lead the trip, who gets first pick of their co-leaders, who gets selected to sit on the board or deliver a presentation, etc.—not because they know how to lead but because of who they know or have led previously. This sort of sponsorship for advancement happens time and again, perhaps not as a result of backroom dealings or bad intentions, but because of how humans form relationship—leaders are people, too, and are naturally drawn to those they prefer to work or be with.

Inheriting a program, organization, or really any place where you may be leading is difficult because you are following someone who previously had relationships with your staff, volunteers, and sponsors. It takes work to learn about these existing relationship, deals, and promises, to come in as the new leader and ensure equity for all. Removing the handshake deals can be challenging in the short term, as those who have benefited may feel they've lost. At the same time, leaders can have more confidence if everyone they work with knows they will be treated fairly—if what the leader offers to one person is the same thing they offer everyone. This confidence allows relationships to deepen and trust to build, and in many cases, for mutually beneficial outcomes to develop. By consistently leading with an eye toward equity, you accrue the currency of integrity over your career.

> **I had made missteps and mistakes, but along the path to becoming more aligned with how I led and the work I needed to focus on, I emotionally released the need to seek approval.**

Integrity in the outdoors can come in many forms. As brands, businesses, and nonprofits address inequity and systemic racism, there will be some who do the work in a merely perfunctory way and some who embrace it wholeheartedly—with integrity. Performative allyship and providing gear or social media promotion rather than financial payment are not consistent with "leading with integrity." Salary transparency and a forthright recruitment and selection process for volunteer leadership and board service are examples of integrity as a value.

For the outdoor-recreation industry to become more inclusive, it needs to change actions, behavior, and structures that have resulted in exclusivity. Integrity points to those of us who are in positions of privilege and power and asks us to step aside so others can have more access and opportunity to the outdoors, more education, and greater advocacy. Integrity means embodying this sense of accountability, consistent action, and transparency.

TAKEAWAYS

- Be 100 percent honest and commit to the extent of your knowledge and authority.
- Demonstrate integrity through the alignment of words and repeated actions.

- Advocate for others and do the right thing, even when there is no one around to praise or penalize you.
- Admit mistakes. Learn from them.
- Don't talk about other people, pass judgment, or spread gossip.
- Build an account of the cumulative currency of integrity. Cultivate the confidence and trust of your co-leaders and participants.

THIRSTY FOR **MORE?**

If you know about it, you are responsible for it, especially if you're the leader. Can you recall a missed opportunity when you perpetuated a situation you could have defused? What was the outcome and what role did you play?

You might be tempted to take a shortcut to feel like you can keep up or fit in. Or you might forward an email or text of ill will or pass along hearsay or gossip. How can you develop a practice of instead stopping, pausing, and checking for facts? This is acting with integrity.

There are many ways to shirk responsibility in leadership, such as not applying for permits, not reviewing health forms, and not filling out all the paperwork. Where do you tend to shirk responsibility in trip leading? What helps you lean into your integrity and take care of these things?

Why is integrity so important for an outdoor leader? Can you see how asking someone to trust you in a new, high-stakes activity (belaying, rappelling, rafting, etc.) is connected to your integrity as a leader?

We all have lapses of integrity. Reflect on a time when you wish you had acted differently. Now identify how you've applied that learning and growth.

We all have demonstrated integrity. Reflect on a time when you acted with integrity and think about why you were resolute in behaving this way.

CHAPTER 7
TOLERANCE FOR ADVERSITY

Leaders make plans; followers follow the leader's plan. But things often change during outdoor experiences, and it is critical for leaders to know how to adapt. The more a leader can tolerate adversity, the better they will be at responding, adapting, and presenting an updated plan. In a difficult situation, a leader can choose to name and understand the difficulty, understand the extent of their knowledge and authority, and be honest with themselves and the people they lead. A leader being vulnerable in this way allows others to see the leader being their full self and opens a space for followers to deepen their own tolerance for adversity. This strategy upends the notion that the leader must resolve adversity for all. Instead, the leader can empower those they lead to lead *themselves* through hardship.

Speaking of which, let's talk about the explorer Ernest Shackleton. Shackleton's ship, the *Endurance*, which was crushed by sea ice off Antarctica in 1915, was found in the Weddell Sea in March 2022, one hundred years to the day after Shackleton was buried (Shackleton died of a heart attack during a return voyage to Antarctica). He had a reputation for being the best person for a tight spot and could improvise amazingly well. His is a great study in leadership and adversity: after the *Endurance* became entrapped, Shackleton was still able to save the other twenty-seven members of the ship's crew, making an epic voyage to fetch help. And while Shackleton did not achieve his goal of being the first to cross Antarctica, he did successfully lead his team to survive in the face of unforeseen adversity—the mark of a true leader.

Navigating the unknown, the uncomfortable, is a primary task for all outdoor leaders. The ability to tolerate challenging times and people is an asset. Change and challenges require the ability to move seamlessly from a determined, communicated, and vetted plan to one that navigates unforeseen (but time- and resource-anticipated) components. It's vital to lean into and embrace adversity with confidence and to withstand doubt (self-doubt and that of others). Being okay with not being okay, and showing this to those who follow, is key. Being vulnerable and transparent as a leader allows others to find the strength to withstand that which may not have been anticipated.

WOMEN AS NATURAL-BORN LEADERS

Despite the many obstacles (including the societal and hierarchal systems created by men that disproportionately benefit men) that women face in leading themselves, their families, their work, and their volunteer communities, women can be natural-born leaders. Women also bring unique perspectives and skills to the collective work of outdoor leadership. As leaders, men and women have similarities and differences, but in my experience, there are two things that women leaders can uniquely amplify: their athleticism and their ability to interact and connect.

Like the difference between men's and women's basketball—a sport I played at the college level—women athletes move differently, using their bodies in sometimes more technical ways or relying less on muscular strength. This in turn can lead to more strategic or intentional decision-making. For example, in women's basketball there is more passing and moving the ball around to open up a good shot, versus the sheer strength men exhibit in driving the lane and dunking. I've seen this also in rock climbing and backpacking: a woman can climb the same pitch or hike the same path, but she'll use different moves than a man. As a result, in leading a group, I've seen women leaders communicate to all what the desired outcome may be, but present different options for getting there; it's more "You may consider using these different holds" than "Here is the move."

I also believe that women have a unique ability to have more personal interactions with and connect to individuals because of lived experience. This is because women typically move into and out of more informal roles than men—for example, leader and follower in a community setting, care provider, consoler, and counselor. In the realms of work, study, sports, and music, it been just fifty years since Title IX, an anti-discrimination law, came into effect. As a result of Title IX, there are now a greater number of formal roles for women, and so generationally there have been significant changes in expectations, roles, and opportunities for women. As a result of their more dynamic lived experience, I believe women are more aware of meeting participants where they are when leading, understanding that people are all on different paths.

When I was first learning how to find my place in this world, I aspired to be an equal among my male counterparts—in guiding raft trips, leading wilderness programs, and chairing boards and leading associations. I thought time, accolades, and being in the right rooms and involved in important conversations were the keys to upward mobility and to being seen and treated as an equal. But, as we've explored earlier, I was wrong. Seeking approval from those who have written the narrative and have held coveted leadership positions and experiences only served to perpetuate the closed-rank gatekeeping of leadership opportunities, both for myself and for those who might follow.

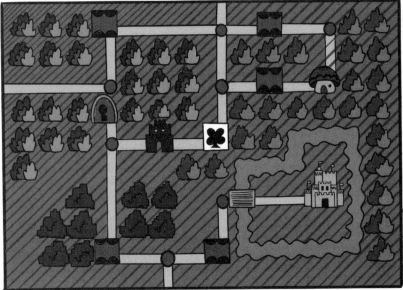

THE EXPLORATION OF LEADERSHIP IDENTITY IS A JOURNEY

The exploration of leadership identity is a journey, one that's constantly punctuated by adversity.

The exploration of leadership identity is a journey, one that's constantly punctuated by adversity. A leader must identify who they want to become and work on themselves toward that end, but ultimately there will be a shift when the leader moves from what they have known or seen as their role into embracing their full potential and utilizing the nuances, gleaned from facing hardship, that make them their best leader or self.

COSTA RICA CHICAS

In 2019, I co-facilitated a once-in-a-lifetime learning expedition to Costa Rica that was intentionally designed for women leaders working in outdoor recreation and education. It was an immersive cultural experience designed to foster professional development, encourage networking, and develop paths for women to transcend in organizations. Trip participants explored—through a women's leadership lens and through facilitated discussion—the intersection of health and wellness within our profession, best practices, and big topics such as the importance of diversity and inclusion, social determinants of health, and the need to build multicultural competency.

Here's how our brochure described it:

La Fortuna/Sarapiquí (May 25)

Settle in and scan the scenery from the convenience of a private vehicle. Travel to Sarapiquí and to the tranquil Cuarto River. Hop into kayaks with a guide and cruise the Rio Cuarto. The calm waters are perfect for birdwatching and wildlife spotting in the forest canopy. This region is known for abundant wildlife and birds, making it the perfect spot for a leisurely paddle while searching for monkeys and sloths. In the evening, join us for an evening yoga session. Zen out after a long day surrounded by the lush jungle and the sounds of rainforest.

Sounds nice, doesn't it? Except that our kayaking day ended with multiple flipped kayaks, a thunderstorm, an anxiety attack, and a lost flip-flop.

This adventure made me think a fair bit about being brave. Being outside without the comforts of technology—or climate control, and without a reliable means of transportation—requires confidence and a willingness to face uncertainty. There is a beauty in that, in which the unknown lies around the next corner and the process is filled with wonder. But for some on this adventure, the bravest thing they did didn't happen in Costa Rica but earlier, when they left behind their kids, their partners, or their pets; arranged to be away from work; and decided to spend their money on themselves to have this opportunity.

In our first four days of adventure, we had swung from ropes into jungle rivers, had seen waterfalls and volcanoes, SUP'ed on Lake Arenal, and whitewater-rafted. Day five moved us away from volcanoes and into the jungle as we headed toward the Atlantic side of the country. On the day of adversity, we changed our lodging from a hotel to remote jungle cabañas. The jungle lodge had an open-air lobby that led into an incredible dining area; we dropped our bags at our assigned rooms and changed into swimsuits for our kayak trip.

We then piled onto a school bus, which drove us past miles of pineapple farms. The landscape was lush, and our banter on the bus was a low buzz, the participants now familiar with and connecting with each other. Eventually, we stopped just past a bridge and came to the Cinco Ceibas Rain Forest Reserve and Adventure Park just as it started to rain. Our river guides were already there, unloading the sit-on-top kayaks— a brightly colored offering of singles and tandems. Until this point, we had enjoyed traveling with our local guide, Aryeri Herrera—chief experience officer, leader, and moderator. Today, as the river guides' safety talk unfolded, there was decidedly more Spanish instruction directed at our predominantly non-Spanish-speaking group than there had been previously.

Moving Through Discomfort and Facing Fear

The rain brought a mixture of emotions—first was the feeling of not wanting to be wet, but then, after realizing we were about to be kayaking, came the feeling of acceptance that being wet was bound to happen anyway. The temperature was comfortable, and the rain was moderately heavy—nothing to be concerned about, we felt, until the lightning and thunder started. Many on the trip were outdoor instructors, and they mumbled about best practices and not wanting to be on water in a lightning storm. The other participants who were leaders, but not in an outdoor context, were unaware of these issues and unconcerned, but they were open to actively and respectfully following the outdoor instructors. After some discussion among our group, we justified our decision by noting that the dense foliage around and hanging over the river would mitigate our exposure to the electrical storm, so into the boats we went.

Down on the river, it was hard to hear each other. The group of kayaks was pretty spaced out, and from my perspective the guides didn't seem too concerned about, well, anything. One participant, who also had experience guiding groups and was comfortable on her kayak, went on ahead while I stayed back to be the sweep.

We were still in shallow water when I heard the first screams after a kayak capsized. It was the dumping, not the depth, that caused the cry. The sit-on-top kayaks were incredibly tippy, and a strong stroke or leaning too far out of the boat resulted in capsizing. As I came up on Jill, I found her drenched but standing in only a foot of water. The river was that depth most of the time but grew to four feet at the deepest channel—you had to navigate away from the sandbars into the channels to avoid getting stuck. Getting out of a sit-on-top kayak can be awkward and walking on a river bottom can be unnerving, but Jill was a trooper and I helped her get back in her boat. The rain continued. We floated easily down the river, with our convoy stretching farther apart.

However, kayaks were now flipping over frequently. Most participants felt a mixture of surprise and fear, shouting when they fell into the water. But for one participant, it was also emotionally challenging. After she flipped out of her single kayak, we decided as a group to pull off to the side to talk about why this was happening and what to do when it did. This participant had had a negative experience on a prior kayaking trip, nearly drowning when her boat capsized. So the two of us decided to share a tandem kayak. We had enjoyed a good connection on the trip, and I was happy to help comfort and reassure her, given my experience working as a river guide. Off we went on what was now a leisurely float trip, drifting downstream in the rain, dipping in our paddles to move away from shore or into deeper waters.

And then it happened. Coming around a corner, the light dimming from heavier rain and a thicker canopy, my partner and I found many overturned kayaks. Women yelled from the water, and there was general mayhem. My partner and I paddled to catch up to assess the situation—the Costa Rican guides were farther downstream. We joined forces and worked to make sure everyone was indeed out of the water—found and not trapped.

Some participants were freaked out. One, Nicole, recalled, "Our [tandem] boat dumped again. When I came up, I was trying to push up the boat because I thought my partner was stuck under it. Then I got stuck between a downed tree or branch and the boat." With her face out of the water but the current tugging at her, Nicole began screaming for help, panicking, until someone came and pulled her out. She said that her partner felt awful about the capsizing, as if it had been her fault, though of course this was far from the case—they'd all been abandoned by the so-called guides.

The kayak trip was all over the place—people being upset about the flip and pinning, the absent guides, the decision to be on the river during the storm. At this point, the only thing I could do was to get everyone into their boats and floating downstream to the take-out.

Processing Challenging Events

Once off the river, the group circled up to process the day's experience. More than a dozen amazing women came together with wet hair, some with red eyes, some with arms around another, and one missing a flip-flop. Each person talked about what had happened. For some, the focus was on the events of the kayaking (mis)adventure; for others, it was on how they felt in the aftermath. We all checked in with each other. This adventure marked the biggest leap several had taken in their lives: they'd felt uncomfortable and exposed, but also alive in a new, vibrant way, having to trust ambiguity and being without the normal constraints and comforts of their lives back home. After the expedition, I became even closer with the members of the trip.

In discussions more than a year later, Nicole remembered, "When I got back to our room, Victoria asked me what happened. I broke down. She stood there, looked me in the eyes, and cried with me. There was no judgment; she just listened, loved, and supported me, and she let me have my feelings. It was amazing. Looking back now, I can identify so much of what went wrong. Sometimes I feel embarrassed about the meltdown, but mostly I accept that what I experienced was traumatizing, not just for me but for the whole group. It was a turning point for me, in some ways. From my lens, this part of the trip was the first time we were pulled from significant comfort."

Individuals can process a common experience differently—both positively *and* negatively. I saw this with the women on the kayak trip, who started processing it right after it happened, then again in a group

debriefing, and years later when they reflected on impactful moments in their lives. At the time of the flip, some responded with action and others with emotion, while others remained unaware of the potential risks. In the group debrief, many shared how the experience felt to them in the moment, with one member connecting the potential loss of a participant to the recent loss of a family friend. Years later, when many of the women connected over breakfast, at least two stated, upon reflection, that the Costa Rica trip was the space and time that allowed them to make significant changes to their lives, including career change and starting a family.

It should be noted that leaders also process events themselves! Following a situation that the group has navigated, leaders will not only personally process and internalize their experience but will need to be intentional about helping and often facilitating the group's experience. After our kayaking debacle, I focused on the group's need to process right after we got off the water, and I recall how important it was for me to create space for each person to share. Then, afterward, I processed the event as an individual, exploring my feelings and understanding of the day's events.

How a Leader's Tolerance for Adversity Affects Others

One thing became clear to me after the Costa Rica expedition: a leader's ability to tolerate challenging times and people can also be a liability. There is a very fine line between tolerating some discomfort, especially when you help cause it (as our river guides had), and ignoring things that are uncomfortable or even unsafe, to the detriment of those you lead. For instance, your participants on a day hike getting a little bit wet because you forgot to tell them to bring raingear is one thing, but failing to recommend they bring raingear on a multi-day excursion during which being wet could lead to hypothermia or other complications is another. In fact, it's foolhardy.

Being on water during a lightning storm, as we were in Costa Rica, is always a bad idea. Water conducts electricity, and being in the water or on it in a boat can be a recipe for disaster. (A good rule of thumb is to not be on or in water until thirty minutes after you hear the last peal of thunder.) In Costa Rica, as the head leader of the trip, I should have done more to set aside my own tolerance for risk and adversity and instead queried members of the group as to where their threshold lay. However, by not voicing concern for getting on the water, especially as an experienced river guide myself, I chose Compliant Leadership— low care for myself and a low commitment to the group. Ultimately, it was not the best decision to go, and we were lucky that things didn't go any worse.

Highly Focused, Concerned, and Hyperaware

RUSS WATTS

Carson Pass is a mountain pass in the central Sierra Nevada, in Eldorado National Forest in eastern California. Wedged between Red Lake and Caples Lake, it has stunning vistas and was a popular gold-rush destination. I was there for a winter-mountaineering trip with my co-guide and ten clients. In addition to the four-foot snow base and sustained winds of five to ten mph, there was constant, light snowfall hindering our views.

Prior to our trip, we had trained our participants in the classroom —for many of them, it was their first trip of this sort. Our first day out, we skied to an area with easy slopes and flat terrain to dig out our tent pads and cooking areas. The wind, our constant companion, helped us to be quick about changing clothes and adding gloves and layers. The day was going well: a solid day of skiing and setting up camp, with an hour and a half left until darkness. As I always do as a guide, I made sure that our clients were together, safe, and prepared for darkness. And then I realized I'd totally forgotten about my co-guide.

I scanned the camp and asked everyone nearby, but no one had seen her for at least twenty minutes. Immediately, my mind shifted to search-and-rescue mode: collecting last-seen moments from our participants and calculating her possible direction of travel. I shifted from being the relaxed, calm, chill guide into being the highly focused, concerned, and hyperaware guide.

Within minutes, the whole group was dressed, with plans for a quick search. We took turns calling and listening, doing a sweeping movement in all directions. As each minute passed and we didn't hear a response, my focus intensified, as did my concern and awareness. I made sure we all followed our agreed-upon timing to go out and return, to check-in. I made sure people stayed warm and in communication with me and with each other.

We focused on the two specific areas that seemed to have the most recent snowfall. The drifts covered some of our older tracks. After what felt like a lifetime but in reality was only thirty minutes, we still hadn't found her—and the daylight was diminishing. I kept my concern for the participants high while holding on to the knowledge that my co-guide would have a very long and painful night out if we did not find her soon.

I asked half the group to stay at camp and melt snow, to begin making dinner and drinks, and stay warm. The ones who went with me seemed energized and were well equipped for the cold. We continued our search and followed the various trails we had not yet tracked down. We called out and listened for any response.

Just as darkness draped us with its final cloak, I saw a figure in the distance skiing toward me. I was simultaneously overwhelmed with joy and consumed by anger. I asked my team to return to camp while I talked to my co-guide. First, I gave her the biggest hug and asked if she was okay. We quickly assessed that she had wandered off and lost her bearing, which is easy to do in such conditions, even for those with years of experience.

We skied back to the camp, and openly and honestly debriefed the lessons learned with the entire group. In all our preparation, we'd been worried about our students. But even the most well-trained experts, including guides, can suddenly find themselves in unpredictable situations. As an outdoor leader, developing your tolerance for adversity is key, because you can never fully control how a trip will unfold—and sometimes the leaders themselves need to be rescued.

Russ Watts (he/his) is a leadership coach (PCC ICF) and integral facilitator, teaching at Georgetown University and Bocconi University; a leadership-development consultant for Global Good Fund and other clients; an avid adventurer, ultrarunner, and sailor; and silly father of two amazing children.

BUILD CAPACITY BY BEING VULNERABLE

Being vulnerable builds capacity, which in turn creates the stamina you need to tolerate adversity. A leader's vulnerability can morph over time and as situations demand. Vulnerability allows leaders to find the strength to withstand that which they may not have anticipated. In the past, I spent an inordinate amount of time trying to appear to be a person who had it all figured out and could not be fazed by anything—in other words, to be invulnerable. But instead, I needed to embrace my vulnerability and begin to lead myself.

Vulnerability allows leaders to find the strength to withstand that which they may not have anticipated.

I texted a friend one morning about a series of curious interactions in which several people wanted my advice. *Why was everyone coming to me?* I wondered. She replied, "You project strength because you are aware of your weaknesses and yet you move forward. Others see that. Your strength comes in part from your core belief that YOU CAN. Others see that belief and are encouraged themselves, inspired, motivated."

Truth be told, I am an incredibly emotional and passionate person. I show my emotions openly—I cry easily, and I can have infectious energy as well as infectious sadness. As I grow as a leader and try to lead with both care and commitment, I have begun to embrace my passion and emotions as allies rather than see them as adversaries. I have begun to embrace my vulnerability.

Tips for Tolerating Adversity

Be okay with not being okay. Embrace adversity with confidence and withstand doubt. We are strange beings, always trying to make sense of ourselves and our surroundings. In seeking comfort, we settle into situations and environments we deem stable and safe. To change our perspective, we must view the world and the way it works from different vantage points, which may include embracing failure and working through fear.

Be transparent. Do what you said you were going to do; if you change course, communicate it to everyone involved. In challenging times, sharing more with those you lead is better than not sharing. Trips and boats go sideways; what was supposed to have been may never become, and it is imperative for a leader to share consistently and openly what the intention is, what happened to alter that course, and what people can expect based on the information and experience you have. Hope is a fragile thing that helps people move through difficult experiences—it's the sighting of a distant shore or the promised take-out point just around the next bend.

Control what you can. Consistency is comforting; complacency is concerning. My dad is fond of this adage: "Most folks are about as happy as they make up their minds to be." We don't have control over others, the elements, and certain situations, but we do have control over our headspace and our actions.

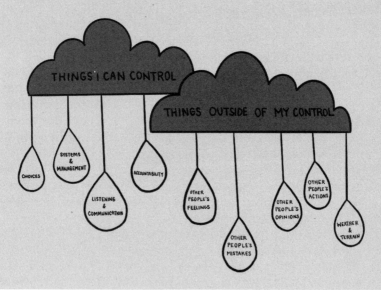

TAKEAWAYS

- Be aware of your tolerance for adversity and of how it impacts your leadership, as both an asset and liability.
- Learn to be okay with not being okay, even though you may feel uncomfortable.
- Be transparent—this vulnerability builds trust and interdependence.
- Control what you can. Release what you cannot.
- Embrace adversity with confidence, and withstand doubt.
- Be vulnerable so you can build the capacity to tolerate adversity.

THIRSTY FOR **MORE?**

It is paramount for leaders to assess what is and isn't working. When things don't go as planned, which complementary abilities will you need to modify your efforts?

Which outdoor experiences have required you to assess your ability to tolerate adversity? What did you learn about yourself and others?

It is easy to avoid things that make us uncomfortable. Identify an area you are intentionally avoiding. Can you become more comfortable with being uncomfortable?

What do you turn to when things become challenging? How do you acknowledge the discomfort yet still find a way to navigate through?

What is your biggest fear in becoming an outdoor leader? What are you doing to address this fear?

CHAPTER 8
ADVENTURE OR ORDEAL?

Outdoor leaders who are curious, open-minded, and have an appreciation for discovery will also have a better understanding of potential situations they may encounter. What things can you anticipate? What things can you avoid? And what things are nonnegotiable? Great outdoor leaders are intentional and present, and they can navigate and control their response to a wide range of situations. Therefore, a leader needs to be self-aware, in order to manage themselves, their emotions, and their energy in a way that is productive, not destructive, for the expedition. This awareness includes being cognizant of your written and spoken words, body language, and presence, since they affect the collective morale and composure.

What may excite one follower can horrify another. When we talk about "outdoor adventure," we should also consider that the spaces themselves may not have been accessible to all participants (because of time and money, for example) but also unsafe (historically, to be gay or BIPOC in the woods has often meant being in danger). The ability to even talk about having an "adventure" stems from a place of privilege—perhaps we sought an artificial challenge in the outdoors, while others' lived experiences in that setting have been of genuine fear and peril. Especially in the United States, histories of colonization, exploitation, and genocide must be acknowledged.

Also, as outdoor leaders, we must acknowledge there is no single "best way to do it"—we must lead in ways that help us continuously learn from others, keeping our minds open to different ways of doing things. And, as we learned earlier, it is vital for you as an outdoor leader to first make sure you *can* lead, so that expending energy on others does not come at a cost to your health or obstruct judgment and decision-making—so that you are poised to lead an adventure, not just survive an ordeal. As a leader, grounding yourself in mindfulness practices and taking a holistic

SELF AWARENESS

SKILLS COMPETENCY

RISK ASSESSMENT

approach to your well-being are just as important as risk assessment and skill competency.

SWIMMING THE STRAITS OF MACKINAC, PART 1

I have swum the Straits of Mackinac twice. The straits, which separate Michigan's upper and lower peninsulas, are 4.4 miles wide. My swims took place in the shadow of the Mackinac Bridge, which until 1998 was the longest suspension bridge connecting Michigan's two peninsulas. I did the swim for the first time in 2015 in the company of eighty-one people. During the crossing, seven swimmers were assigned to each safety boat, and we swam with our pod from the upper peninsula to the lower peninsula. My pod got a little caught in the current, and that 4.4-mile swim turned into almost 7 miles, according to my GPS.

I have a very high pain tolerance but a very low tolerance for poor planning or uninformed decision-making. In preparing for the swim, I planned and trained so I could swim farther than the stated 4.4-mile distance, and so being caught in the current, nearly doubling the swim, while uncomfortable, was a known risk I was able to muscle through. Being a leader requires deep research—e.g., understanding weather patterns, snowpack, and snowmelt; locating water sources; considering the impact of altitude; looking into recent animal activity; finding locations for definitive care; and compiling numbers for local police and rangers—as well as training, packing, and testing for the proposed adventure, and an understanding of what could cause the adventure to deviate or derail.

Open-water events are challenging to plan, host, and execute as a result of many of the variables listed above, as well as the compounding effects of exposure to the water (the potential for hypothermia), difficulty in seeing swimmers and the fact that they spread out due to different pacing (support boats), the inability to "stop" because of the possibility of drowning—it's not like a footrace, where you can walk if you get tired—and the long distances covered. For these reasons, I never swim alone in open water, I always share where I am swimming and when I expect to return, I tow a swim buoy to be seen more easily and to use as a potential float should I get tired, and I swim early in the day before motorboats hit the water.

SWIMMING THE STRAITS OF MACKINAC, PART 2

The second time I swam the Straits, I was a shipwreck—truly, I was a mess. It was early August 2019, and my siblings and I were just becoming aware that our father was starting to navigate dementia. I didn't take this news especially well, and while I had trained for the swim and knew I could do the distance physically, I was mentally out of sorts. I did not sleep well the night before, did not pre-race fuel well, and I even forgot my goggles in the van. Realizing this right before the ferry—from which we'd jump into the water and start the race—left the port of St. Ignace meant my husband had to run back to the car (at 4:45 a.m., mind you) and then race back and toss the goggles up to me on the deck. My nerves and emotions were already getting the better of me.

The ferry ride across the straits takes about twenty minutes. In the early-morning light, the Mighty Mack bridge was all lit up and the lights from Mackinaw City were still flickering. I train with a wonderful community of open-water swimmers in Michigan, and a handful of them were also doing the swim. We huddled together amongst the four hundred other nervous swimmers on the ferry's deck, and then, as instructed, jumped into Lake Huron. The first order of business was to swim to the shore of the lower peninsula, get out, cross over the timing mat, and then return to the water to start the swim north.

I jumped from the ferry, but I was already a hot mess. My goggles filled with water—my own tears—as anxiety washed over me. I am one of the stronger swimmers of my training group, yet in the initial 150 yards to shore, I could not get enough air or take a full stroke. I watched as my friends pulled away from me. Once on shore, I knew I needed to make some decisions—namely, should I start the swim or not?

In considering this decision, my second question was, would I become a liability for someone else—the race director, or the lifeguard who might have to help me, or the limited resource of the support boats? I knew I could swim the Straits—I had done it before—but *should* I?

LEADERS ARE PEOPLE, TOO

As I wrote earlier, a leader needs to be self-aware, in order to manage themselves, their emotions, and their energy in a way that is productive and not destructive for the expedition. However, leaders are people, too, with the same emotions, fears, and issues we all share. The key for a leader is understanding how their emotions manifest in times of duress and the effect this has on the group. To be clear, it is not desirable for a leader to remove or suppress their emotions; instead, they need to recognize that their presence in the moment can build or destroy trust in their ability to lead.

A leader needs to be self-aware, in order to manage themselves, their emotions, and their energy in a way that is productive and not destructive for the expedition.

As a very passionate and emotional person, I cry easily and I cannot mask my emotions. I recognize that when others see me cry, it can be off-putting or difficult, but over time I have embraced this part of my personality.

As a leader, I now share in advance that I may show this emotion, and I reassure followers that when I do cry, I am fully functioning and not lost or overwhelmed. At the same time, I'm very goal driven, and I've learned that I must check my energy, motivation, and expectations of others who may not be as driven. Although highly motivated people can inspire others into action, expecting followers to assimilate to your disposition is not a sustainable leadership trait. Swimming the straits that day, I found myself manifesting both these sides of my personality—crying openly with anxiety over the race and my father's failing health, but also driven to keep going, given how much effort I'd put into preparing. However, I knew that if I was to continue, I needed to make sure it wasn't an ordeal—for myself or anyone else.

I thus came up with a plan, and it was simple: make it to the first abutment on Mackinac Bridge and assess if I wanted to continue. If I did, I would swim to the second abutment and make another assessment. In the straits, the first 500 feet is in roughly 10 to 15 feet of water, which is so clear you can see the bottom, and then it drops off to the channel, where freighters can pass. There is current, too—water moving from Lake Michigan into Lake Huron through this constriction. The various bridge abutments—huge cement pillars, the first at 500 feet, and the second at 1,800 feet—would be ways to mark forward progress. They also offered a place to stop and snack (I had GU packs duct-taped to my buoy) because they would cut the current and make an eddy I could rest in.

There were heavy safety protocols in place for the swim, which included requirements from the Coast Guard (concerns of terrorism related to having boats near the bridge) as well as race policies which dictated that swimmers stay east of the bridge, but not by more than 200 yards, so the support boats could track us. (It's tremendously hard to discern something or someone in a body of water—be it a hat, a dog, or a person—especially from a boat or the shore.) We all wore wetsuits, and each swimmer had a required swim buoy, but add in the early-morning light, waves, and the churn of four hundred swimmers, and it became a recipe for a near-miss—or a total miss.

Creating Space for Authenticity

DEIDRA GOODWIN

"Leadership" is a funny thing. When I feel like I'm leading the *least* is when some of the best results emerge. Earlier in my career as an outdoor leader, I attributed these good outcomes to luck. Now, having grown as a leader, I attribute them to authenticity, which can be hard to center in the real-time moments of leading.

Once, while I was standing in a plowed parking lot at Grand Teton National Park Service visitor center, with the range gleaming in the bright late-winter sun, the NPS Academy members started an impromptu snowball fight. Straight ahead, there were groups taking selfies, and slightly right of that stood uniformed rangers, having an excited conversation while watching it all unfold. I took it all in, nodding to myself in that way you do when you're thinking, "I'm not really sure how this all worked out, but this is the best possible thing I could have imagined."

I think it's hard to see leadership when it is happening right in front of us, unless it is in the stereotypical way—out loud, overseeing *all* of the things. That method isn't true to me, despite how hard I've tried to make it be in the past. Instead, my style is to observe and catch things before they're noticeable, and to dart around in the background making minor tweaks. *What does it look like if I choose to give myself the space to focus my energy instead of scattering it to reach everything?*

Most important is that observation piece—checking in not only with the participants and other facilitators but also with myself. Asking the same questions: *What's going well? What's missing? Do I need to react to this right now?* My strongest leadership outcomes arise when I give myself the time to answer these questions.

Deidra Goodwin *(any/they/she) is an experiential and outdoor educator whose career has spanned different sectors of the industry: campus recreation, youth programming, commercial guiding, and conservation. Deidra is passionate about the power of reflection not only in personal development but in professional growth as well.*

SELF-AWARENESS > STRENGTH

This is key: leaders do not have to have more strength, stoicism, or bravado than others on an outing. Whatever personal journey you are on, as an individual or as a leader of a group outing, it is not imperative that you are the strongest or fittest. It is critical that I express this point because leaders are often typecast in movies and other media as being the bravest and the most stoic. This simply is not true. The most powerful strength leaders have is their knowledge of what they can, and more importantly can't, do—precisely so they don't negatively affect the rest of group. This was a lesson I took to heart that day on the Straits of Mackinac; I knew I needed to be *self-aware* as I cast off into the water.

The swimming that day was difficult, but over time I found my rhythm, my fears faded, and my confidence grew. The current in the shallow water was stronger than I had anticipated after the second abutment and into the main channel, and I found myself unable to get anywhere close to the next abutments. I needed to swim at a 45-degree angle to make sure I stayed within the 200-yard boundary. It was when I left the second tower that I had to make a key decision: go for it, knowing the longest part of the swim with the strongest current was in front of me, or turn around and swim to the support boat.

It wasn't hard to imagine floating away—floating east into Lake Huron with my orange buoy and wetsuit, knowing it could be hours before

someone would (1) notice I was missing, and (2) start to look for me. I'm not implying I would have perished. Rather, I knew full well that I *could* have and that it was my responsibility to be self-aware enough to acknowledge this possible outcome.

When you work in the outdoors, you can't guarantee safety, but as a leader you look to minimize risk. I had devoted countless hours in the gym and the water across my seven months of training, and I was physically fit. I had completed this crossing a previous time, and I knew I could do it again. I know I perform well in stressful situations and that I have a tenacious ability to move through the grind. I knew I could do it if I chose to move through it. And so that's what I did.

SUPPORT OTHERS BUT AVOID OVEREXTENDING

Leaders must take care to avoid overextending or expending too much energy when they nurture others in crisis, because that can come at the cost of their own personal health and energy. They might lose their capacity to lead others.

Helping others on open-water swims—be it while training or during an event—means keeping an eye on each other and verbally encouraging each other at rest breaks. As a leader, I often find myself walking the tightrope between mindful guiding of others, as on these open-water swims, and encouraging people to take care of themselves. As a mother, I know how to mother. It's the many ways of caring for others and seeing what a person needs—for instance, a layer or a warm drink—by repeatedly asking them, and it's comforting. However, it's all too easy to cross over from nurturing into neglecting your own needs, to your detriment. This can include sharing an extra layer so someone else is warm but then getting too cold yourself or taking weight off a struggling hiker but then making your load too heavy as a result.

While a certain "stick-to-itiveness" is a positive attribute, the ability to determine what is not working and seek an alternative is a more admirable leadership quality.

It's challenging not to overextend, especially for women, who have traditionally been expected to take on nurturing roles. However, in an outdoor environment, where there can be traumatic accidents and precarious situations, overextending can be extremely risky. There's a saying in lifeguarding—"Better one than two, better him than you"—that captures the reality that trying to help someone in a dangerous situation may cause two casualties instead of just one. So, as an outdoor leader, consider how overextending yourself, perhaps courting things like dehydration, poor thermoregulation, and fatigue, can impact your ability to lead your group safely and competently.

Averting a Dogsled Disaster

STACY BARE

Once, as a trainee guide, I got a dogsled stuck around a tree. It could have been worse.

There were twelve people on that weeklong trip in the Boundary Waters—two each on three dogsleds and six people on cross-country skis. We alternated daily between the two modes. The first two days, I had been nervous and made many little mistakes, but by day three everything came together. I felt confident and relaxed about my ability to guide us through the frozen north. On one of the final days, I was with a client in the last sled of the group. While we were following a tricky route over a large island between frozen lakes, our sled slid off the trail and jack-knifed around a tree, leaving us floundering in deep snow.

We felt strongly that if we could just push the sled away from the tree, we could get it back on the trail. The dogs' pulling, however, meant the sled wasn't budging. Because I was inexperienced, and the dogs could read my body language, the sled team's instinct was to move forward because they knew we hadn't yet reached our camp for the night.

I left my partner at the tree and trudged ahead through high drifts in hopes of contacting the rest of our team. Unable to find them and concerned about the cold as well as the significant delay, I made a plan with the client, who was a military leader and a veteran of multiple deployments. I unhooked the dogsled line, thinking I could keep tension on the dogs while my client freed the sled.

What a miscalculation! The dogs immediately bolted down the trail, dragging me along bouncing face-first in the snow. Disaster was narrowly averted when they came to a halt just as I was deciding, out of desperation, to wrap my body around a tree as an emergency anchor.

I sat dumbfounded, mere inches from smashing into the tree, and heard the client screaming in alarm at my near demise. Meanwhile, the dogs just stood there calmly.

I held onto the team while the client maneuvered the sled into place. After reconnecting the dogs, we investigated why they had stopped sprinting so suddenly. As it emerged, there was a small branch, just a quarter inch in diameter, that crossed the trail right at the lead dog's shoulder height and had brought him to a dead stop, along with the whole team behind him. I'd gotten incredibly lucky.

After five to ten minutes of sledding, we regained visual contact with our group. When we got close enough to speak, they asked where we had been. There could be only one answer: "We both had to poop."

Stacy Bare (he/him) *led the first successful ski-mountaineering ascent and descent of Mount Halgurd, the tallest mountain in Iraq. He has also led expeditions skiing or climbing in Afghanistan, Kyrgyzstan, and Angola.*

He is a National Geographic Adventurer of the Year and a military veteran of conflicts in Bosnia and Iraq, also serving as a humanitarian explosives-ordinance-disposal officer in Angola and Abkhazia, the Republic of Georgia.

COURSE CORRECTIONS

To avoid having an adventure turn into an ordeal, a leader needs to be able to assess what is and what is not working and have the complementary ability to modify the effort—to adjust their plans on the fly. Plans are imperative. They provide a direction between where you are and where you want to be or go, but they also must be modified and updated as you move along your path.

The Straits of Mackinac have been dredged so container ships can move from the East Coast through the Great Lakes to Chicago. In these deeper waters, the currents are stronger, and as the Upper Peninsula came closer with each of my strokes, the current and waves continued to push from west to east. Past the last abutment, the bridge comes down to the land, the bottom becomes visible, and a seawall extends into the water. Getting to the seawall meant I would have a break from the currents. We swam along its east side, and then swam under a bridge cut into that seawall, aiming for the park where the race finishes, roughly 500 yards distant. Because the water was moving from Lake Michigan (on the west side of the bridge) to Lake Huron (on the east side), and because this channel under the bridge was the water's only outlet through the seawall, there was a significant upstream current in the 50-yard stretch under the bridge.

We swimmers had been working hard for two hours at this point, exposed to the cold water, the currents, and the waves. Under the bridge, the current was impressively strong—so much so that the safety kayaks were struggling to paddle against it. There was also a volunteer with a rescue buoy standing on the cement footing, encouraging the swimmers. It was clear to many that they simply could not manage—they were not strong enough to swim against the current, and risked overexerting themselves if they tried. As I made my way into the current, I noticed these other swimmers getting out of the water, walking over the bridge, and re-entering the water where the current wasn't as strong.

We all have egos, and leaders can have outsized egos that blind their better judgment. While a certain "stick-to-itiveness" is a positive attribute, the ability to determine what is not working and seek an alternative, as these other swimmers had, is a more admirable leadership quality. Out on the straits, I knew I might have to be adaptable as well.

Swimming the section under the bridge, with the finish in sight, I remember feeling the same as I'd felt at the first abutment hours earlier: doubtful I could make it yet determined to do so. I knew I had the physical strength to power through the current, but I'd also need to stay composed emotionally—and be prepared to bail out and walk around if it didn't work out. As I broke past the current and my strokes returned to a more comfortable rhythm, I felt strength and confidence fill my head and my heart. I crawled onto the shore, stumbling on wobbly swim legs through the finishers' gauntlet. I looked for my family, and when I found them, I felt comfort, safety, love—and presence.

On reflection, I had never had an experience like this during which my personal leadership journey occurred at the same time as my physical journey. I had moved through all the leadership quadrants, and I'd led myself across the straits.

Saying Yes to Adventure

I'm drinking coffee after having watched the sun come up on a Bahamian island. A mere forty-eight hours earlier, I was drinking coffee in Michigan when I got a text from my little brother at 7:30 a.m. If I could get to Fort Lauderdale by 5:30 a.m. the next day, there was a spot on a plane and a place for me to stay in the Bahamas for a week. Seriously.

It is always easier to say no. Maybe "easier" isn't the best word, but it's certainly less arduous and stressful to decline opportunities that are not fully baked. Saying yes makes us vulnerable; we risk a lack of control or being in charge. We don't want to be a burden on others, so we fret, and we say no to things that could be a yes. But I always start with yes—it's exciting to move toward something that was previously unseen, and how often, really, does life present us with these opportunities?

My ability to respond to opportunity, quickly, was supported by experience (knowing what to pack and where things were) as well as structures I'd already put in place (Global Entry, a current passport, a general readiness to travel). These result from value alignment. Travel is something I find fulfilling, and I'm invested in it, with the clothes, bags, packing systems, etc. I was designed for this—or, I have designed myself to be open to this. The feeling of adventure, the lifting off of the plane, the unknown connections, the wondering if I have the right things and making do with what I have—these are what it's all about for me.

CAVING WITH TREPIDATION: THE NOVICE MINDSET

My boyfriend (now husband), Justin, once took me caving in Jewel Cave National Monument, South Dakota, at the end of my first summer working as a rafting guide. I had been on cave walks before but not actually caving, and I felt trepidation as we prepared for our trip. Justin—who'd been working at the monument all summer as an interpretive ranger—his best friend, Bryant, and I were going to do one of the wild cave tours; it would last three to four hours and required that we be physically fit. We each got into our coveralls, fitted our helmets and headlamps, tucked away an extra light source, and descended in the elevator. We started along the walking tour with its motion-sensor lights, and then stepped off the main trail and ducked into the first room, descending into darkness. We scrambled along the cave floor, walking/bouldering/scrambling over rocks on an unseen path. Each room we entered showcased something new: its sheer size, a geologic feature, or perhaps water. We marveled at this subterranean world; we squeezed through passages.

Caving was a wild experience immersed in darkness. I could almost feel the weight above me, devoid of sensory input aside from whatever our headlamps lit up and the voices of our fellow cavers. It is hard not to be fearful if you can't see an obstacle or where you could get hurt, and at the same time, the darkness itself was a source of primal fear.

Justin led the way, familiar with the unseen path, having covered it many times already that summer for work. He pointed out things that were helpful to know—how long the low spot would be, for example—and made recommendations for navigating any obstacles. At the top, before entering the cave, we'd all been asked to demonstrate that we could crawl through a cement box that was approximately the size of the tour's tightest point, ten feet of sinuous passage called the Otter Slide. With space that only allowed for one hand stretched in front and the other hand down by our side, Justin, Bryant, and I wiggled and laughed through the box, though neither Bryant nor I really understood we would have to do this 300 feet below, in the dark.

When we reached the Otter Slide, Bryant went before me, and then it was my turn. Alone in the gloom, on this side of the experience, I felt the scariness of the darkness and I began to fret about getting stuck. As I wriggled into the passage, it felt terribly small, but once I committed, going forward was the only option. The rock pressing on my back and stomach felt suffocating, and I began to panic, fear taking over my mind and tears running down my face. I can't recall how I was able to navigate the Otter Slide, but I made it.

I wonder, for me, if the cave tour—moving through an unfamiliar space in complete darkness, underground, with tight constrictions, and with limited knowledge of caving technique—had been more of an ordeal than an adventure. I juxtapose this with my second race across the Straits of Mackinac, which, while stressful, felt much more like an adventure because I was on familiar ground (well, water!). If I had become stuck in the Otter Slide—because of my actions or fear—I'm sure I would have found a way through. But to this day I'm still not sure the cave tour wasn't an ordeal, and depending on who I share the experience with, and my feelings at the time, I'll often describe it as an adventure *and* an ordeal because both things are simultaneously possible.

TAKEAWAYS

- A leader needs to be self-aware, in order to manage themselves, their emotions, and their energy in a way that is productive and not destructive for the expedition.
- Leaders do not have to have more strength, stoicism, or bravado than anyone else. Self-awareness is the superpower you seek. Leaders must be aware of how their words and actions create or deflate the collective morale and composure.
- Leaders, and in particular women leaders, must avoid overextending or expending too much energy when nurturing others in crisis. This impulse can often come at the cost of their personal health, energy, or ability to lead others.
- A leader must be able to assess what is (and what is not) working and be able to change course.

THIRSTY FOR **MORE**?

What is a strength in your identity that you are working to harness?

Which techniques ground you in times of adversity?

What constitutes an adventure for you?

Reflect on a time when you were able to manage yourself and your emotions during a challenging situation. When you look back at that situation through a self-awareness lens, what do you know now that you didn't know then?

CHAPTER 9
MAKING GOOD DECISIONS

I am rarely uncomfortable outdoors, especially if I know I've prepared and have the right equipment. The times I'm most uneasy are when I have ceded my decision-making to someone else. I may worry they haven't done their due diligence, haven't prepared, or haven't taken care of the equipment. I doubt their ability. This chapter builds on the notion that in an outdoor environment, the *right* decision does not necessarily exist. Instead, you make the *best* decision based on the myriad factors at hand.

Decisions have a progressive quality to them—when a leader consistently makes choices based on experience coupled with real-time inputs, they tee their group up for success. On the flip side, when leaders build on a weak foundation of poor choices, including even such fundamental things as not letting the group get enough rest or drink enough water, they set the group up for failure. However, there is an upside to failure: it's a means to grow positively, and, in fact, avoiding failure removes the opportunity to learn (and therefore the ability to make better decisions in the future). True empowerment for outdoor leaders comes when they understand the key to making good decisions is having the chance to make poor ones—and then learn from those outcomes.

WILDERNESS MEDICINE: THEORY TO PRACTICE

Everything outdoor leaders need to know about decision-making is taught in a wilderness medicine course. Wilderness medicine (also known as remote, expedition, or austere medicine) is the practice of medical care in locations where definitive care is delayed. It empowers individuals to render first aid where it may be difficult for others to reach and evacuate the patient, or where they have limited equipment, face environmental extremes, and need to call on strong decision-making, creative thinking, and improvisational skills. An individual with wilderness medicine training will prioritize supporting basic life functions: opening airways, checking for breathing and circulation, and protecting the spinal column, as well as preventing the patient from environmental exposure that can result in issues like hypothermia or dehydration. Wilderness medicine programs teach basic anatomy and physiology so a first-aid provider can ideally stabilize and support acute injury and illness until the patient can be evacuated.

Rendering first aid to someone in a wilderness setting is complex. In an accident, you may need to immediately stop a bleed and then clean the wound to prevent infection, but there can also be complicating factors and related questions to answer first: Do you have a first-aid kit and, if so, which items is it stocked with? Where is the person physically located—dangling from a climbing rope, in a snowbank, on the side of a river? Where on their body and how they are injured? Is it an open wound or is bone protruding through the skin? Can the patient move on their own? Can you transport the person out or will help have to come to you? Are others in your group also injured and in need of care, or will they be able to assist you in evacuating the victim?

Accidents happen and unforeseen obstacles arise; as an outdoor leader, all you can ever do is make what you feel is the best decision given the information you have at the time. I've been teaching wilderness medicine for more than fifteen years and leading groups in the outdoors for thirty, and over that span have come to see that there's little to no safety net when working outdoors: the environment can be remote, there can be limited access to resources, and evacuations are difficult. I do the best I can to manage risk, but I simply can't guarantee safety. Rivers rise. Rocks fall. Wind, rain, sun, and snow promise beauty but also potential peril. Even on my best day or best trip, a cry for help will decide my primary tier of decisions.

I have also lived this reality as the patient of a wilderness accident. I decided to become a wilderness medicine instructor after a rappelling accident because it was a way for me to navigate my emotional stress/ PTSD as I sought to process what had happened. I was also becoming more anxious, believing I was having premonitions about unforeseen and unrealized accidents. As I prepared to be an instructor, attaining my EMT license, attending an intensive two-week staff training, and spending a year traveling to apprentice for wilderness first aid (WFA) and wilderness first responder (WFR) courses, I recognized that it was decision-making— making the best decision based off the current information—that applied to both leadership *and* wilderness medicine.

THE "TRIANGLE" METHOD

When I taught for the Wilderness Medicine Training Center (WMTC), out of Winthrop, Washington, we used a mechanism of injury/illness pedagogy for field assessment and treatment in the wilderness. WMTC uses the following triad for patient assessment: size up, stabilize, and SOAP (subjective, objective, assessment, and plan). To go deeper, the three triangles are: (1) size up—determine the mechanism of injury, make sure the scene, rescuer, and others are safe and assess resources; (2) stabilize— address respiratory, circulatory, and nervous-system threats; and (3) create a SOAP note and evacuation plan—do a head-to-toe patient assessment. WMTC teaches this same model for every incident—it allows a rescuer to systematically identify the issue, address basic life-support problems, and then create a treatment plan including evacuation. While I taught students this triad for wilderness medicine, I believe it also can help outdoor leaders be better at decision-making.

Scene Size-Up: Assessing the Situation

Look for the whole, not the holes—in other words, consider the integral situation before you spring into action. In a tense situation, people act with urgency, and this urgency may or may not require a leader's action or involvement to prevent further misadventure. It's important to stop and assess what's going on: What could have contributed to the situation? Do other hazards remain? How many people have been or may be affected? How will this affect those who are not currently injured but may be at risk or will need some attention?

In wilderness medicine, this is referred to as "scene size-up." Before choosing to act and provide patient care, leaders need to assess if that's the best course forward. For example, we can't provide care on the bank of a river if the river is rising—we need to get the patient and ourselves away from the raging waters before we become patients ourselves. It takes discipline to pause and not act right away, especially with the urgency of other participants in a stressful situation. Being able to ascertain the issue—the source and not just the symptoms—allows us to more safely and skillfully assess and treat the injured party.

This was all driven home during a recent trip to Iceland, during which Justin and I very quickly realized how ill prepared we were for the country's elemental nature. During our first hour there, we found ourselves in a February snowstorm, trying to navigate by our rental car's one working headlight as we peered through a windshield choked with snow. We made it to our first night's accommodations, driving slowly and relying on humor and our experience with Michigan winters to get us through. We were fortunate enough to stay with two Icelanders, Hanna and Thor, whose son had helped us plan our weeklong adventure. The next morning over coffee, with the wind howling outside and snow pelting the windows, our hosts insisted that we modify our itinerary. They showed us an app that listed roads closed in real time, informed us there were only seven hours of daylight, and described the ice-rink-like driving conditions that made studded tires a requirement.

> **Being able to ascertain the issue—the source and not just the symptoms—allows us to more safely and skillfully assess and treat the injured party.**

Culturally, Icelanders respect their country's changing conditions and will modify their plans to accommodate—doing a classic scene size-up.

After a morning of discussions and hearing more about the very real risks of things like being stranded for days until help arrived we decided to change our itinerary. Our hosts' persuasiveness and local knowledge helped us to modify our itinerary, to make sure we could safely see Iceland's big landscapes and still return home.

When You're a Hammer. . .

When you're a hammer, it's easy to fall into the trap of seeing every problem as a nail—to jump right into action and start problem-solving. But it's critical to assess *everything* before you devise a treatment plan. How often do we give our precious time and attention to things that are not essential to the core issue?

One of the best ways to acquire information about things that might not be obvious is ask: What are we potentially not seeing or not aware of that may be contributing factors? With gaps in knowledge because of our unconscious bias, skilled leaders will be inquisitive and question others about things the leader themselves cannot see. Leaders should try to understand as much as possible, as well as be approachable so that others feel comfortable sharing sensitive feedback with them.

Stabilize: Prioritize, Then Act

Assessing, prioritizing, then acting is essential to administering basic life support. While broken limbs are painful, these injuries are not as dire as arterial bleeds. Meanwhile, there may be more than one issue for more than one patient, and you will need to determine what and who needs your attention first. Critical systems come first, including establishing and maintaining an adequate airway, making sure the patient is breathing, stopping major bleeds, and determining responsiveness— we must fix the critical life issues of airway, breathing, and circulation before we address any secondary problems. Tending to a broken leg is pointless if the patient is no longer breathing.

Look also for hidden killers/life threats: a common scenario in wilderness medicine classes is a patient with a wound that is visible on an extremity but who is also suffering from something else not easily seen, such as internal bleeding. Once the scenario is over and the class debriefed, many rescuers realize they missed the internal bleeding, which is a critical concern. We then talk about making sure we look for injuries beyond those which are visible or present readily.

Justin and I used to participate annually in a local fifty-mile relay race called Dances with Dirt, in which five teammates navigate fifteen different segments with a mixture of trails, swamps, and rivers and where missing a colored direction ribbon can add miles of travel. We filled our last position with Ashley, a fit college athlete who was up for the sort of type-two fun ("fun" only after the fact) that the race demanded. Trouble presented itself, however, after Ashley hobbled in after her first two-mile segment. She was, for some reason, wearing men's dress socks and proceeded to throw up, eventually sharing that she hadn't fully recovered from a late night out. We tended to Ashley's uncomfortable blisters, dehydration, and nausea; while her injuries were far from life-threatening, they certainly could have gotten much worse had they been left unaddressed (and had Ashley continued racing). Then we assessed the remaining segment of the race, reallocated the miles among the four of us, and continued on.

SOAP: Subjective, Objective, Assessment, Plan

When a patient is verbally responsive or better—with major bleeds stopped, breathing adequately on their own, and protected from the elements—the next step is to perform the secondary, SOAP assessment—a four-part information-gathering and planning protocol—and to document and redocument these steps as needed, for the caregivers in the chain after you.

Subjective Information

Subjective information comes directly from medical forms and the patient themself, and as such may or may not be trustworthy. It can include things like a recounting of the accident, a list of symptoms, and the patient's medical history.

Objective Information

This is information you can verify by measuring it, taking vital signs (heart rate, breathing rate, blood pressure, etc.) and carrying out a thorough head-to-toe examination, looking for things like swelling, bruising, visible wounds or fractured bones, etc.

Assessment

This is a compilation of your subjective and objective evaluations, in which you list all possible problems you're facing based on your findings, being as thorough as possible. For every problem you identify, you list how you plan to treat the issue. For example, a wound would require cleaning and dressing within two hours, bandages need to be changed over time, and the patient needs to be assessed for signs and symptoms of infection.

(Evacuation) Plan

To determine the urgency of evacuation, you first assess the level of risk to the patient as well as to any rescuers. For example, if you have a patient with a collapsed lung, evacuation is a high priority and you may consider traveling at night even though it could result in injury to the rescuers. Another example is someone with a broken arm. If the arm is splinted, it is not a mortal threat, so even as uncomfortable as your patient may be, there's no need to expose your rescuers to risk—for example, traveling at night. One great paradox in wilderness medicine is that you have no time at all but also all the time in the world. You must immediately remove people from water if they are drowning, clear snow out of an avalanche victim's mouth, and open an airway after a lightning strike, but after you've stabilized the patient, you'll need to be patient. The work to plan and orchestrate an evacuation can take anywhere from hours to days, during which you'll need to support the patient as well as others on your expedition.

Here's a situation in which leaders had to make that call—whether to evacuate a participant or not. In 2001, Justin, our two friends Bryant and Joe, and I set out to climb the Grand Teton. We decided to use a guide service due to our lack of familiarity with the climb, and frankly, because I hadn't consistently practiced building rock anchors in some time. We were joined by another climber, Derek, whose wife had bought him the trip as a gift.

Following our co-ed guide team, we started the hike up to the Lower Saddle. As we walked, Derek shared a bit about past adventures and climbs he had completed. He had strong opinions about how things are done and how they work, including his insistence on which gear was the best and not having a female guide. Derek appeared to be a fit guy, but as the miles continued and the slope grew steeper, his pace and his comfort decreased. Not in the role of leader myself but being aware of what I personally thought about Derek, I observed how the guide team managed the group. About midday, after a rest break, Justin, Bryant, Joe, and I were invited to continue on with the female guide, leaving Derek with the other guide.

Our group of five eventually reached the Lower Saddle. There, we rested and watched the sun set over Idaho, and then prepped for an alpine start the next day. Hours later Derek arrived, complaining of fatigue and foot discomfort. The guides brought Derek food, checked out his feet, and encouraged him to drink water. Before we went to bed, Justin, Bryant, Joe, and I discussed how Derek was going to impact the next day's climb, which had technical sections, but also recognized that it was the guides' decision as to how our group would continue.

The next morning, headlamps on, we set off up the talus slope with two new guides from the company at the lead and sweep. Just like the day before, Derek was slow and voiced his discomfort. When we got to the first pitch, the guides shared with us that they were modifying the trip; clearly, Derek wasn't doing well. They'd decided not to evacuate him but to see how far he, teamed up with one guide, would be able to climb safely. Meanwhile, the four of us would move ahead for a summit attempt.

ABCDE: Airway, Breathing, Circulation, Disability, Environment

I've shared that I became invested in wilderness medicine after experiencing a significant mountaineering accident on an expedition (see chapter 13). I like the wilderness medicine decision-making process: it's simple in extraordinary circumstances, and, without the burden of technology or access to expertise, the layperson can become an advocate or activist. Decisions must be made based on the information at hand—what you can see, what the patient tells you, what the medical form discloses. You can't see the future, and you can't stall or be indecisive.

Airway, breathing, circulation, disability (refers to head/neck/spinal-cord precautions), and environment—these things need to be evaluated and supported, or your patient will die. Everything hinges on the vital life functions of breathing and circulation, and on attaining or maintaining an environment that is not further endangering your or the patient—this is where decision-making can really show leadership. Bleeding needs to be stopped. Wounds need to be cleaned. Bones and joints need to be splinted. Spinal precautions need to be observed in handling a patient to prevent further damage. Body temperature needs to be stabilized by removing wet clothes, adding dry layers, and reducing convection and conduction.

A patient assessment is an invitation to make decisions. If you aspire to become or are already an outdoor leader, take a wilderness medicine course. It is as much about the ability to stabilize and evacuate someone as it is about having a process to guide clear decision-making in stressful situations.

DECISION-MAKING IS DIFFICULT

Prior experiences, including failures, will help you make more-informed decisions. And most leaders make a lot of poor decisions. I don't have any issue with making poor decisions. The mistake happens when poor decisions are made but the decision-maker doesn't take ownership of or learn from the negative consequences. This feels a bit like parenting: I help my kids learn how to make decisions (something they prefer not to do), and when they do (at last!) make that decision, they can use the resulting experience to guide their decisions in the future. My husband and I take this somewhat unconventional, hands-off approach because we believe it better helps our kids grow as people. Yes, it can be maddening to see them make what we feel are poor choices, but ultimately it is our children, and not us, who must live with—and learn from—the consequences.

When I'm leading in the outdoors, I try to base my own decisions both on being practical and on prioritizing fun. I'd rather build in a rest period before a summit. I'd rather break a long drive into two shorter chunks to give people time to recover rather than cramming ten hours of driving into a single day. And I'd rather enjoy nightfall sitting around a fire, and then crawl into an already-set-up tent with a sleeping bag unfurled and the mat inflated, than drive all day and set up camp, haphazardly, in the dark. So I'm willing to make other decisions—such as breaking up that long drive or making similar changes to an itinerary—in planning for these experiences.

Unremarkable, Unmemorable Decisions

ABBY ROWE

I've worked as an outdoor educator for more than twenty years. I've been responsible for at least fifteen hundred students, either directly as a trip leader or one step removed as a program director. When I was approached about sharing some thoughts on "good decision-making," I was surprised I could not recall any really great decisions that stand out in my professional career as an outdoor educator.

My second and more recent career has been as a first respondor and instructor of wilderness medicine. In these roles, my relationship with decision-making has changed. I generally receive immediate and positive feedback for appropriate interventions. I've reflected on this dichotomy a lot in the past few years. I realize how much easier it is to perform a risk/benefit analysis when responding to an emergency versus preventing one, as is often the role of the outdoor leader.

That is the tricky thing about good decisions: they are often unremarkable and unmemorable, defined most by the lack of chaos or crisis. They are rarely acknowledged or celebrated. Good decisions are often made up of many small decisions, such as appropriate route and food planning. The human learning cycle often comes from making mistakes, and as a result we spend a lot of time analyzing bad decisions and identifying how to avoid similar ones in the future. And while that is a necessary and important part of the process of developing good judgment, good decision-making would develop more quickly if we focused more on identifying and analyzing those "unremarkable" good decisions.

We need more tools to define success. We must create a practice of asking: What decisions made today were successful, and how can I make similar ones tomorrow?

Abby Rowe (she/her) was an instructor, course director, and staff trainer for Hurricane Island Outward Bound as well as the director of the Outdoor Leadership Program at Colgate University. She spent more than twenty years as a full-time outdoor educator. Abby is the current owner and president of Wilderness Medical Associates International and works as an Advanced EMT in Maine.

DECIDE—AND WORK WITH—THE CONSEQUENCES

We outdoor leaders are responsible for our own choices. We need to be open to input, but ultimately, it's up to us to make the tough decisions. Without fail, we must also be okay with the consequences of our decision-making—good or otherwise—and never lay blame on other individuals or factors.

For example, if you decide to travel fast and light—preferring to shoulder a lighter load—you'll have to be okay with not having the camp chair and extra layers, or with eating a dinner of energy bars. In this case, it wouldn't be fair to expect the group to provide or share their chairs or food or layers. To be clear, we all forget things—matches, socks, rainflies—and in these cases, everyone on an expedition should be quick to problem-solve and assist. But if your tendency is to think only of yourself and not the effect you may have on the group, you alone should shoulder the consequences. Ultimately, in an outdoor experience, your choices will affect the group.

Ultimately, in an outdoor experience, your choices will affect the group.

RIGHT DECISION OR BEST DECISION?

One thing I find so refreshing and rewarding in outdoor leadership is the opportunity to make the *best* decision rather than focusing on the *right* decision. I was greatly influenced in my formative years by high expectations and achievement standards. With grades, schools, sports, manners, everything—if results were not achieved, it was attributed to me not making the *right* decision. However, in the outdoors—with countless fluctuating factors like nature, elements, landscape, ability, and human nature to consider—it's impossible to make a singular right decision. You must instead make the *best* decision with the best information at hand.

While I was leading a trip for high school students in Alaska's Talkeetna Mountains, we had many river crossings in cold, fast-moving water. As the trip leader, I knew the stakes: even a safe crossing of a massive, braided river channel could result in cold exposure and wet boots, leading to serious complications like frostbite and hypothermia in a remote location. So while we'd made route-finding decisions *prior* to the trip that seemed like the right ones, *during* the trip—out in the field amidst the ever-changing rivers—I knew we'd have to revise our route and instead make the best decisions on the ground. Thus, we often deviated from the planned route to scout for the best crossings, which added both time and mileage to the day's hike. While this process might have seemed burdensome and conservative, it paled in comparison to the time and miles we would have had to add to resolve a rescue and resulting traumatic or hypothermic emergency. As that trip showed me, possessing the widest array of information helps with better judgment.

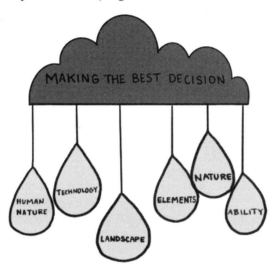

The Complexity of Adult Decisions

LILY DURKEE

I have been whitewater kayaking since I was nine years old. Learning to kayak as a kid has advantages with building technique and managing fear, but it also has disadvantages in terms of decision-making and leadership. For example, I learned to roll when I was ten and had a solid combat roll by the time I was twelve, giving me confidence on the river that still stays with me today. I also received formal coaching in slalom, so my forward and corrective strokes are powerful and efficient. However, when I was a kid on river trips, an adult was always there to facilitate the logistics and make tough decisions. I never had to think about setting a shuttle or checking a gauge, and I was only allowed to paddle runs that my coach said I was ready for—I never had to make that decision myself.

Some "slalom kids" never quite make the transition to paddling as an adult, usually due to burnout. I didn't paddle for two years after quitting competitive slalom. Coming back to paddling, I quickly learned how to check the gauge of my local run and for rivers farther away; I learned what levels were good for play and when to stay away or run the sneak lines. I started making my own choices about who to paddle with, when to step it up, and when to play it safe.

Then, when I was twenty-three, I left the DC area for Fort Collins, Colorado. For the first time in more than ten years of paddling I had to learn new, local rivers and find new paddling friends. My first season paddling in Colorado ended suddenly after a run down the Bailey section of the South Platte. I had done the run before at 150 cfs lower, and I assumed I could easily handle higher flows. For the most part, I was right. However, when we were coming into the last big rapid, I missed the set-up eddy on the left. Confident that I remembered the line, I straightened myself out and went over the first drop. I was surprised at the size of the hole at this level, and I flipped. I felt a pop in my shoulder. I pulled my skirt. It was my first swim in four years, and it was a bad one—I was slammed repeatedly against rocks, and my friend had to fish me out at the bottom.

"You should try to paddle to the take-out," I remember him saying. "There aren't any real rapids left."

Whether it was the shock of dislocating my shoulder or my desire to impress this paddling friend, I agreed. I got back in my boat, and I watched my friend paddle away. I was left at the back of the group. We approached a rapid, I had to brace, and I felt my shoulder dislocate again, then clank back into place. Grimacing in pain and on the verge of tears, I clumsily caught an eddy. I then informed the group that I would walk to the take-out.

Two years later, I felt another pop in my shoulder. This time, the rapid was much smaller, and I realized I could roll up. I floated over to my friends—a trusted group with whom I had paddled numerous times since my bad experience on Bailey—and told them my shoulder had subluxed, and I needed to get out. My friends were sympathetic, and they did not hesitate to help get me safely back to the car.

I paddle only with trusted friends now, and I listen to my body. My physical and mental well-being are so much better because of it.

Lily Durkee is a PhD candidate at Colorado State University studying ecology, evolution, and conservation. She is also the founder and president of the 501(c)(3) nonprofit organization Diversify Whitewater. She has been kayaking for fifteen years, and hopes to paddle for the rest of her life.

CELEBRATE THE FAILURES: LEVERAGING DECISIONS ON MOUNT RAINIER

I am always willing to try new things, all while being uncertain of the outcome. If I fail, I will stand up and try another way. I also find it flattering that others view me as someone who is not flattened by failure but rather who leverages it, and that they seek to emulate this approach. Being supported this way has certainly been helpful in my taking on outdoor adventures that might result in failure, and I'm grateful for the many privileges I enjoy that let me do so.

Soon after we were married, Justin and I were invited to climb Mount Rainier as part of a non-guided trip with other outdoor professionals from a college outdoor program. It seemed like a good thing to do, having done nothing like this, and so we started with yes.

The last time there were glaciers in Michigan was the last ice age, which ended approximately twelve thousand years ago. The glaciers gave Michigan its topography—the Great Lakes and other bodies of water, the sandy soil, and the kettles and kames that populate the landscape. What the glaciers did not leave were large mountains like Rainier or places to practice mountaineering. So, Justin and I trained for Rainier by walking the stairs at the University of Michigan's Big House (the huge football stadium) while wearing weighted backpacks.

In June 2003, our random group of academics, recreation providers, IT workers, and the high school son of the expedition leader all met up at the Seattle-Tacoma airport. We also invited along another friend—a competent American Mountain Guides Association (AMGA)-certified guide—as much for his personality as for his expertise. We had our checklists, and we had all brought gear or rented boots, crampons, and ice axes for the adventure.

We laughed and joked in the parking lot as we ate lunch and packed our gear a final time. It was beautiful as we set out from the trailhead, amidst the blue sky, the snow, and the stands of conifers. We hiked and moved along a worn trail. Just after lunch, we set up a station to learn and practice self-arrest skills on a broad, gentle snowfield that had enough angle for us to practice, but no serious repercussions if we did not have the skill mastered. I had done self-arrest drills twice in the Wind River Range of Wyoming, but I was far from an expert and I welcomed the refresher. Afterward, we trudged on and set up camp.

FIRST NIGHTS ON THE MOUNTAIN

We hiked to our first camp, at around 10,000 feet on the 14,411-foot mountain, and set up. Justin was not feeling particularly well, and I remember pitching the tent and getting him situated as I worked on other things like dinner. We had a variety of tents and people, but everyone was responsible for their own setup. I remember thinking, "Now that we are married, of course my husband is getting sick on this trip," and also realized my fear of not being fit enough for the climb paled compared to the reality of one of us falling ill. Many of us have a fear of being the weak link in anything. Most groups can readily accommodate and understand the need to move at a slower pace or adjust, but everyone dreads being the cause. There is a certain sigh of relief—on a hike, a walk, a run, or a swim—when someone else says, "I'm going to go easy," so that the whole group then backs off a bit.

The first night on the mountain was not that cold—a relief, since this had been my biggest worry. But in the morning, Justin was *not* well at all; in fact, he was throwing up, likely from altitude sickness. It didn't seem life-threatening at this point, but it was miserable for him. I packed up our gear, and we adjusted the weight distribution for the day. We hiked on, now getting into real mountaineering steps but not yet roped up. Kicking steps into snow and following the climber in front was new to me—and it was incredible. I felt like I was designed to do this: carry weight and just move, methodically, step after step. Up we went.

We got to our second camp, situating it in a place that was not in an avalanche or rockfall path. The sun continued to beat down—it was a comfortable temperature and I was unaware of the risk of falling ice and rock as the massive, crumbling stratovolcano warmed. We ate and hung out, with the plan of going to bed early and then heading off early in the morning, when it was cooler, to climb through a more technical section. Justin would not make the summit attempt—he felt better, but he was still sick and so would wait at camp. I went to bed excited for the morning!

That night, the two most accomplished climbers left to check out the intended route and evaluate the ice and rock. They came back in the early morning, having passed through the technical and dangerous icefall area. They shared that it seemed too dangerous to take up our large group, knowing that the day was supposed to bring more clear skies, and thus heat—and rockfall and avalanche risk—to Rainier's glaciated upper slopes. Some in the group decided to try anyway, to see how far they could get. Others decided to wait at camp until they returned. I decided that, even though summitting was a goal, the climb seemed too risky; for me, it was not the right time to do it. I could always just come back. Ultimately, only the two most accomplished climbers summitted that day.

REFLECTIONS AFTER RAINIER

There is something magical about an expedition, being with a group of strangers, and getting close to them throughout the adventure. On Rainier, what affected me the most was my time spent with the group—preparing for the trip, talking in the parking lot, eating lunch up on the mountain, cooking and sharing other meals, and feeling insignificant as we looked out together from our perch atop a particularly steep pitch.

Questions of self-doubt—*Can I keep up? Will I get along with the group?* —are answered during an adventure as it develops. If everyone were better at accepting the uncomfortableness of newness, in any sort of endeavor, they could have a more fulfilling experience. All the gumption in the world comes not from competence, but confidence—not in achievement but in the ability to try, to learn, to adjust.

Outdoor experiences can be transformative for individuals and for groups. When I reflect on the Rainier trip, I am proud we tried something we had never done before and worked through our self-doubt and nervousness in the face of the unknown. Justin's health remained stable when he stopped pushing to higher elevations, and it improved dramatically on the descent. His altitude mountain sickness certainly had been uncomfortable for him, and this was the first time I had experienced communicating with a large group about balancing an individual's health needs with the group's desire to summit. But not requiring everyone to push for the summit, even though that was the intention for the trip, was the best decision we made as a group. Even those who tried to go a little farther but ultimately turned back felt like that had been the best decision for them. It was not the trip we'd expected, but it was nonetheless a grand adventure and a positive process. And it had a good outcome: we all came home alive!

TAKEAWAYS

- Assess the situation. Gather all the information you can using every avenue possible (checking paperwork, asking participants what they know, asking about events that led up to the here and now, understanding what duress the person may be under, understanding weather, fatigue, etc.).
- Prioritize, then act. Not acting is a decision.
- Make your decision, and then move forward with the consequences.
- Be open to input, but ultimately make decisions based on your own knowledge and values.
- Right decision or best decision? Make the best decision you can; arriving at the "right" decision will always elude you.
- Celebrate the failures—they allow for future successes.

THIRSTY FOR **MORE**?

Do you remember a time when you made a poor decision that affected other people?

How involved are you in group decision-making? If you are not the decision-maker, can you support the decisions that others make? Or do you judge how they could have done better?

Have you been positively or negatively affected because of others' decision-making in an outdoor setting?

CHAPTER 10
LEADING CHANGE

Leadership is a choice. Leading others well inspires them to change their thinking, and it changes their behaviors, resulting in positive outcomes. As a leader, you can either create change or respond it. Change management requires extraordinary leadership in which you lean on trust, communication, and sharing your vision; it also requires you to be ready to encounter and mitigate resistance. Change can be simple, complicated, or simply complicated! People are motivated to change when they feel they could benefit, but will resist change if they believe they will lose their advantages.

A leader can support change by helping a group achieve something they otherwise might or could not do, like kayak a raging river or mountain-bike a technical trail or scale a glaciated peak. Change can uplift and advance individuals and groups in the outdoors, instilling in participants aspirations to visit wild, new destinations and a yearning for adventure.

INTENTIONAL CHANGE

When I interviewed to become the first executive director of the Association of Outdoor Recreation and Education (AORE), I gave a presentation to the board, and I led with a sentence about what I hoped would be my legacy: "I will champion for the advancement of the outdoor professional." A short video by the bestselling author Daniel Pink, which had been used for marketing his book *Drive: The Surprising Truth About What Motivates Us*, had recently inspired me. Pink shares that motivation comes when you ask yourself two questions: (1) "What is my sentence? These words state what your legacy would be," and (2) "Was I better today than I was yesterday?" His premise is that we can lead our own lives by repeatedly focusing on what we set out to do, then reflecting on whether we're acting to support that intention.

We can lead our own lives by repeatedly focusing on what we set out to do, then reflecting on whether we're acting to support that intention.

This is what leading change is about. There are so many things to change—politics, programs, and policies, as examples—that can contribute to a better world. I like change. I have always struggled with how best to leverage my privilege and opportunity. If I am looked at as a leader, I should attempt to be a change agent rather than a complicit beneficiary of privilege and position.

Why is change so difficult? From what I've seen, it's often because individuals in power both consciously (they don't want to change) and unconsciously (they cannot see how the status quo benefits them) don't want to see change, because they're the ones who benefit the most from the structures and systems that were developed to support the majority and its decision-makers.

REMAINING RELEVANT: INSPIRE CHANGE BY COMMUNICATING YOUR VISION

Leading others is all very complicated. To be relevant, a leader must have the information, resources, and the network to help move themselves and others forward. A leader must also keep these tools honed and ready to use, which means staying abreast of and/or cultivating change.

Change is the opportunity to improve. However, as I wrote earlier, not everyone wants this opportunity, because it poses a threat to power structures and to the status quo. Individuals must first want to change, and they must believe or trust the leader they are choosing to follow. To become that trusted leader, you need to learn to clearly and proactively communicate your vision for change, and then be flexible about how you get followers on board, as every person and situation will be different.

Over my years as a leader, I've learned that the best way to implement positive change is to convince others to believe this change is of their own making. This is not a new concept. I may be more successful than others in leading change because I connect with people, listen to their needs and interests, find common ground, and make suggestions, but I also let them take ownership so they want to make the change themselves.

As an example of this philosophy, AORE and Sierra Club Military Outdoors are establishing a Center for Veterans Employment in the Outdoors that informs transitioning service members of opportunities for education and employment in the outdoor fields. The vision is that AORE would become a leader in veteran employment in the areas of outdoor recreation, reaction therapy, outdoor adventure and experiential education, outdoor education, outdoor behavioral health care, and industry-related fields such as product design and retail. AORE has an opportunity to develop strategies that will positively impact the outdoor community, improve access to the outdoors for marginalized communities, and be a national leader in cross-sector collaboration. Our nation's veterans have demonstrated leadership skills that are transferable for employment in the outdoors, yet there is no clearly defined path, support structure, or capacity built for this potentially impactful workforce. This is what AORE can do, intentionally, to support veteran employment outdoors.

Learning How to Foster Change

COURTNEY ABER

Years ago, I started a new position running an outdoor program. We determined that the youth, when signing up, could choose which gender they identified with. Another program in our organization adopted the same policy, and we were excited about having a space for youth to be their authentic selves. Then the first openly trans participant signed up, and our CEO was not on board with the plan.

I was asked to meet with the CEO and another program representative. The CEO explained that, yes, as an organization we supported allowing youth to choose their gender, but that any trans kids would need to sleep in a separate cabin because our programs were not set up to support them. I shared my deep conviction (in the imperfect language I had at the time) about the importance of not being separated; the program staff also shared their conviction that we could manage it. We also suggested a few minor ways we could change the program to accommodate. But the CEO wouldn't budge. I left the meeting thinking he was an old, out-of-touch jerk. I felt quite righteous in my anger; I was fighting the patriarchy and restrictive gender norms, and it felt pretty good.

Problem was, there was still a young person who wasn't going to get what they needed and deserved from our outdoor program. If anything was going to change, I could only start with me. Getting past my own judgment was going to be important.

I found out more about what our CEO cared about. He needed more options and information than I'd provided in our first meeting, and he wanted to understand how this change would benefit everyone. I came to learn he was committed to equity, but this was a new arena for him, and he was learning. Honestly, I realized I was learning too, and I studied more data on trans youth and best practices for meeting their needs.

Eventually, that young person did participate in our programs, sleeping in a cabin with others. It was not an easy process, but our organization began to make changes to our systems and advocate for those we work with to do the same. It took many people acting as change agents, including the participant's family, who had the grace to educate us in both subtle and strong ways. It also took a full year to make it happen—I wish it had been quicker and that it had been easier for this kid to join us.

Later, the CEO who I had thought was a jerk became a friend of mine—someone whose opinion I respect and value. Although we don't always see eye to eye, I now understand how his compassion shows up in the world. The biggest lessons for me were that if I want to foster change, I need to find out what others care about and why, and I may need to change my style to meet theirs. I also learned that change usually takes more time than I want it to, and more courage than I may feel in the moment.

Courtney Aber (she/her) is the national director of YMCA Bold & Gold, an immersive outdoor program that brings youth together across the divisions of race and socioeconomics to create opportunities for them to learn about each other and themselves.

CHANGE MANAGEMENT REQUIRES EXTRAORDINARY LEADERSHIP

A leader is often asked to change an organization and the way work is done there. Each organization will have structures, systems, and people who understand and perform various roles and tasks, report in a certain manner, and receive feedback or outcomes in ways that are familiar. Even if how the organization operates is frustrating, or individuals have challenges with each other, it's understood that the organization operates in a certain way. Thus, it's not uncommon for change to be met with opposition, and it can be difficult for a new leader to determine whether this reluctance is based on the suggested new ways of operating or if it's just change itself that is uncomfortable.

AORE hosted a three-day virtual Outdoor Recreation Inclusive Summit to help attendees recognize and actively change exclusionary practices within outdoor recreation and education. This was AORE's third Inclusive Summit in two years, and I'd participated in all of them, each time learning more about my own limited views around inclusive outdoor recreation and how I might improve them.

As a white woman leader in this space and as someone who hosts events, I'm often torn between those who think I am not doing enough (most certainly!) to create inclusivity and those who think using AORE's resources to support JEDI work is not necessary. In discussing the huge dissonance in the membership's views, a member of the board of directors put it eloquently by saying that some members felt the AORE was missing out on attracting would-be members by being late to the dance in doing JEDI work, while other members seemed to be completely unaware of JEDI issues and felt no need or pressure to change and learn.

Anticipate resistance—it's an opportunity to lead. So, at these events, instead of focusing on those members who resist opening themselves to JEDI work, I decided instead to focus on thanking those who were participating, adding this into my opening speech:

If you are just starting or learning about JEDI and inclusive practices, thank you for being here.

I hope you learn some things, and I hope you reflect on your role and find ways to be more inclusive in your outdoor facilitation.

If you have or have had access to professional support, and have been applying JEDI and inclusive practices in your work, thank you for being here.

I hope you will meet others who may help deepen your understanding, connect with the various speakers, and become more involved in associations they lead or support.

If you are in a position of power and leadership in your organization, thank you for being here.

I hope you will seek ways to hold yourself accountable to elevate those you lead in facilitation and your policies and procedures.

I hope you will consider how you can mentor, invite, volunteer, and support others in their learning of JEDI.

Broadening Collaboration

TALDI HARRISON

In March 2020, the early days of the COVID-19 pandemic, the United States was in lockdown. With indoor activities curtailed and so much unknown about the virus, many Americans turned to outdoor activities for their mental and physical health, some of them for the first time. Those of us in the outdoor industry fielded questions about how people could get outside safely during a pandemic. As public lands prepared to reopen in summer 2020, a year that would see record visitation, it was clear we needed broader collaboration between outdoor users, outdoor businesses, land managers, nonprofit organizations, and the public to provide guidance about how to get outside safely. By May 2020, we launched the Recreate Responsibly Coalition as a collaborative space for collective problem-solving between a diverse network of stakeholders invested in keeping our public lands open, safe, and accessible for all.

The early days of the pandemic sparked an intense itch to just *do* something, yet there was no clear sense of what to do or how to do it. What was clear was the outdoor community's passion to help the public access our public lands for their health and well-being in a time of great uncertainty and suffering. The ever-changing way we worked, now by weekly video calls, enabled us to unite a national coalition, collectively problem-solve, and co-create guiding principles for how to recreate responsibly. Grounded in a shared purpose, these weekly meetings fostered a sense of trust, communication, and communal vision. We all learned as we went, not just about COVID, but also about equitable access, public land-management issues, and large-scale coalition building.

Within months, more than fifteen hundred organizations had joined the coalition. Recreate Responsibly had no paid staff, and no one organization owned the movement. It operated on volunteer fervor, which incidentally fostered a creativity and a freedom in how people came to the table, ready to employ their gifts and skills. I found when individuals arrived authentically and felt integral to the effort, their commitment to the enterprise and to the team grew. As it grew, so did their willingness to take on more responsibility and risk.

COVID changed everything: how we worked, communicated, and spent time outside. Yet in responding to those changes with a shared vision and a united team, we created a community of practice and learning that was able to adapt to the uncertain terrain of a world grappling with a pandemic and produced meaningful guidance that helped millions of Americans recreate responsibly.

Taldi Harrison (she/her) is the director of community government affairs at REI Co-op. With more than fifteen years of experience in federal government affairs, coalition-building, and philanthropy, Taldi works to increase equitable access to the outdoors and ensure that the United States takes meaningful action to address the climate crisis.

BE A COMPETITOR (EVEN IF YOU AREN'T COMPETITIVE)

AORE was loosely established by outdoor educators in the 1980s and received its 501(c)(3) status in 1993, allowing it to support college, university, military, and nonprofit outdoor-recreation programs. These programs exist to instill positive outcomes like leadership, self-responsibility, decision-making, and servant leadership for eighteen- to twenty-four-year-olds at a critical developmental point in their lives. Through AORE's history, the organization has tried to support its members by offering a network in which to share, learn, and grow.

As the outdoor industry started to understand how overlooked and underrepresented populations cannot easily access public lands and recreational opportunities, AORE likewise began considering how best to support individuals in these populations. Speaking candidly, AORE has always depended on colleges and universities for its financial base,

Key Challenges around JEDI from a Nonprofit Lens

There may be challenges to an organization's growth and awareness around diversity, equity, and inclusion, including how the organization completes the work and understands the major issues. I asked an independent contractor to capture key challenges, and they noted:

Critical of progress. People—members and conference attendees—may be critical of the nonprofit's JEDI work. A chief complaint is that the organization says a lot but does little. In other words, there's more theory delivered than practice.

Afraid of stepping forward. The nonprofit's members and volunteers seem intimidated by diversity work. Few are willing to step forward and contribute to this topic, let alone serve as content and thought leaders. There is a genuine fear of fumbling and making a mistake, to the point of nonaction.

Consultant or bust. The directive has consistently been to hire a specialized consultant on this topic. Short of that, it's either "not worth doing" or interest simply fizzles. The perception is that if the work is not done externally, then there is no validity or value to it.

Funding is the only answer. Since consultants cost money, there are typically annual requests to fund a JEDI consultant. If funding is not allocated or grants are not acquired, the perception is that the organization can't do the work, and all momentum is abandoned.

Awaiting the perfect storm. Finally, there seems to be an overwhelming "all or nothing" mentality. In other words, if all the stars (or ideal conditions) don't align (e.g., hiring a consultant and finding funding), all confidence and interest are lost and little to no action is taken.

and when those funds are decreased or diminished, AORE starts to lose revenue. Thus, AORE can't help remove financial barriers for underserved populations when this monetary and member support dry up.

Because the mainstream outdoor industry has been focused on white, able-bodied, and affluent recreationists (read: potential customers), identity groups that enjoy getting outdoors have had to establish their own nonprofit organizations. AORE will never be able to serve the needs of all these identity groups adequately, nor should it ask these groups to assimilate into how AORE membership chooses to recreate—we won't be competitive.

But what AORE can do is help the predominantly white, majority male–led college and university outdoor organizations that comprise our membership base learn to expand their JEDI knowledge and then apply that to leading intentionally and appropriately. AORE can be a competitor and catalyst in creating longitudinal change in these higher-education programs by supporting members with actionable JEDI work, assisting them in building DEI program audits, having diverse staff and leaders, implementing DEI program policies, and developing leadership and succession planning. This will result in better-run programs in which everyone can participate, as well as the creation of staff trainings and leadership roles that better reflect on-campus and community diversity.

Is There One Best Way?

I had a once-in-a-lifetime opportunity to travel to China to present about the value of outdoor recreation at various colleges across the country. I was part of a contingent from the University of Minnesota that has established exploring sports as a means for international understanding. I did not know what the experience would be like in a part of the world I had neither experienced nor studied, and I was nervous.

Imagine speaking in front of hundreds of college students and professors in an auditorium thousands of miles from home where you don't speak the language and each sentence needs to be translated for your audience. I'd been told that the Chinese government had expressed interest in learning how to be the best outdoor educator and in learning how to do so at scale; they thought the work AORE was doing as an association and at a college-recreation-program level could provide some insight.

I shared that there was no singular best way to be an outdoor leader, and that the components that led to successful experiences represented an ever-evolving combination of technical, teaching, and leadership skills taught in a very fluid environment. While I really believe in the power of outdoor experiences, I was frustrated that I couldn't offer one "best" way.

The hosts treated our group like royalty, in so many ways. They showed us the highlights of their cities, from parks to museums to places to eat. I met dignitaries and Olympians. As the tour went on, it became more evident the hosts really wanted a road map, a clear direction, on how to make sure they could be the best at outdoor recreation, but the beauty of outdoor recreation is that there will never be a single "best" way to experience the outdoors.

WHO GETS TO BE CONSIDERED A LEADER?

Outdoor leaders and leadership are changing. Take the "Women in Leadership" chapter in an earlier book on leadership, *Outdoor Leadership* by John Graham, for example. It explores, from the author's perspective, how women can also be considered outdoor leaders. As I re-read the chapter, I was frustrated with the misogyny in outdoor recreation, while I also recognized that there are many current and future leaders—beyond male and female labels—who are actively trying to change the literal face of and faces in the outdoors. Here is an excerpt from the 1998 book:

A man's world? Women make just as good leaders as men, and the basic principles of good leadership apply to both genders.

Women lead differently than men. Each gender tends to excel in areas in which the other doesn't.

Each gender can learn from the other. Both women and men need to see the differences in their leadership as strengths rather than weaknesses in the other gender—and a rich basis for learning from each other.

The ideal leader combines traits generally regarded as the predominant strengths of one gender over the other. Good leaders use every aspect of their beings to lead.

Women leading outdoors—and in. The training, experience, and self-confidence women gain as leaders in the outdoors can help them change constraining relationships at home and break through glass ceilings at work.

Leading Change

The more I thought about that "Women in Leadership" chapter, the more I realized how fortunate I've been to have had the opportunity to co-lead change—to expand the narrative to allow for new results—with many people, of different genders and identities. Considering that, I'd like to propose the following rewrites to the first three excerpts above (we'll dive a little deeper in the section that follows for the final two items):

- **A *leader's* world.** Anyone can be a good leader, and the basic principles of good leadership apply to all genders. In chapter 7, I noted that woman may lead differently than men because of their different lived experiences. Similarly, by raising awareness of the lasting impact of toxic masculinity and gender roles, we can name the fact that being a man doesn't make you a natural or competent leader. Left unchallenged or unquestioned, incompetent male leaders tend to assume positions of authority in group settings, even if they haven't built the capacity for good leadership.

- **Differences in leadership are a result of choice.** This book is built on the concept that leadership is a choice, and good leaders make better choices repeatedly, regardless of their gender. You can only be a good leader if you work on it, and this may mean unlearning what you've been taught your entire life in order to learn new things that you've never or rarely experienced.

- **Leaders can learn from other leaders.** The leaders I have admired the most throughout my career—regardless of gender—have been the ones who knowingly seek ways to improve themselves and their competencies as a leader. I believe outdoor skills can be acquired, and I feel most favorably inclined toward leaders who have worked hard to become better at communication—they read leadership books, listen to podcasts, send notes of encouragement and reflection, and have candid and clear discussions.

Learning from Each Other

Each of us has a different leadership style, and each of us excels in areas where others don't. One of the most effective things a leader can do— both for their own learning and in how they show up for participants—is to step outside their typical or perceived area of expertise, and lead in a new arena. For instance, for a male co-leader on a backpacking trip, this might include leading the bathroom discussion and overseeing food purchasing, organizing, and kitchen setup—areas typically assigned to women. I've seen this put into action a couple of times, but one that stood out is when my co-leader Dave and I took high schoolers into Alaska's Talkeetna Range. There are many things that must happen on any adventure, and while a monthlong expedition to Alaska (two weeks sea kayaking and two weeks hiking) may not be in your immediate future, the gift Dave gave to those students—our working dynamic—was incredible. I've drawn on that experience here, in rewriting the final two bullet points.

- **An ideal leader considers the care and commitment continuum and looks to be transformational.** Introducing backcountry behavior to novices is a heavy lift. It reminds me of a plane that is taking off: whether you have 25 or 250 people on board, you still need to go through all the safety protocols.

  In Alaska, following the shakedown of gear and preparation to head out, Dave took the lead in addressing bathroom basics to a nervous crowd. He was thorough and used plenty of humor as he discussed challenges the women on the trip might face when urinating in the backcountry, and with all the care in the world he took the time to explain, and even act out, ways to avoid peeing on themselves or their clothes. He addressed menstruation and packing out toilet paper. His delivery was candid and full of compassion; it demonstrated to the group that he was aware and approachable, and that participants of all genders could choose to discuss with either of us anything that may historically have been gendered in a male/female co-led team.

Organizing food is another area in which, while it was historically assigned to women, male leaders can apply their leadership skills, including communication, listening, and group dynamics. This includes helping a group plan and purchase the food, communicating clearly what the caloric needs are and which cooking resources the group will have, listening to and accommodating dietary preferences, being competent in cooking, planning a variety of diverse and nutritious meals, and being able to manage a kitchen in the field. Perhaps your typical male leader has never had to consider these tasks before, but they can be easily learned, and his taking them on frees up his co-leader to address logistics, other gear, and technical items. It might initially be hard for a male co-leader to see what he may never have been—or needed to be—aware of, and, simultaneously, it may be difficult to unlearn that behavior. But all genders can learn from each other. People need to see the differences in their leadership as strengths rather than weaknesses in another gender—and as a rich basis for learning from each other. As we—people of all genders—continue our leadership journeys, we can work on being more aware. What a great opportunity for us!

- **Women—and other nondominant cultures—leading outdoors and in.** The training, experience, and self-confidence people gain as leaders in the outdoors can transfer into their personal lives, work lives, and relationships. Leading outdoors gives quick and true feedback and expedites growth and understanding which can, with reflection, be easily transferred to leadership roles and positions people are pursuing.

TAKEAWAYS

- Change can uplift and advance individuals and groups in the outdoors.
- Leaders remain relevant by inspiring change.
- Anticipate resistance to change; it's an opportunity to lead.
- Change requires extraordinary leadership; people crave consistency.
- Leaders **must** communicate a compelling vision.

THIRSTY FOR **MORE?**

A tangible vision and a clear direction are critical for leading. Leaders ask when improvement or growth is needed:

- What is the desired outcome?
- What problems might you encounter?
- What operations, systems, or structures will be affected?
- What actions do you need to take?
- Who will be affected?
- Will this change be in alignment with the values of the organization?
- What is the goal?
- What is the problem?
- What is the truth?
- What is the change?
- What is the action?

CHAPTER 11
AN AUDACIOUS AND COMPELLING VISION

Where do you want to go? And who do you want to be your leader? "Vision" means seeing the essence of something not quite in focus and what it could be, and then working toward that thing. It's the thought of something more, something difficult to pin down but easy to paint in colors, words, and feelings. Identifying and agreeing to a common desired outcome—one that is exciting and achievable, yet still presents a challenge—is paramount to bringing together those whom you lead.

Today's outdoor leaders must bring their values to the job as they connect people to outdoor spaces. This requires recognizing barriers that have existed (and may still exist) and crafting a better future in which all can connect to the outdoors. How do we achieve this? We do so by sharing our vision for this desired future state with our followers and fellow leaders, through communication, community-building, and quests that combine fun, adventure, and learning opportunities.

WHERE ARE YOU HEADED?

Have you ever been asked this question? Maybe it was when you were turned around on a hike or while out cycling, or maybe your mentor or friend was the one asking. Did you know the answer? Could you share your intention—your goal? Was it a physical destination you had painstakingly planned out, or was it more abstract—a way you aim to be present in the world?

One thing is certain: if you don't have a vision, you won't reach your goal. If you don't have something you are working toward, there is little hope for forward progress. In that way, vision is much like open-water swimming, something I've been doing for a large portion of my life and that has offered transformative experiences I work to apply in my leadership.

I've always been a very physically active person, and while I've played my share of basketball, volleyball, and softball, I also fell into rowing in college. I thrived in rowing until back surgery modified my Olympic aspirations. I started open-water swimming after that so I'd have an athletic endeavor my body could tolerate.

Fortunately, Michigan has plenty of swimming opportunities—water literally surrounds the state.

Outdoor experiences aren't limited to rock climbing, paddling, mountaineering . . . or open-water swimming. You may be learning from birding, standup paddleboarding, a hike on the beach, or a trail run. The point is that, with whatever outdoor pursuit, you are learning and growing with a vision to be better tomorrow than you are today.

Vision Starts with *Yes*

I like to start with yes; it's my preferred answer. Should we go on this adventure? *Yes*. Can we work together? *Yes*. Would you like to participate? *Yes*. Would you like to learn more? *Yes*. A good leader can say *No*, but I always like to assume something is possible. Somehow.

From a day hike or afternoon bike ride to swimming around an island. I like preparing for the adventure, gaining the fitness and diving into the planning, and then just being in the moment. As a mom, it's been important to me that my kids share in this ethos as well.

One of the biggest *Yes* things our family did was drive to Alaska in 2018. With a grade-schooler and middle-schooler, work demands, financial limitations, and obligations we couldn't skip, we had many reasons to say *No*. It took a lot of planning, saving, prioritizing, and gumption, but I'm so happy we made this trip a priority and I think very fondly of it to this day.

That time with the kids in those wild places was priceless, as were visits with friends we met up with along the way and being present in such magnificent places. The wildness and remoteness of the trip and the way our family team worked to set and break camp, cook, clean, grocery-shop, and live in close quarters was a gift that continues to provide joy.

Six weeks is a long time for an adventure, and if you asked Gretel, a painfully long time to be in a twelve-passenger van with her little brother and parents. Still, photos from the trip include our family having fun at silly roadside attractions in small towns, checking out things like a twenty-foot-high buffalo, the world's largest beaver, moose, teapot, and Easter egg. We listened to audiobooks, and we panned for gold in the Yukon. The kids became Junior Rangers in many national parks. We did laundry at dusty laundromats and ate ice cream on the steps as we watched families come to "town" for groceries. We navigated car repairs on the Kenai Peninsula and eye infections in Wrangell–St. Elias. We heard wolves howl and watched whale flukes fade under the water. We rode in a Cessna and, from the air, watched a glacier calve. There were tears and there were fears to overcome, but we collected stickers to put on the van and we found ourselves relishing our time with our children in a way we will always be thankful for.

And it was all because we said *Yes*.

GET COMFORTABLE BEING UNCOMFORTABLE

Open-water swimming is one of those athletic pursuits that, after you see it, you talk about how crazy those people are. Open-water swims can be cold and long, goggles can leak, and arms and necks can chafe with or without wetsuits. You're often swimming for hours to get to a finish line that you can't see. It's uncomfortable, and most people don't enjoy being uncomfortable. Exercising visionary leadership can be challenging as well; it's not always comfortable to share your vision. There are, in fact, many parallels between open-water swimming and visionary leadership:

- **Learning what you can and can't control:** On a swim, water temperature is one factor that's impossible to control. To manage the discomfort, you can wear a wetsuit, booties, and gloves. In leadership situations, there will often be too many facets to manage, so leading requires making a decision using as much information as you can ascertain, but certainly understanding you may not have all you desire.

- **Learning to be accountable to yourself:** Swimming is monotonous. It takes stroke after endless stroke for hours many times a week to build stamina for a long swim. Cold, early mornings can be unpleasant for training, but having the discipline to be consistent and follow training plans, without skipping days, means you can count on being able to finish a long swim. As a leader, making a strategic plan is one thing, but consistently completing the tasks, especially the monotonous ones, is another. The monotonous tasks are just as important as the vision.

- **Learning perspective:** There is simply no way to be able to see the finish of an open-water, point-to-point swim, such as when crossing a lake, swimming a big river, or traversing a chain of lakes. In order to make forward progress, a swimmer sights on the next visible buoy, similar to reaching a benchmark or progress point while advancing a leadership mission.

- **Learning to be more present:** Long-distance swimming is just that: long! The hours in the water can seem endless, making you wish it was all over. To combat this, you can make yourself be present—seeing where you are, rather than imagining where you want to be, looking at the bubbles that follow each stroke as it breaks the water, swimming over a turtle or following a fish, seeing stunning rocks below in clear waters. Catching success in the present, while immersed in the process, can help motivate you onward to the desired future end state.

THE POWER OF THE BHAG

I'm a big fan of the big hairy audacious goal (BHAG), a term Jim Collins and Jerry Porras coined in the book *Built to Last*. The BHAG is long-term—ten- to twenty-five-year timeline—and guided by core values and purpose. Looking this far ahead is a way to perceive a goal beyond the immediate barriers that seem to separate us from it, such as not having enough money or time or fitness. With a BHAG, I dream big, I make big plans, and I have every intention of achieving them. Sharing the vision and building a team that will support the process is critical. For example, my swim group focuses on the big, open-water swims, which are usually over 5 kilometers long—more than 3.1 miles! Being in this group means I must show up and be accountable; we give each other the support to train year-round. We spend weekends doing three- to four-hour swims in local lakes or we drive across the state to swim in Lake Michigan.

There is freedom in open-water swimming, where there are no limitations of lap lanes or pool walls. But to navigate this freedom—all this open water—I need sight. Sighting is looking up and forward, trying to choose a buoy or a boat, or perhaps a cottage across the lake, and then swimming toward it. This continual process of sighting—looking up, choosing a point, and working toward it, adjusting as needed—applies equally to leadership and decision-making. Any long swim has a sequence of events that unfold. After the initial shock of the water, the doubt and the questioning are replaced with something else: calm. But it takes time to get to that calm. It takes going through a fair bit of discomfort, negative self-talk, and duress. Then, time passes, and I realize I'm not thinking at all. I'm just swimming.

I've found my power, and I can watch the clear blue bubbles come off my fingertips with each stroke. The sun cuts in and gives me the ability to see the bottom, the rocks. The water, like my head, is crystal clear.

Where the Fun Happens

VICTORIA LOPEZ-HERRERA

I never considered myself "outdoorsy." My vision of someone who was outdoorsy was a person with the means to own cool gear, travel to amazing places, and do adventurous things. The picture in my head was of a group of fit, well-equipped white folks. I'm not those folks. I am a Latina with curves from a lower-middle-class family. Being outdoorsy was what other people did, so I wrapped that picture up and stored it away.

Then I had an opportunity to travel to Costa Rica for an adventure trip with a group of women. While preparing for the trip and envisioning what it would be like, I thought, *Maybe I can be outdoorsy*. This amazing trip put me in uncomfortable situations and forced me to confront the picture I had created in my head about being outdoorsy. It was the beginning of a long journey of exploring what "outdoorsy" meant for me. I had to confront and modify the vision I had referred to for most of my life. I dove into my ancestral roots and remembered how we stewarded the land and its gifts of healing, growth, and life. Time is cyclical, and we are connected to our family and other-than-human relatives. I realized, for me, that being outdoorsy could mean going outside my front door and stopping to feel the breeze, hear the animals, or connect to the earth. This opened a new perspective. I was able to pull out that old picture and revise it.

As a leader, I'm someone who naturally looks into the future by way of observing patterns and making connections. Thus, I find it easy and enjoyable to create a vision for a team. My mind is in constant motion, and I'm always thinking about what is on the horizon. However, once I have committed to a big picture, it can be difficult for me to adjust, and I sometimes get in my own way by being inflexible. But sharing a vision doesn't have to include how we get there; rather, it can simply inspire others to join in the journey and for us all to be open to new experiences and unforeseen events along the way.

I must create space for others (and myself) to bring their whole selves and offer freedom from old narratives. I take morning walks. Each night, I envision waking up, double-knotting my shoes, and walking out the door. I don't know which path I will take, but I know I'm going to be outside breathing in the beautiful air and connecting with the earth. And, once I get home, I know I'm going to feel a hell of a lot better. A vision can always be in place; how we get there is where the fun happens.

Victoria Lopez-Herrera *(she/her/ella) is a partner, mother, sorority woman, and Xicanista. She has worked in higher education for more than twenty years and has served on the board of directors for the Association for Outdoor Recreation and Education. Other board services include Gamma Phi Beta Sorority and NIRSA Leaders in Collegiate Recreation.*

CONNECTING TO PURPOSE AND CHAMPIONING THE VISION

To move to a place that is not yet realized—in the full sense—such as a location on a quadrangle map or a goal for your organization, a leader must guide those who will be instrumental in achieving that success. The vision for AORE is "a vibrant community where everyone can connect to the outdoors." That is the end game, and if we achieve it, we will have met our BHAG. This vision, which was created by the board of directors, is our guiding light, and we work to uplift those who connect people to the outdoors, in whatever way they choose to do so. The very essence of vision is something you move toward but never quite achieve, because it's always morphing. It's the thought of something more, something difficult to pin down, yet easy to paint in colors and with words.

I am passionate about the idea of everyone being able to connect to the outdoors. Being outdoors has positively transformed my life, and I hope that everyone else has positive outdoor experiences. I like doing things outside because I feel free and alive, and I marvel at nature. I like how everything is seemingly in order, in its rightful place, but ironically, I also love the enormity and chaos of nature, and how these make it impossible for humans to always be in control. I am fortunate to have made a lifelong career out of outdoor leadership, and introducing others to adventure remains forever my purpose. A huge part of this process is clearly and inclusively championing my vision.

Vision is the desired future you are inspired by and motivated to create; mission is the method that supports this vision.

It is in this crucial moment when vision is crafted and curated, put forth, and pulled apart. The vision, at first, is a mixture of emotions and

musings: "Wouldn't it be nice . . . ?" or "Can you imagine . . . ?" It's a time when anything goes—not brainstorming per se, but co-creating a vision, building a community of individuals and perspectives that are different from my own worldview, presenting a vision to this group, and asking them what resonates, as well as what I have missed. In this way, I can incorporate perspectives I might not have considered, as well as learn about potential barriers I may not have been aware of between us and our desired outcome—our ultimate vision.

One trap to be aware of is the tendency to get lost in mission nuance as opposed to the vision. Vision is the desired future you are inspired by and motivated to create; mission is the method that supports this vision. So while visioning might be you saying, "I want to spend more time outdoors and feel comfortable and confident," mission nuance would be, "I am going to hike a three-mile trail or lead four trips for kids in my community." The problem with the latter is that it's so specific, you may not realize this exact goal, and thus get discouraged or distracted from your vision. Vision is thinking, "We want everyone to connect to the outdoors," not, "We get people outside." Can you see why the first statement would be more inspiring or visionary than the second?

A Team Vision

In college, I was an athlete at the University of Michigan, and I had the chance to be a part of the transition of the women's rowing team from club to varsity status. That was the vision. When I transferred to Michigan, rowing was a club sport, which meant fundraising, traveling in fifteen-passenger vans to the regattas, sleeping on church floors, and using and maintaining boats that were old and outdated. Standing on the shoulders of the women and men who came before us, our club program performed competitively on a national level against fully funded varsity programs. My sophomore year, rowing with six seniors, we won the Dad Vail Regatta and received a berth to compete at the Royal Henley in England. We continued to have compounding successful results at big regattas, which demonstrated our speed as a program and our ability to compete at a varsity level; in the athletic department, the women's team was elevated to varsity status. This changed everything, giving us resources such as new boats, funding to support student athletes, access to athletic trainers, and charter buses instead of vans. It also removed fundraising pressure. This upgrade eventually accelerated Michigan rowing into the top ten annually at NCAA competitions and launched the careers of many Olympic and world champions.

CREATING A POSITIVE FIRST-TIME EXPERIENCE AND THE NEED FOR A STRONGER INDUSTRY

There is a place and the space for everyone to be outdoors. Regardless of how someone experiences the outdoors—through a specific program, in a particular place, by learning a new skill, or by contributing as part of a community—an experience facilitated by a competent leader can provide myriad health and wellness, emotional, physical, and interpersonal benefits. We have come to understand, anecdotally and through empirical research, that it is good to be outdoors. Young people who are increasingly disconnected from the natural world experience depression, obesity, and attention deficit disorder. Exposing children to the wonders of public spaces and wild places can help change negative health trends and cultivate the next generation of conservation stewards. We have also come to acknowledge that the ways people experience the outdoors are fluid and more expansive than originally imagined. As outdoor leaders, it is our job to be open-minded and flexible when introducing people to nature.

The key to getting people to spend repeated time outside is a positive first-time experience. Everyone should have the opportunity to access public lands and waterways and experience the positive outcomes. To provide these facilitated outdoor experiences, it's important to develop outdoor professionals and the outdoor industry. The vision is that outdoor professionals become fully respected, valued, and compensated for their work and expertise. The financial impacts of the outdoor economy are huge, and its contributions to the GDP are significant. Now is the time to elevate the outdoor profession and professionals who will be our key advocates and ambassadors.

Career opportunities for outdoor industry professionals are countless, but often poorly remunerated. Outdoor facilitators—those who provide the rafting, climbing, caving, or paddling experiences, manage the risks, and have the technical training and competency—deserve fair and adequate compensation, professional development, training, and certifications, to name just a few. We need to invest in facilitators so we can ensure everyone is safe and happy when they go outside.

A transformative leader who's grounded in care for their group and has a high level of commitment will create and cast the vision for change. A visionary leader invites followers to contribute and co-create a better future, and they share the positive results of this desired future. With a clearly defined, described, and imagined vision—such as more support for outdoor facilitators—the individuals in an organization or members of a team can make decisions that consistently result in moving the vision forward into reality.

How I Grew into My Vision

NIKKI SMITH

What is vision? We often think some great idea will pop into our heads, and it will be clear and guide us through all the challenges we might face as we bring that vision to life. Like many of the ideas we romanticize, however, the reality is that vision alone isn't enough, nor is it always easy to find and follow.

I was always into art, and when I was five years old, my dad, an amateur photographer, gave me a point-and-shoot film camera. I took horrible photos, but my dad saw something, probably more in the act of me taking pictures than in the images themselves. He decided to blow a couple of them up and entered them in the Utah State Fair, where I won a blue ribbon for one of the photos. Even though I liked photography as a youngster, it didn't connect immediately. Our house was full of *National Geographic* magazines. I remember reading each one, looking at the photos, and imagining these faraway places. Still, I grew up in a family that didn't have much money, and for us travel outside Utah was extremely rare. My cheap point-and-shoot didn't look like the big, beautiful cameras and lenses the pros used. At the time, I couldn't conceive of being a photographer who traveled or photographed for *National Geographic*. I had to develop my experience in the world. I slowly realized I could try to make photography a career in my early twenties.

At that point, I developed my vision, but that vision alone wasn't enough. I spent years seeking feedback, begging professional photographers to review my work. I lugged a light table and magnifying loupe around for people to view the small rectangle images sandwiched in a slide sleeve. After years of getting told my work wasn't good enough, I started to create images that experienced photographers respected. So, I'd made it—right?

Unfortunately, there was still more work to be done. I had begun work on my vision, but had truly only built one facet of my expertise. I still had to learn the business side of photography: pricing and negotiations, marketing myself, and—one of the most important—building relationships and understanding my clients' needs. Each brand or magazine had a vision of their company and how they would portray that image in the photography they used. A good photograph wasn't enough; it had to be a good photograph that shared a worldview, lifestyle, or vision that matched the company's needs.

This understanding and additional skill base is something I will never stop growing and learning with. Technological changes, societal changes, and trends in photography mean that even the best photographers need to continue to learn and grow to keep their vision alive. There will be tough times and extraordinary times, but you must keep going to see a vision fulfilled. In my forties, I was officially named a National Geographic

Adventure Contributing Photographer. Looking back, I can see how many forces aligned to help shape my vision and the skills I developed to realize it. But I had to have faith in that vision and do the work required to put myself in that vision: to be like the photographers I saw in magazines as a child, to open windows into worlds, lifestyles, and people that are meaningful to me.

While she could not picture it back then, I know the little girl imagining these faraway places while looking at the pages of *National Geographic* would be so proud of us for not giving up on dreams she didn't yet understand.

Nikki Smith (she/her) is a photographer, educator, writer, and athlete based in Salt Lake City, Utah. Her work focuses on building a more inclusive, diverse, and safe community within climbing and the outdoors.

TAKEAWAYS

- Leaders, it is *not* about *you*. It is about *them*. A vision connects others to a shared cause in a way they both feel and support.
- Be clear about where you want to go; what may be obvious to you isn't obvious to everyone.
- A leader champions their vision, co-creating compelling and audacious goals with those who follow.
- Start with saying *Yes!*
- Never stop communicating the vision.
- Encourage group members to be more than they are as you move forward, together.

THIRSTY FOR **MORE?**

What is your personal vision as an outdoor leader?

What is the current vision where you lead?

How is your success connected with those whom you lead? How do you create mutual understanding?

In your desired future state, what outcomes are important to you? And what outcomes can you let go of—and why have you been resistant to releasing these outcomes?

When was the last time you participated in conversations that challenged your thinking or came from a wider perspective? If you cannot recall a conversation that didn't push you to re-examine how you lead, why are you avoiding or not prioritizing growth in this way?

CHAPTER 12
MAKING MISTAKES

I make a lot of mistakes, but I've realized mistakes are opportunities to learn and grow. Now that I know better, I can do better—to improve my skills as an outdoor leader, I can learn to appreciate my mistakes and be open to giving and receiving feedback. Other important attributes for a leader are humor and grace, the ability to get back up and try again, and cultivate a culture of learning. It's also important that a leader use risk assessment and managing risk through near misses to become more aware of the gravity of recreating in a potentially dangerous environment, thus avoiding future mistakes, some dire or even potentially life-threatening. The ultimate outcome is accountability to and ownership of that which can be prevented, as well as knowledge gained about how to mitigate or manage escalating circumstances.

No leader is perfect, but if you fear making mistakes, you will never lead; you will only follow. My list of past mistakes includes things like not having the right equipment, performing a skill poorly, reading the map incorrectly, tying the wrong knot, forgetting the fuel, and many others. But the biggest mistakes by far are those I made by *not* making a change when it was warranted. The mistake of listening to the insecurities in my head about why I should or should not proceed, instead of weighing the actual pros and cons. The mistake of not seeing at first how I was wrong, and the mistake of taking too long to apologize for this. The mistake of not considering another perspective, and the mistake of not asking for help. I've made these mistakes on every outing I've ever led. However, as I've learned, they can be countered with humility, vulnerability, and reflection; these come from my focus on care—for myself and the group—as well as from my commitment to leading mindfully.

LEARNING IS AN ITERATIVE AND IMPERFECT PROCESS

Franklin Delano Roosevelt is said to have said, "A smooth sea never made a skilled sailor." Regardless of the attribution, I cannot think of a quote that's more applicable to learning from your mistakes as a leader—challenges that result from a leader's mistakes are, when harnessed, the most powerful wind of change. The knowledge from each mistake made builds on lessons learned similarly in the past, until you eventually accrue an iterative body of learned wisdom that strengthens your ability to lead.

Critical to this process is letting go of the idea that a leader needs to be perfect. Mistakes happen, ranging from big ones like safety oversights—forgetting the first-aid kit or medicine for a preexisting condition, a missed command on the mountain, or deciding to deviate from the intended hiking route and not having an emergency response plan—to smaller ones like locking keys in your car at the trailhead or forgetting the rainflies (which turn out not to be needed). There have been so many times (more than I can count!) when I, as a leader, have made mistakes that I've long since realized I will never do things perfectly 100 percent of the time. Nonetheless, I strive to be that leader who has a reputation of listening to feedback and working to improve. If I'm to grow as a leader, I know I must also remain open to hearing about my failures, owning the impact I've had, and intentionally changing my behavior.

IMPOSTER SYNDROME AND QUELLING DOUBT

Have you seen those shirts that read "~~female~~ engineer," "~~female~~ athlete," "~~female~~ climber," "~~female~~ doctor," et cetera, with the word *female* struck through? Have you ever considered the significance of putting the gender in front of these titles, and the significant difference it makes to simply call someone an "engineer" or "leader" or "climber" or whatever and not also emphasize or include their gender?

While the above example was about female empowerment, we could really apply it to any label we give people: "Black leader," "Asian mountain biker," "Trans climber." I have to ask: What if society could recognize the constraints and limitations it puts on people who aim to lead past and through these barriers? Perhaps those in the majority—instead of being concerned about underrepresented people being a threat to them—could instead realize they don't need their own programs, because all programs have already been for them?

Continuing to use women as an example, the need to create more learning opportunities for women was brought to my attention by members at my association, AORE. Women were interested in coming together and sharing what they knew and how they felt about being female outdoor leaders. Many common issues and challenges came to light—things these women faced in their work environment—from their male supervisors and male participants. These women shared their need to always feel perfect, to be "on," to do more, to tolerate injustices including harassment, misogyny, and bias. One of our first conversations was about observing how, when working with male co-leaders, the men did not feel the need to share, and the participants did not inquire about, the depth and breadth of the men's certifications and trainings. The women, however, would start by listing theirs; perhaps classic impostor syndrome–fueled self-doubt had provoked these women's need to show that they somehow "belonged" in the leadership space, whereas the men simply assumed they did.

I could relate to many of these challenges, and I was also aware that I had in the past modified my presence to better fit in with the men I was co-leading with, using humor or athleticism and competition, tolerating more than I should, and taking on more work than those around me. I realized that perhaps this had not been the best approach; here were these younger women who followed me telling me that, while I had assimilated, they (and I) should not have to, and that we could all lead just as we were—as our full selves. It was both a brilliant and challenging discussion, one I learned a lot from.

Silencing doubt is hard—it's a work that's ever in progress, and many old tropes about gender and race and sexuality remain. Around the time of the 2016 elections, I realized many differences I was seeing and feeling as a woman leader. Women leaders might be called "aggressive," while the same behavior in a man would be called "assertive." A woman might be "bossy," while a man with the same presence is "strong." Even as society becomes more aware of these systemic and institutional biases, it is important for leaders to recognize their own growth and development, and to be grounded in that process. Leaders of all genders can continually be aware of and seek feedback on how their bias influences their decisions and sponsorship or advancement of others, including those they lead.

Failures in the Field

JENN VELIE

Whether it was in childhood competitive sports, music recitals, or school, someone always tried to cheer us up with the idea that it takes many failures to achieve success. But as children, did we even know what that meant? What was a failure, and how did we identify it as such? Was it because a game was lost? What if you played well—was that still a failure?

For many of us, reflecting on failure causes us to picture missing the playoffs, making a life-altering critical error in our decision-making, or letting down someone we care about. But failures can often take smaller, more subtle forms. I've had hundreds of failures in the field, all of them various poor decisions that have negatively affected myself and those around me. Many of those failures have shaped me into the human I am today. From them, I've learned when to push the boundaries, when to respect Mother Nature, when to read the crowd—the list goes on.

Years ago, I was invited on a 116-mile bike-packing trip with some new co-workers. I wasn't much of a cyclist, nor had I ever been bike-packing. I knew it wasn't going to be pretty, and I only had a couple weeks to train, but I was set on making it happen.

I trained, and I had the bruises to show my incompetence on a mountain bike. We loaded up the bikes, made the drive, and headed into the woods. Day one was one of the hardest things I have ever done. I was not in shape for this adventure, nor was I expecting to hike my bike so frequently. A section of the trail had recently experienced a horrendous windstorm, and there seemed to be more downed trees than trees standing. We hiked our bikes for about four hours, trying to find a way through. We were lost, cold, soaked, and had no clue how long it was going to take us to find a place to camp for the night. Finally, hours later, we found a spot and set up camp. Although the day had been rough, I'd had a blast in a type-two-fun way.

The next morning, we were set to pass through a little town where we planned to grab breakfast from a diner—a quick bite and then head off. About two to three hours into our ride, I felt sick. Minutes later, I was off the bike to use the bathroom. I was off my bike about every ten minutes after that, becoming severely dehydrated. The temperature had dropped, a storm was rolling in, and I was becoming a liability to the rest of the crew. Three of our crew headed up separately, to try to get ahead of the storm.

I was exhausted, dehydrated, malnourished, and cold. I can be very hardheaded, and I was set on finishing the ride, even if it took me an extra day. We landed on a forest service road, and the wet sand felt like glue, bogging down my wheels. One of my best friends pulled me aside and said, "We need to call it." Devastated, I fought back and was angry. I kept riding, even though I could have walked faster. About two hours later, I saw a vehicle coming down the road. I was thirty miles from the finish and couldn't make it—so I jumped on the lagwagon.

In the moment, I felt vulnerable and embarrassed. At this point in my life, I hadn't been in the field with a group for a couple years. I had completely crumbled. My failure was humbling and helped remind me that we are truly never in control. While it was easy to think that my trip-mates were judging me, they all reassured me that they weren't, and that they weren't holding this "failure" against me in any way. This experience helped me realize the real failure would have been not giving up, pressing on until I collapsed and put the rest of the group in the position of having to rescue me. Sometimes it's okay to give up, and to admit when you've reached your limit.

Jenn Velie earned her bachelor of science in from the University of Central Florida before completing her masters degree in education from Georgia Southern University. She has over seventeen years of experience in the outdoor industry in the retail, higher education and guiding/instruction sectors. Jenn is operations director at Whitewater.

WHERE I WENT WRONG

My dad shared with me, after hearing that I had been asked to write this book, that readers would be more interested in learning about my leadership mistakes than my triumphs. I agreed. Credit also goes to Dad for this "Where I Went Wrong" section—like most learning, I have found that I gain the most understanding after intentional reflection.

Mistake No. 1: Believing That High Achievement Is Required for Acceptance

You can climb, you can hike, you can paddle, and you can bike, but can you also do all these things without bragging about the number of summits, the grades of the climbs, the number of rapids, or the epic rides you've completed? Because, ultimately, this list of accomplishments has little to do with your ability to lead.

In fact, almost everyone can think of a person they would call a great leader, but who did not have (or care to share) an accompanying list of credentials and accolades. It is the person who is always on time—prepared and ready—who is taking care of and assisting others, because they have already led themselves. These **It's how the team works together that ultimately determines if the goal will be met.** are the people who should be admired and looked to for leadership, because they have achieved something most appointed leaders have not—self-acceptance.

They find their success by knowing what to do and how to do it, knowing what they need or want to work on, and knowing how critical interdependence between group members is—that it's how the team works together that ultimately determines if the goal will be met. If every member is not ready and contributing to the expedition, the expedition will fail. While there is an expedition leader, the achievement of being accepted as a *competent* leader comes only with participants trusting your leadership choices.

Do not confuse competence and achievement. You can still be a competent outdoor leader without having completed epic, sought-after summits, climbs, rivers, and so on. The belayer is just as critical to a successful climb as the lead climber, and the paddle crew is just as crucial for the success of the raft on a gnarly rapid as the river guide. Everyone has a role to play.

While an outdoor leader may coordinate the group, success is achieved because everyone does their part.

Mistake No. 2: Neglecting to Offer an Apology

I have become aware that I make two main types of mistakes. First, there are the mistakes made due to my poor planning or oversight with logistics or in missed communication. Second are mistakes that hurt someone's feelings—mistakes I usually remain unaware of until the person I've hurt, or someone else, shares the impact of my words or actions. In both cases, I am slow to apologize—or I don't apologize at all—because I need to be right.

What I should do instead is make a proper apology: name what I did, take responsibility for my actions, express remorse, and most importantly verbalize the ways I intend to not repeat the error. When I owe someone an apology, I need to make that apology as soon as I can, even if the transgression took place years prior. What I have learned is that asking for forgiveness and then moving forward will ultimately allow me to build stronger relationships, establish trust, and become a better leader. It's not the mistake that is the issue; it is the inability to learn from it and do better.

Mistake No. 3: Not Asking for Help

Earlier in my evolution as an outdoor leader, when I was more focused on not disappointing others, I often chased accolades and achievement—the only thing I knew how to do was to become invincible. For me, that meant being the best, not letting anyone get close, and relentlessly pursuing excellence. I was consistently defensive when questioned, threatened by those who would challenge my work or intentions. I felt that any feedback was criticism that I was not enough, was not doing things right, and that I was a failure. But really, what I failed at was owning my mistakes and asking for help. The fear of being seen—letting someone past my façade of strength and composure—made me a compulsive, anxious mess. I was intolerable, really.

Today, in contrast, I learn from and work with those I am leading in more intentional ways. While I may hold the title or distinction of "leader" (boss, parent, captain), the best way I can lead is by asking others how they see themselves best contributing their skills or perspective to the task or conversation at hand. By asking for help—insight—I can make better decisions that will benefit the group or the initiative. I now actively look for the tension or missed connection, and reach out proactively, with genuine curiosity, to ask what I may be missing. And, where and when I do make mistakes, I'll acknowledge them and apologize (see Mistake No. 2). Everyone can lead—in fact everyone *is* a leader when they are leading themselves. If they don't take control of their intentions, set dreams, or identify who they want to be and what they want to do, they will end up following someone else's intentions and dreams. The only requirement to lead is to start.

Mistake No. 4: Not Being Candid

One of the best professional speaking sessions I attended was Shari Harley's "Candid Culture." Her message—"Ask more, assume less"— left a lasting impression on me. In particular, I loved her driving idea that: *Candor is not bad news, and a candid culture is not about saying hard things. Candor is asking more questions at the onset of relationships.*

When I was a new leader, I certainly did more telling than asking. While telling may be appropriate when teaching a new technical skill such as climbing or paddling, I missed the opportunity to ask questions about how those I led preferred to learn and why they were participating. These people came to me for an experience, and yet oftentimes I shied away from candid feedback because I was fearful they would not want to follow me. I did not realize at that time how two-way, open candidness can create a more trusting and fulfilling relationship. I was not fully practiced in giving constructive feedback to help move a challenging conversation or relationship forward. I missed opportunities to create candid relationships between me, as a leader, and those who followed.

Talking out Loud

RACHEL SCHMIDT

Just say it out loud. No matter the situation or the company, say it out loud. When we don't, we make assumptions about *everything* and *anything*— what others know, don't know, think, don't think, on and on. When we say it out loud, we establish the foundation for true success. When working with anyone, whether it's someone I have known for years or just met, on the smallest project or activity or the biggest adventure or campaign, I always say, "I talk out loud."

I talk out loud so you know what I am thinking, so you know the direction I am going and why. I follow that up with letting that person know I'd like them to listen to me and hear what I am saying, so they can educate *me* about areas where my thoughts may pose issues, or I can educate *them* about something they have never thought about. If they listen, they may hear something that sparks inspiration to build upon my thoughts or may take us to even greater success together.

You know what they say about assumptions. The adage is there for a reason: the second you assume something of someone—assume they know how to rig a boat, read a line through a rapid, make a move in a rapid, get out of trouble, or help you get out of trouble—is the second you fail at being a leader. I have spent my life running rivers, and I love running rivers with groups of friends. To my fellow river rats out there, you know how excited we get to draw a permit on a coveted river, and how we get just as excited to get an invite on someone else's permit. If you are the permit holder, you control who is in the party; if you are the invited, you do not—and this is where it gets tricky. Just because someone can row a boat or is willing to run a river does not mean they should. We should never *assume*.

Many people don't voice what they think, know, or wish to question out loud due to insecurity or fear of rejection, or they might desire to hoard knowledge as power. They may make assumptions that the people they are with have more experience, or know more about a situation or topic, and worry that if they think, ponder, or ask questions, they'll appear "stupid" to their more experienced peers.

There could be nothing farther from the truth. If you take the lead and start talking out loud—whether you are scouting a rapid and planning lines or discussing an issue and developing plans to solve it—you are opening the door for others to learn or share, and that makes us all stronger. Share what you know and ask questions about the things you don't know, because chances are you know more than you think, and others likely have the same questions. If we openly work together, we will be better prepared to tackle the unforeseen moments of life and make it through together.

Rachel Schmidt (@mtraerae) is a lifelong Montana resident. She was chosen to create and direct the Montana Governor's Office of Outdoor Recreation, and she continues to work on conservation and recreation-economy issues, specifically around public lands, water, and wildlife. She also enjoys river rafting, camping, hunting and fishing, lake surfing, skiing, and traveling.

A FIRST CHANCE TO MAKE A SECOND IMPRESSION

In sharing my perspective and experiences in leadership, and reflecting on mistakes I've made, I have a hard time recalling specific examples from my adventures. To be clear, many things have gone wrong under my lead, but there are two main reasons I can't recall them: (1) many co-leaders, as well as supervisors, have made up for, stepped in, or resolved issues, for and with me, and (2) making mistakes along the way meant adjusting actions, packing lists, expectations, checklists, etc. in the moment before things spiraled out of control, so that these mistakes were barely blips on the radar. (That is why it is common practice to debrief and ask for feedback after a trip—it's important to note the things that went well so they can be replicated, as well as the pressure points and issues that needed to be resolved and will likely come up again in the future.)

One of the biggest mistakes I have made rather consistently is not fully appreciating the varied experiences of those who follow my lead. During the pandemic, I reconnected with former rowing teammates from college. While we are now at many different places in life, what brought us together originally and keeps us connected now is our shared team experience. In our monthly meetups, we covered various topics and issues, including how we have experienced or navigated leadership in our lives after athletics.

It was during these conversations that I first started to hear that the experience of the others—at the same event, on the same team, after the same goal—was entirely different from mine. I heard stories and anecdotes of which I'd never been aware—like how little feedback or coaching other teammates had received. More embarrassing was when I shared something important to me, and thought it was equally important to others, only to learn that it hadn't been. The more I listened, the more I realized that, even though I may have been seen as a leader on the team, things I valued and thought were priorities for all were push points for others—including their difficult experiences with coaches and other frustrations. This gap in my awareness represents one of the most significant mistakes I have made in my leadership, and as I became more curious about it, I began to see how I'd done this in other situations as well.

Over the years, I have reconnected with others to reflect on some highly transformative experiences in my life: my co-workers from Great Northern Whitewater Rafting outside Glacier National Park where I worked three summers as a rafting guide, and the other students on my NOLS Instructor

Course. Whether it's been catching up over a beer while traveling through towns or reconnecting on a float down the Middle Fork Salmon River, I've learned a lot that I didn't know before about the positive and negative impacts we can each have in communities of people working toward a common goal.

THE FAILURE LAB

Many people support my leadership journey. Some have grown alongside and with me for decades, while others have come into my life by design or happenstance. There is one thought leader I admire tremendously: he's thoughtful and kind, intelligent and reflective; he also aspires to do big things. I can count on him to share a good book, a podcast, and a new connection, just as much as I can count on him to send a message wishing me a good day, reminding me to be gentle, or sharing a friendly joke about my favorite sports team. Recently, he introduced me to the Failure Lab, and I could not be more excited about diving into and sharing this concept with others, because, ultimately, where I went wrong and how I responded in my leadership will be more memorable than where I went right. On its website the Failure Lab (see Selected Bibliography and Resources) defines itself as:

- A call to become a more thoughtful and empathic human.
- A reminder that the journey to success is continuous and not straight.
- An invitation to connect through shared human experience.
- A challenge to develop the skills necessary to become more comfortable being uncomfortable, to embrace continuous growth, and to dive into the sticky, complicated experience of being a human who interacts with other humans.

In the Failure Lab, selected individuals work on developing their story—one that culminates in an event at which they publicly share a tale of personal failure. The storyteller does not share the lessons learned or how the issue was resolved, but instead invites the audience to consider how the story connects with them. How can we all be more empathic and vulnerable as individuals and leaders?

This model of sharing failures and our mistakes as individuals and leaders, and then inviting others to lean in and learn, invites curiosity. Getting curious allows for creativity and sets leaders up to expand their care of the group. It supports high commitment, which is the basis for strong leadership.

TAKEAWAYS

- Learning is an iterative process. Build a body of wisdom from your mistakes.
- Leaders make mistakes. Own the impact of your mistakes and change your behavior next time.

- Understand and deal with impostor syndrome. You don't need achievement to gain acceptance.
- Offer an apology. Learn how to give a good apology—it's an excellent skill to hone!
- Ask for help. Ask for support. Ask to grow, not just to know.
- You are enough—as you are. If you have the skills or experience, or are willing to learn them, you don't need to be accomplished at the start. But you do need to start.

THIRSTY FOR **MORE?**

What are two or three things you have learned because of a mistake you made? How do you apply this knowledge going forward (and not repeat the mistake)?

Describe a time when you accomplished a goal that could have been realized differently.

Is there a mistake you feel you can't recover from? Why or why not?

What steps can you take to move forward and work toward recovery? What do you perceive as the value of holding tight? We can learn, remember, and let go to have more care moving forward. So how can you learn, remember, and let go?

What are your biggest trepidations about being a leader? How are you actively working to overcome these?

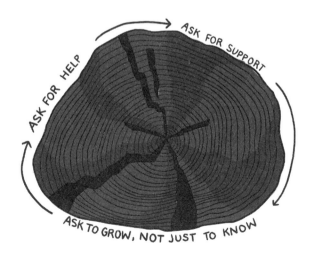

ASK FOR SUPPORT

ASK FOR HELP

ASK TO GROW, NOT JUST TO KNOW

CHAPTER 13
LISTENING

Time in nature allows us to truly listen—to people and to wild places. To listen, without distractions, to what people are saying is empowering as a leader and builds the strongest possible relationships with others. It's a key transformative leadership skill.

A leader who listens and stays true to their core values in words and actions is better able to be of service to others. You in fact cultivate success by listening to your followers' needs, interests, and wants, changing the relationship dynamics and fostering trust. As a result, you create an active and empowered followership. Most people have a story, but often we're too busy telling our own story to really hear anyone else's. Fortunately, the quiet, wild places we find outdoors—and the hyper-focusing reality of the risks outdoors versus our limited backup and resources—are conducive to slowing down and listening.

Most people have a story, but often we're too busy telling our own story to really hear anyone else's.

SIMPLE YET COMPLICATED

It is both simple and complicated to be a good listener. Listening is difficult because we tend to want to talk—about ourselves and our expertise—in our constant, all-too-human search for validation and approval. Listening is framed as understanding and having the ability to be receptive to messages from others, and, as with most other leadership qualities, it is often overlooked, negated, or left unmastered.

It can be challenging for leaders to listen to people when they are expressing feelings, both positive and negative. It's hard to resist the urge to talk or offer input or solutions ourselves—to rush in to fill the void of silence or awkwardness with our own words—but when done well, listening requires a pause and potentially a course correction, to adjust to the newly gained knowledge or perspective. (I don't offer specific strategies for becoming a better listener in this book—it's a big topic. See the Selected Bibliography and Resources for some of my favorites.)

In an outdoor context, a leader needs to listen not only when communicating with the group but also when participants approach them individually to communicate their needs, fears, and worries about their abilities. People are complicated, and while we may ask for and support open communication on an expedition, a tired, scared, or hurt individual may not be forthright in sharing their needs.

VERBAL AND NONVERBAL MESSAGING

Some people express in words exactly what they mean. But a lot of communication can happen via what is *not* said—and most of us communicate in a variety of ways. We also process information differently; everyone has a way that works better for them. One of the challenges a leader faces is learning how to share information—either one on one or with a group—when communication styles vary so widely.

1. **Outdoor leaders must be attuned to both verbal and nonverbal messages.** Observing dynamics in a group is an easy thing to do, but it's also an easy thing to overlook. For example, try observing who is moving along the trail together or sitting together at breaks, or who does or does not help in the kitchen. Consider also who comes early to check in and who works to be seen as a leader—and how that person is seen by the group. These are all subtle clues to potential dynamics that can lead to near-miss or strained interpersonal connections.

   Taking the time to speak one-on-one, from a place of genuine care, opens space and builds trust for future conversations.

2. **Confirm or correct what you think you've observed by having conversations with individuals in the party.** The first couple days of an adventure can be filled with big emotions and major adjustments, even if everything is going well. Taking the time to speak one-on-one, from a place of genuine care, opens space and builds trust for future conversations.

Creating a Culture of Listening

KAYDEN WILL

Creating a culture of listening starts from the very first moments. Learn people's names, remember details about them, and show them that you hear them, see them, and value their contributions. When I meet my students, I repeat their names out loud, both to help me remember and to let them know that I value them. As instructors, we can make sure that we have a meaningful conversation or check-in with every student within twenty-four hours of their arrival to begin building the foundations of trusting relationships.

I often think of a group of young teens that I backpacked with in Idaho for two weeks. The early check-ins revealed that about half of them were excited to be there and had chosen the course themselves; the other half had been signed up by their parents and thought they were going to summer camp. Understanding these differences in "why" helped our instructor team set aside its assumptions and shape the experience to meet these various sets of expectations. Although challenges and the need for deep listening continued along the way, at the end of the expedition, course evaluations showed positive outcomes for every student and the initial differences in motivation had diminished.

Establish forums for listening. This might be a daily check-in with the instructor team over evening hot drinks, an evening meeting with the full group, a post-hike debrief, or a group council to address emerging concerns. Establish ground rules to help each person develop the skills to both speak and listen. By explicitly teaching the communication skills that students will need to give and receive feedback, everyone can have ample opportunities to practice listening and sharing their thoughts before inevitable conflicts start to arise.

These skills can be applied in all sorts of situations. I was working with a group on a ten-week expedition in which several students broke a foundational rule and were being dismissed from the program. Rather than having them simply leave, we called the whole group together for a listening circle. For over an hour, each person had a chance to talk without interruption or judgment about how they were feeling, allowing them to take ownership for their roles. Although the students still left the program, everyone found some level of understanding and growth.

Lean into the value of paraphrasing. Confirm that you know what someone means by repeating it in your own words and affirming that your understanding is correct. "What I hear you saying is. . . Am I understanding you correctly?" Often, we have a tendency to fill the silence with advice or to interject our own stories, but consider that the best response may be the reflection of their own words, the gentle offer of a question, or the simple knowledge that someone is quietly and compassionately listening.

Kayden Will (she/her) is a learning specialist and wilderness orientation director at Proctor Academy, where she continues to practice the leadership and listening skills she gained working as a field instructor and program administrator for NOLS and several other organizations.

FOSTERING GROUP TRANSFORMATION AND INTERDEPENDENCE

Can you imagine a situation in which the people you lead not only know what is expected of them, but can also see ways to contribute to the group's success? A healthy foundational relationship, no matter what level of expertise or ability participants bring to the table, makes each individual feel like a valued and contributing member of the group. An empowered individual has opportunity in front of them; they can set

their own course and determine their own actions and decisions. To help followers achieve these things, a leader needs to listen while holding the following intentions:
- Trust and verify
- Maintain confidence and trust
- Value opinions (but maintain perspective)
- Solicit feedback

Trust and Verify

Listening is perhaps better framed as the art of asking good questions. If you can ask focused questions and be curious, your participants will give you the information you seek. Your leadership clout is based on their trust in you, which you cultivate by making yourself available and open to feedback and input, and by allowing space for their perspectives. However, you also need to verify any facts and information that you gather from them.

Do you know how to assess someone's competency before you take them into the wilderness? Does experience in a summer outdoor school or on a semester outdoors reflect their whole ability? Do you assume your belayer, whom you just met, knows how to belay outdoors if they have only done it in a gym once previously?

Verifying that someone can belay before your feet leave the ground is simple enough and can be done in the moment and in person. But there are other types of information you'll want to compile from qualified sources, in a timely and updated fashion, *before* making any decisions. Weather patterns are unique to certain areas, just as water levels can vacillate and avalanche conditions can turn. Finding out on day thirteen of a trip that a bridge over a major river you must cross washed out last season has ramifications that could have been avoided by seeking out this key information earlier. Certainly, verifying terrain or technique is imperative for an expedition's success, but so is verifying information directly with the source. Information that is shared with the leader or overheard about someone or something—slanderous or praising alike—requires a leader to pause and consider if the information is truthful and adequate; decision-making based on incomplete or biased information can be hurtful to the group's trust in the leader as well as to the trip's desired outcome.

Early in my career as AORE's executive director, I was often met with comments that were uninformed and incorrect, things along the lines of "Some people said. . ." or "Members are saying. . ." I spent an absurd amount of time attempting to respond to these comments—often defensively—when I really should have requested that individuals bring their feedback directly to me. Receiving information from the source rather than relying on hearsay would have allowed me to do two things: first, to fully hear and seek understanding of these individuals' perspective and information, and second, to demonstrate good leadership by showing that I was a good listener and could be open to and grateful for feedback, regardless of whether it was positive or negative.

Maintain Confidence and Trust

My dad likes to share a metaphor about toothpaste and gossip that he learned at summer camp—gossip is like toothpaste: when it comes out of the tube, it's out and impossible to put back. I think about this when someone confides in me: if entrusted with someone's personal information or a delicate situation, I have learned it's not mine to repeat, unless they tell me they want their story to be shared. A leader who's a good listener can be a repository for information that is observed or shared, and once verified, perhaps acted upon. There are ways to do that with grace and to avoid sharing that which doesn't need to be shared. Leaders can become adept at conveying what others *need* to know, not *all* there is to know.

Maintaining confidentiality is key to building a reputation as a trustworthy leader, and perhaps to being invited to partner on future projects. If a leader's focus is on getting what they want at the expense of others, they may share private information to move forward quickly. However, the gossiper's actions most decidedly will catch up with them—and probably sooner rather than later.

Sometimes someone just needs to vent and isn't looking for help in solving a problem. Sure, listening to someone vent isn't always the funnest, but if your followers trust you won't share that information, it may allow them to move through whatever barrier they're facing. In this way, you take on more of a coaching and less of an advisory role. And while it's perhaps more time-consuming in the short term, this leadership approach will lead to longer-term returns for your participant, including increased self-confidence and increased faith in you as a leader.

Value Opinions (but Maintain Perspective)

Have you, as a leader, ever been told that you don't listen well? I wonder if it's because listening is a skill that can also be complicated by bias, position, privilege, and gender stereotyping. As a woman leader, one thing I have struggled with is being told—by men—that I don't listen well, particularly when working with a group of men. If I choose *not* to take a man's recommendation, I am "a bad listener" or I am "not listening." It's challenging to convey that I, in fact, did listen to his suggestion but decided that what he had to say did not support the direction or action I'd chosen.

Have you observed in a group setting who speaks first, who speaks the most, whose ideas may be shut down, and who is talked over or undermined? Do you notice who listens intently and who is not invited to share? If you work with a co-leader, are you mindful of how much you talk versus how much you step back, listen, and let them lead the conversation?

Having a wide range of opinions is important to good decision-making because, even (or especially) as leaders, we don't all see or experience issues the same way. Asking others their opinion on an issue or how they might address a situation provides a wider lens, allowing you to make a more informed decision. Just be aware that when someone is asked what they think and how they would proceed, and the leader chooses not to proceed that way, ill will can follow—we all place importance on our own opinions. Certainly, it's a challenging situation to ask for differing perspectives, but you, as the leader, ultimately decide which course to take.

Solicit Feedback

With verified information, a culture of candid communication, and various perspectives sought and heard, the leader will be able to make the best decision. One last step can assist in both transparency and buy-in from those you lead, and that is seeking appropriate feedback, which allows you to make any final adjustments. Feedback facilitates picking up or considering something important that was overlooked, or perhaps didn't earlier seem feasible for whatever reason.

What could be more fun than being tethered to a partner when swimming with shoes on and running in a wetsuit, alternating between these two disciplines for thirteen miles? In 2022, I did just that: a swim-run on Orcas Island, Washington, with three friends. The event began with a mile run and then a swim in the Salish Sea, a short but incredibly cold second leg. Then we started up the first of what seemed like countless miles uphill on rough terrain, where my lack of running fitness required my co-racer Liz, a very fit runner, to walk with me on the steep gradient. The second swim was across a freshwater lake, and while it was relatively short, it became evident that I needed to adjust my pace for Liz, just like she'd accommodated me on the run. Our two other friends moved at a faster clip and soon separated from us.

The longest swim of the event was a half mile along the length of an alpine lake, complicated by whitecaps and wind. While both Liz and I struggled to swim in these conditions, it was clear that Liz was not as experienced at navigating rough waters. We slowly and safely crossed the lake, adjusting our pace as we swam, and then moved on. I ran slowly and walked at times, my pace further slowed by a recent bout of COVID. Liz and I both soldiered on, miserably, until we came to the last swim, which required us to again cross the long, whitecapped lake. We gave each other feedback, sharing that we both had no intention of stopping, but also acknowledging the foolhardiness of swimming this stretch in our fatigued state. In the end, we told a race official that we intended to run the trail that circumnavigated the lake instead. At the lake's far end, we reconnected with our friends as they came out of the water, and all four of us ran the last mile to cross the finish line together.

When giving feedback, your participants may tell you what you want to hear, but not what you *need* to hear—for example, telling you that everything is fine with a plan when you can sense that something is off with the group or an individual. A leader can have an outsized position, and followers may conflate their respect for and fear of you. While you may not be able to entirely fix this dynamic, listening sincerely to what they have to say, and pressing them to go further as needed, is the best course. Feedback can be challenging to hear when we are emotionally invested in a decision, but a good leader will always listen, understand, reflect—and then act.

Listening to Understand

BRANDI FOSTER

In the late 1990s, I was the coordinator of a Montana university program meant to bring more racial and ethnic minorities into the healthcare fields, and I ran an enrichment camp most summers for thirty to forty teens of diverse backgrounds from across the country. As part of the curriculum, we spent several days hiking, camping, and learning in Glacier National Park. We had hosted this camp for years, and had a solid agenda with set schedules and defined outcomes.

One of my favorite activities was having a friend of mine, who was an ethnobotanist from the Blackfeet Nation, lead the students on a hike and talk about the use of plants for healing and food, along with some historical and contemporary stories of his tribe. The goal was for students to see how much of traditional medicine comes from nature and to appreciate the role Indigenous communities around the world have played in contributing to society's knowledge of plants and their uses.

One year, we had a large cohort of students from inner cities—places like Chicago, Detroit, and Baltimore. Most of these students had never slept in a tent, cooked over a fire, or hiked in the mountains, let alone in a place as grand as Glacier National Park. It was difficult to keep them focused on any task, partly because they were so overwhelmed by these new experiences—some students didn't appreciate Mother Nature the way I had hoped, and others were distracted by the foreign environment. None of them seemed overly interested in listening to someone talk about plants. I dreaded having my friend ignored or, worse, disrespected by my students.

I decided to talk with them beforehand, and asked what they wanted out of this experience and how they felt being in this strange, new place. I listened to these young people open up about how scary the quiet was, how disconcerting the open spaces were, how it was hard to think of themselves as having options that were different from what they had always known. Truly listening to what the students were saying meant we'd need to reconsider how we ran the hike the next day if it were to be meaningful.

Fortunately, my friend was also an amazing teacher, and when I told him what I learned the night before, he was able to alter his approach to focus less on the plants themselves and more on interdependence, community, and perspective. The students knew they had shifted the conversation and engaged with questions, stories, and laughter. The best part, and the thing I remember most twenty years later, is how they first showed, and then told, me what they truly needed to learn in that moment. Listening to those whom I was meant to guide and trusting in what I was hearing allowed us all to have a more meaningful experience, one I hope they still carry with them wherever they may be.

Brandi Foster (she/her), a native Montanan and an enrolled member of the Iowa Tribe of Kansas and Nebraska, has been working in higher education for more than twenty-five years and has been learning from nature for more than fifty. She lives in Washington State with her family.

MY RUN-IN WITH A ROCK

When I was twenty-five, I had a run-in with a rock while I was learning to rappel on a NOLS Instructor Course in the Wind River Range of Wyoming. One afternoon, three other students, an instructor, and I went to a sixty-foot cliff to learn and practice technical high-angle descent. That morning, we had learned and practiced snow anchors. We were a highly connected, motivated, and high-functioning group. The approach to the rock outcrop was up a snowfield, and before we started, we examined the site for loose rocks and other potential hazards.

Up on the cliff top, we set up appropriate anchors and talked through strategies and considerations for managing technical descents. A fellow student on the program, Jennie, and I were the first to descend and used a counterbalance rappel, role playing that one of us was the student and the other was the instructor. We worked our way down about thirty feet to a small ledge, "walking" our feet down the cliff as we descended.

As we left the ledge, we needed to make a transition past the lip to clear an overhang below. As I was transitioning, hanging in space and entrusting my full body weight to the system, I felt myself swing into a gully. The next thing I remember seeing was the shape of a rock between my legs—my mind captured it as a parallelogram—falling through the air and down. I had been hit on my lower legs.

Later we determined it was a 250-pound boulder about a foot and a half by two and a half feet in size. I didn't immediately realize I had been hit until I saw that my right pant leg was torn open and missing. I saw bone and fat and blood. I yelled up that I had been hit and I was bleeding.

Jennie, out of sight around the gully's edge, yelled to ask if I was okay, and I told her I was not.

The instructor, Peter, descended on another rappel rope, reached my location, clipped into me, and then coached me down the remainder of the rappel. Peter and Jennie assisted me away from the base of the cliff, and then assessed the injury: an eight-inch-long by two-inch-wide by three-inch-deep laceration on my right medial calf and a puncture wound on my left shin. Peter administered first aid to address the wounds and alerted the rest of the expedition as to the accident.

We were fifteen miles deep in the Wind River Range near Timico Lake. Peter and three other members of the expedition hiked through the night to the trailhead to start the emergency-response plan and request a helicopter. The rest of the expedition worked to make me comfortable: cooking and trying to feed me, discussing splinting, and assessing evacuation strategies. A small group built a shelter where I was, which kept me warm, and they gave exceptional patient care—reassuring me, comforting me, drying my tears, quelling my fears, and cleaning the wounds to prevent infection.

It was a rough night. The pain was remarkable; my legs felt like they were on fire. The swelling continued, and I started to lose feeling in my feet. Not knowing what might happen was challenging. Would I lose my leg to infection? When would I be evacuated? Was my leg broken? I didn't know how long it would be until I had definitive care, but I did know that the longer my injuries went unaddressed, the more complicated repairing the damage could be. I assumed we'd start a self-evacuation, which is time- and labor-intensive. I remember a feeling of elation as I saw a helicopter come up the valley toward us, and the team let me know it was for me. I realized I was going to make it.

I was flown to a regional medical center and was in surgery within twenty hours of my accident. The wounds were cleaned and dressed, and miraculously I had no broken bones. The medical staff also managed for compartment syndrome, encouraging blood flow to my feet and lower leg to keep the blood from becoming trapped and increasing the swelling. I did hyperextend my knees and legs, so for months had to keep my legs extended straight as I used a wheelchair and crutches to get around. But I am happy to report that I made a full recovery.

So that happened. I've been open about discussing my accident, as I think it is one of the best things to have happened to me. When I returned home, I began processing. I struggled with contemplating my mortality and what might have been had I been hit on my head, bled out, or lost my leg. One way I processed the experience was to become an EMT and work to instruct wilderness medicine courses. This let me use my voice to teach others wilderness medicine, encourage people to act, and embody what is usually the faceless patient in an outdoor-adventure accident. Deep down, most outdoor leaders fear bad things happening on their watch. Having had a backcountry accident myself, I strongly feel that telling my story and sharing the lessons have helped me to heal and process my own mortality.

A PATIENT'S PERSPECTIVE

I don't remember getting hit by the rock, but I do remember looking down at the damage it had wrought. And while I don't recall feeling pain right out of the gate, I do remember recognizing the severity of the situation. Once I'd been rescued off the cliff face and moved to a patch of ground away from the rock outcrop, I became quite emotional. There, my leader did a secondary patient exam to see if there were other injuries. I realized my trip was done—I would not complete it. I had a wave of feeling at peace, of knowing that everyone I loved knew that I loved them in the event I did not make it out.

Deep down, most outdoor leaders fear bad things happening on their watch. Having had a backcountry accident myself, I strongly feel that telling my story and sharing the lessons help me heal and process my own mortality.

This was the twenty-third day of an Instructor Course. We had hiked, climbed, and lived together in these mountains for more than three weeks. An expedition of this length is a breeding ground for building confidence and comradeship, sharing dreams, and disclosing personal issues with newfound friends. I had recently become engaged, and as we'd hiked the miles, I thought about what my married future would be like and what would come next.

An expedition of accomplished outdoor leaders all trying to become instructors presents a unique scenario. More than a dozen participants had worked hard to be accepted into the program, and we each had our own leadership style, comfort level, expertise, and weak spots. Each of us had taken part in or led an evacuation in the past, and now, as I waited for my own evacuation, I had a chance to observe everyone in action. Various teams had been assigned: People back at camp boiled water and made sure there was food, while the rescuers had their needs met, physically and emotionally, with what we had. Others administered first aid, checking my vitals and discussing how to clean and dress the injuries. And still others considered how to build a splint and move me from the snowy slope where I waited to prepare for an evacuation. Meanwhile, Scott, the lead instructor, was gathering feedback and information so he could make the best decision on how to proceed.

Everyone worked so hard to keep me comfortable and calm. A handful of people tended to me, holding my hand, wiping my tears, and telling me stories through the night. Reassuring. Caring. I believe I was a good patient, willing to help with sarcastic jokes and even offering to take my own vitals. But the most helpful thing I could contribute was answering

questions to the best of my ability—how I felt, what the pain was like, what made things better or not. I can't imagine better listeners than my rescuers, both as individuals checking my vitals and completing paperwork (SOAP notes—see chapter 9), and as a team, working together to assess and create a plan for my evacuation. We all think we are good listeners, but being the patient gave me a fresh perspective. I realized we all had to listen, patient and rescuers alike.

TAKEAWAYS
- It takes courage to listen. You learn by listening.
- Be attuned to verbal and nonverbal messaging.
- Listen so others can fully express their ideas without interruption.

- Listen, then trust and verify.
- Listen to maintain confidence and trust.
- Listen to and value opinions, but also maintain your perspective.
- Listen, make a recommendation, and then solicit feedback to find out what you may have missed.
- Be curious but not judgmental.

THIRSTY FOR **MORE?**

Ask others for feedback on what kind of listener you are. How might you incorporate their feedback to become a better listener?

Do you know a good listener and, if so, what makes them good at it? Consider sharing with them that you have identified them as a good listener and ask how they've developed this skill.

When is the last time you really felt heard? What made you feel this way? What made you feel you could trust the listener with that knowledge? How can you make others feel more heard by you?

As a leader, how do you create and hold a space that welcomes and elevates listening?

CHAPTER 14
CONFIDENT, COMMITTED, AND COURAGEOUS COMMUNICATION

The thread that unites all aspects of outdoor leadership is effective, consistent communication. Effective communication is clear, kind, and candid. In contrast, ambiguity, oversight, and carelessness with people and their ideas and values foster conflict. The success of an expedition so often rests on what can be conveyed with words—or in the nuances of conversation. Different scenarios require different messaging, but a leader who relies on a clear vision, accountability, and direct and open conversations will be able to motivate, empower, elevate, achieve, and— perhaps most important—readjust.

ADVENTURES IN RAFT GUIDING

A rafting trip is an expedition of communication. Being a whitewater rafting guide near Glacier National Park during my college summers was one of the scariest things I had ever done—not so much the rafting but being responsible for people's safety, in a raft, through rapids, on a glacially fed river in a remote environment. I had always wanted to work out West, and I found four rafting companies in Montana right outside Glacier National Park. The Meryl Streep movie *The River Wild* had just come out around that time, and when applying to each company, I did some "head art" with the movie-promotion image, putting a cutout of my head onto Streep's body. It landed me an interview, and I secured the job.

Water requires the utmost respect and can be devastatingly powerful, while words that are communicated poorly (or not at all) can be equally catastrophic.

Rafting really is an easy job. Easy to mess up, that is. You have this awkward inflatable tub that most of your clients have never sat in, much less paddled, and you must direct them to work as a group to avoid hazards, including rocks, moving water, eddies, and logs. It is a train wreck waiting to happen. YIPPEE! Yet raft guiding, like trying to improve your communication skills as a leader, is a learnable (and teachable) skill. These skills require exposure, experience, repetition, and feedback to gain confidence and become effective. It would not be a stretch to say that both skills, if done poorly, can cause disaster. Water requires the utmost respect and can be devastatingly powerful, while words that are communicated poorly (or not at all) can be equally catastrophic.

Before I went out to Montana, I had never rafted. I showed up with all my gear and joined the other new staff in guide school—a multiday adventure during which we learned how to read the river, swim the rapids, navigate strainers (logs that can trap a swimmer), and right flipped rafts in super-cold water. We repeatedly ran the stretch of the Middle Fork of the Flathead River that we'd be guiding. We took turns giving the safety speech and learning how to navigate the various rapids. We learned the history and some of the local flora and fauna to help round out the client experience. We learned how to prevent accidents, and we learned how to resolve situations that had escalated.

Defining Rapids

- Class I: Fast-moving water, small ripples. Self-rescue is easy.
- Class II: Straightforward rapids with clear channels. Swimmers are seldom injured.
- Class III: Moderate rapids, irregular waves. Complex moves. Group rescue helps swimmers avoid long swims.
- Class IV: Intense rapids, maneuvering critical. Self-rescue is difficult, and scouting is advised.
- Class V: Long, violent rapids, drops, strong currents, and hydraulics. Swims are dangerous, and rescue is difficult.
- Class VI: Usually not run due to unpredictability and danger.

The Flathead has mainly class II and III rapids and, at a certain water level, one technical IV—but this all really means nothing to a first-time paddler. Once the paperwork is done, life jackets fitted, and wetsuits given out with instructions that the zipper goes in back (not the front), everyone loads into the big school bus. The driver, sharp on the corners, names the peaks visible in the distance in Glacier National Park.

THE SAFETY TALK AND PUT-IN

Guiding is all about entertaining and managing people—them and their expectations. At the Moccasin Creek launch site, before putting in, the guides tumble out of the bus and give their paddling instructions. Guides rarely know anything about the clients: their paddling history, their sense of adventure, or their fitness level. Your raft can be a mix of anyone and everyone.

Standing by the creek, clients feel the cold glacier runoff for the first time. The guide runs through how to hold a paddle, the basic commands, and the safety talk, including what to do if you fall out of the raft. In this case, you either: a) if you are close, grab onto the rope that encircles the raft until someone can pull you in, b) if you get separated from the raft put your feet downstream, in the "lazy boy" recliner position, and use your hands to paddle away from rocks, or c) listen for the guide and look for the "throw bag," which would be tossed to you and give you a way to pull yourself back to the boat. Following the talk, we also point out that we won't be returning to the put-in (this is not a lazy river), and people can't leave their bags there. It's amazing to me how some people just don't quite understand how rivers and waterflow work.

The boats push off. I'm sitting in the back of the boat, high and dry with my guide stick, working on my Chaco-sandals tan, and learning the guest names as we float down the creek. In the creek, I explain again what happens if someone falls overboard, helping them understand that they must turn around and grab the raft, followed by a demonstration on how to pull someone in. I show them how to place their feet downstream if they are separated from the boat in a rapid, relaxing in a recumbent position so they can push away from objects until I can either a toss a throw bag (a bag of floating rope) in their direction or they can get to shore and crawl out of the river.

At the confluence where Moccasin Creek spills into the Middle Fork of the Flathead, there's a strong river eddy line where the two bodies of water churn together, each with a different color. Here, I give the command to turn the boat to the right so we can enter the main flow at an upstream angle. The boat hits the current and turns quickly to the left, clients jostle and laugh, and we enter the main river. The first part of the float is mild, with Glacier National Park on the river's right. I launch into my comedic spiel in the hopes of garnering tips at the trip's end, explaining the elevation at which the deer turn into elk, how heavy the mountains are, and providing various other answers to questions that clients usually ask.

ENTERING THE WAVE TRAIN

As we work our way down the river, Tunnel Rapids presents itself and we enter a little canyon. Tunnel is a fun little introductory rapid, with a big rock lovingly called Can Opener situated right at the bottom of the last wave train. Done correctly, this is how the run goes: we start at river left, follow a couple wave trains down, make a move to river right, and skirt around Can Opener, the final move of a lefthand turn to pull away from a small undercut section of rocks at the bottom. Pretty straightforward.

On almost every trip I have guided, however, participants stop paddling as they enter this first rapid. And that can have consequences if we hit the Can Opener or if someone falls out. Guides try to convince clients to sit

on the outside tube and use strong paddle strokes that will keep them in the boat. Participants, however, like to sit in the middle tubes where their paddles can't reach the water—a recipe for disaster.

The first couple of strokes are generally fine, and then everyone stops paddling once a wave comes over the bow and they get splashed with cold water, at which point not running into or wrapping on Can Opener becomes a major concern.

One day, we entered the wave train, and I watched as a client—Caitlin— fell into the middle of the raft. At the time, I didn't think too much of it since we were only being jostled a little. I knew that some people get a little hesitant paddling, and I was working to guide the weak paddling crew to avoid the hazards. Then I noticed that Caitlin had curled into the fetal position and lay immersed in the water that had collected in the bottom of our non-bailing boat.

A FAILURE IN COMMUNICATION

After we were through the rapids, I tended to Caitlin, trying to figure out what was going on. Her husband had stopped paddling and had helped her to sit upright so she wouldn't inhale more water. Then he told me she had epilepsy. His wife was having a seizure.

I had a situation on my hands. Before we headed into the next rapid, I used our agreed-upon river-communication signal to hail the other guides in their rafts. I got the attention of the lead guide, Kevin, who maneuvered his raft closer to mine. We agreed that our only option at that point was an evacuation. We were able to get my boat to the riverbank and walk up the embankment to the train tracks, and then radio for an evacuation.

The situation was frustrating. Caitlin and her husband had failed to disclose her condition at the outset. This made it impossible for the guides to make the necessary accommodations, like putting her and her family in an oar rig, which would have given the guide more control of the experience and ensured the boat was self-bailing so there wouldn't have been standing water in the middle. Once we were out on the river, in a semi-remote environment amidst cold glacier runoff, we couldn't simply adjust on the fly. Had Caitlin, for whatever reason, fallen out of the raft rather than into it, she very well might have drowned. And it would have been on my watch, all because of a failure to communicate.

No Task Too Small

JESSICA (WAHL) TURNER

As much as you work strategically and smartly to grow responsibilities and achieve leadership positions, sometimes it's the little things that don't go unnoticed.

When I was very early in my career supporting the First Lady Michelle Obama's Let's Move! Initiative, we were working to bring the programs to Bureau of Indian Education schools and reservations. The launch of Let's Move in Indian Country! took place at the White House with partners I had helped bring in to support the program. I had been working with Tribal leaders, community groups, big corporations, and White House senior staff to integrate traditional healthy food and physical activities into how agencies supported youth. I toured the country with several cabinet secretaries, arguably a very outsized role for a twenty-four-year-old fresh out of grad school.

The day of the program launch event, which took place on the White House lawn, couldn't have been any hotter. It soon emerged that we needed a different event setup and agenda, and so we had to keep the kids entertained while they waited in the heat. I moved the chairs in my sweat-stained dress and played with the kids in my heels, hustling about to ensure the event came off perfectly. Years later, I was shocked to learn from a Fortune 200 corporate partner and senior White House adviser that what impressed them the most, and initiated a mentorship and friendship, was not my role in planning, presentations, research, or coalition building; it wasn't the things that were easily visible or the big, bold programs. It was the fact that I never hesitated to dive into what needed to be done that day—the fact that no task was too small.

Two years earlier, when I had just started my grad-school practicum at the Bureau of Land Management (BLM), I learned an important and similar lesson. My first day was Inauguration Day, the same day the new administration leadership moves into their offices and is in immediate need of staff support. My boss at the BLM offered my help to the Department of the Interior Secretary, so I walked a few blocks from the BLM office to the Department of the Interior's headquarters. There, I was assigned the very basic task of creating lists of stakeholder contacts, Googling them and compiling contact information and email addresses from scratch.

I dove right into the necessary tasks and went above and beyond, because if you are going to do something, do it well—right? When my two weeks were up with the Secretary's office, I was surprised that my should-be boss from BLM told me that the Secretary's office had asked to keep me on detail. Four years later, I had moved up in roles and responsibilities in the Office of the Secretary, all because of a great spreadsheet and attitude.

Whether you're a student-outings volunteer, an environmental professional, or an outdoor guide, there really is no task too small. If someone needs help with the mundane, the boring, the monotonous, show that you care. Help them out, and it could end up helping you out, too.

Jessica (Wahl) Turner is the first president of the Outdoor Recreation Roundtable (ORR), America's leading coalition of outdoor-recreation organizations. Jessica has over a decade of experience navigating the halls of the White House, Department of the Interior (DOI), Capitol Hill, and outdoor-lifestyle businesses. Jessica received her bachelor's and master of arts degrees from Georgetown University, and is a passionate outdoorswoman.

A TWO-WAY STREET

Communication is a two-way street—to be effective communication, it simply must be a conversation. Guides cannot guarantee safety in outdoor activities. Instead, guides look to manage risk, all while knowing that between the outdoor landscape, the weather, and the rigors of physical exertion, things can and do happen. Guides try to clearly state what they plan to do: hike four miles with two thousand feet of elevation gain, raft a wild and scenic river with eight Class III rapids, climb a 5.9 multipitch climb with a difficult, talus-field and scrambling approach. If participants are unfamiliar with these activities, guides try to explain what they're like, including the time commitment and exertion levels, as well as how involved everyone will have to be. And they try to make this a conversation: instead of asking, "Does anyone have any questions?" they lead with, "What questions do you have?" and work to address and reduce any assumptions.

Many components go into the messaging and marketing of whitewater rafting trips: for example, the classic image of smiling people holding their paddles overhead after they have navigated a rapid with a great standing wave. Then there are the rapids splashing against the boat. And perhaps the words "wild" and "adventure" and "fun" are overlaid on the photo, along with the rapids' rating (I through VI) as further enticement to take the trip and earn bragging rights. However, marketing a river as "gentle" when its rapids may be unsuitable for novice paddlers can lead to misalignment in expectations and ultimately a risky situation. Good communication in messaging—whether while promoting a river or speaking to a group about activity levels and risks—allows participants to also evaluate if the adventure is a good fit for them.

Junctions: Checking In

Picture the classic trail junction. You've been hiking along, enjoying the walk, and you come up to a wooden sign at a fork in the trail. Sometimes it has grooved-out letters, painted yellow, with thick arrows pointing in different directions. The mileage to your goal, if listed, is always farther than you hoped. The space is usually open or clear, with the various trails being obvious.

I have been taught, and I teach, that the group stops at every trail junction. Even if the expedition is spaced out, and it may take some time to wait for participants to gather, you never proceed down the trail until everyone is at the junction. This removes any misdirection and keeps the group together. It also allows for everyone to check in, addressing issues like hot spots on feet, adjusting people's loads, hydrating, and refueling with trail snacks.

It's such a simple thing to do: bring everyone together, check in, and then press on, whether it's at a literal trail junction or a metaphorical one—some logical stopping and gathering point in an outing or group project. When we do this in a work or volunteer environment, it can make all the difference. But if we skip bringing the group together along the journey, misdirection, miscommunication, and missed outcomes will result.

THE IMPORTANCE OF TOTAL HONESTY

Be 100 percent honest: You set followers up for failure by not first addressing what needs to be said in a candid and clear way, especially when it comes to policies and procedures you have been hired to follow for an outdoor organization. For example, if clients are required to wear life jackets and helmets on the river, then they must wear them. If your group is attempting a summit, it's possible not everyone will be able to continue; an individual's hiking speed and other factors may mean that you need to tell them the summit isn't theirs this time. Failing to truthfully address a client's ability, or inability, to participate for fear of disappointing them is not the way to proceed in remote environments. If someone is led to believe they will have a certain experience or option to participate, and they are denied that and not apprised of this potentiality in advance, then you have not been clear; in fact, you have been cruel.

> **Be 100 percent honest: You set followers up for failure by not first addressing what needs to be said in a candid and clear way.**

When it is time to go rafting, participants check in, paying and filling out a liability waiver and a release form, both of which are common in the outdoor industry—you've probably signed one, even at an amusement park or jump park. These forms essentially lay out the potential hazards and risks you may be exposed to, and clearly state that your safety is not guaranteed and that you understand and release the service providers from liability.

These forms also include an area to disclose any special needs or health accommodations that the guide should know about. This would have been the perfect place for Caitlin, the woman in my raft, to disclose that she had epilepsy, so that we could have made the relevant accommodations *beforehand.*

Followership and the Anticipated Experience

Just as leadership is a choice, followership is a choice as well. A leader who is 100 percent honest communicates the anticipated experience, but followers should strive to be just as clear about where they are at as well. Clear is kind; unclear is unkind. The author and researcher Brené Brown has moved this messaging forward in her work and observation that leaders often are unclear due to their fear of being uncomfortable or of making their followers feel uncomfortable. Simply put, a leader avoiding uncomfortable communication is being unkind to their followers. Clarity is key, for both leaders and followers: telling half-truths or avoiding tough conversations often results in us being unkind and unfair when we assess the actions, input, or involvement of others.

In 2018, I was on an expedition in Ecuador where one of the activities was canyoneering. In this case it meant rappelling down a series of waterfalls. Cold, wet, rappelling—three things I've stated that I don't particularly care for. Knowing it was the planned activity for the day, I had not slept well that night before, and my stomach was in knots as we got into our wetsuits and climbing harnesses.

Practicing active followership, I pulled our leader, Julio, aside and explained that I had had a serious rappelling accident years before and that, while I knew how to rappel, it was only with great hesitation that I was choosing to participate. I had confidence in the rappelling guides as they set up each anchor and double-checked my harness and carabiners. Two others in the group were close friends and knew of my accident, and honored my emotions and offered words of support and gentle ribbing to make me smile as I began my descent. A picture taken halfway through the rappel shows my tears and fear as the water crashes down around and on me, and yet I stuck it out and did it. My honesty in communicating my fears and experience helped Julio lead while understanding my need for reassurance and extra safety checks. This in turn gave me the confidence to follow rather than choose not to participate at all.

LEAD BY EXAMPLE

Leaders say more with actions than with words—people are always watching. While leaders do not have to be perfect, they still have a responsibility to those they lead: to follow the rules and protocols, and not act as if they deserve special treatment. This includes bringing the proper safety gear and the right layering system, packing the backpacks correctly, helping at the campsite, and making sure others have enough to eat (leaders eat last). As ambassadors for the outdoors, leaders must be aware that their every action will surely be emulated and amplified. Did you choose not to get a permit?

Leaders say more with actions than with words—people are always watching.

Then why would your followers get a permit for their next adventure? Did you talk badly about a participant or another guide? Then why would others trust your word in a critical situation?

Rafting guides give the safety talk before clients ever get in the boat, where they'll be distracted by dealing with life jackets and figuring out how to hold a paddle. It's even better to give the talk with the raft on the river, so you can do a hands-on, leading-by-example demonstration of key concepts like how to pull someone in, do a highside (when everyone in the boat physically moves to the high side of the boat to avoid wrapping the raft on a rock or flipping), or hold a throw bag. When introducing new concepts, physically demonstrating exactly how they look and work allows participants to see and connect your words to the desired action. It's easy to hear, "Grab them by their life jacket, and pull them into the boat," but literally grabbing their shoulders with your knees on the stern and leaning back to pull them in is a much stronger and more memorable example.

CONFIDENT, COMMITTED, AND COURAGEOUS COMMUNICATION

It's also all too easy to miscommunicate and to have missed communication, lead to bad outcomes—leaders miscommunicate by failing to express themselves clearly and miss key communication by avoiding conflict and difficult conversations. However, leaders can have a much more positive impact on participants and on trip goals when they share information and direction *confidently*, commit to communicating *consistently* as the experience progresses and participants' needs and the dynamics change, and communicate *courageously* by addressing individual and group behaviors or giving feedback to maintain accountability and expectations for the group.

Confident Communication

Understand the information and the situation at hand, and then confidently communicate a decision. On the Flathead River, we had no option but to evacuate Caitlin, as we did not have a way to get her safely down the river, given that she might have another seizure. We knew her family would be upset—both because of the financial aspect and the embarrassment of stopping the whole float.

I took her husband aside and let him know that Caitlin's safety was my first priority, and following that was the safety of the rest of the participants. I simply could not move forward knowing that she—and the others—could be at risk. I told him we would walk her and the raft up and out to the road, where we'd be met by a bus. While I could not offer a refund at that time, I suggested we could find a more suitable option for their family to enjoy the river.

Hard things can be delivered with compassion and vulnerability if they are said from a place of care, positive intention, and authenticity.

Those who choose to follow you seek someone who is confident in the situation and able to communicate key information. Confident communication is empowering and offers choices; choices build trust and confidence in challenging situations or in times when the world seems unclear. Confident messaging is not boastful or directive; instead, it's thoughtful and it simplifies complicated situations.

As a confident communicator, you can make your messaging the most impactful by having an awareness of the current situation, reflecting on past decision-making (and those lived outcomes), and understanding the nuances of the group you're leading. Like many other skills, delivering confident communication takes practice. Take advantage of any opportunity to communicate—whether written or oral, group or individual—and be open to feedback on how your messaging lands to build confidence you can use in the future.

Committed Communication

Regular, timely updates keep followers informed and flexible so they can accommodate changing situations. This is committed communication. I will confess that I am still working on this area of my leadership, as I'm not naturally great at ongoing communication. Committing to more regular updates to the membership of AORE does not always feel like the best use

of my time, but ultimately, when I think about the change I am leading, the need to commit to more timely communication trumps my personal work-ethic insecurities.

Since I'd guided the Flathead River over three summers, it was easy to forget that, for my participants, rafting the river was a new experience. I knew how the river-level changes impacted the rapids and subsequently how to best move through them, and I knew which channels got thin enough to stop the boat and where there were potential strainers. During Caitlin's evacuation, after I had spoken privately to the family and things were underway, I not only needed to communicate with the remaining paddlers that we'd keep going down the river, but I also needed to boost their morale for the challenges ahead—with which I was intimately familiar. I explained to the other participants that if much of my attention had been focused solely on managing Caitlin and watching out for her safety, I would have been ineffective in navigating the remaining rapids and protecting everyone else on the rafts. Engaging with the group was difficult because of the high emotions and stress, but committing to sharing with them why I'd made the decision to evacuate and how this would impact the rest of their float helped alleviate any unspoken concerns and assumptions.

> **Commit instead to timely communication, and you may find that small updates delivered at the appropriate time allow the group to more easily adjust or accommodate, by breaking up this new information into more-palatable chunks.**

Timeliness is a key facet of committed communication. To me, it means addressing issues as soon they arise and you have information to share. It does the group a disservice to tell them that you missed the trail hours ago or to wait until the end of the day to bring up an issue that's been impeding forward progress. Commit instead to timely communication, and you may find that small updates delivered at the appropriate time allow the group to more easily adjust or accommodate, by breaking up this new information into more-palatable chunks.

Courageous Communication

Say the hard things and address conflict. It is difficult to say the hard things to people whom you lead—to hold them accountable for their mistakes. It's human nature to avoid people and issues we don't like, though the momentary peace we get from our evasiveness will only resurface later in the form of underlying worry, angst, resentment, and interpersonal implosion.

However, hard things can be delivered with compassion and vulnerability if they are said from a place of care, positive intention, and authenticity. Addressing an individual who is not following the group expectations can feel like the most challenging thing you'll ever encounter, but opting for inaction means that you've essentially abdicated your leadership. That day on the Flathead, I had to do something especially difficult for a young guide: summon the courage to speak privately to Caitlin's husband about evacuating her. Sure, it was not the easiest conversation in the world, but it was a necessary one that, in the end, led to a good outcome for all parties.

Intentions and Assumptions

State intentions but remove assumptions. Leading requires technical knowledge such as familiarity with the terrain and route finding, as well as managing the interpersonal aspects of the group. For example, say you're leading a group hike, and you've been clear in your messaging of what the hike will be like, what terrain and elevation changes to anticipate, the time it will take, and so on. You will also want to share at the start of the trip that the group will stay together and will not split into subgroups of faster and slower hikers. You've communicated your *intentions* and addressed *assumptions* for the outing.

You've set off from the trailhead and you're moving along when the usual unforeseen and unseen factors—things like the group's pace, trail conditions, shifting weather, etc.—start to come into play. Soon, you realize the group is slowing down and attitudes are deteriorating. Now the group is starting to divide into those who want to move more quickly to reach the campsite (the intended outcome) and those who are moving more slowly, who feel unsafe or fatigued and want to stop to set up camp.

If you as the leader failed to clearly articulate intentions for the day, as well as how things will be handled when issues arrive, trouble will ensue. If people assumed that the group would be okay splitting into two camps—literally setting up two campsites—then as a leader you will find yourself trying to convince the faster hikers that they can't go on, or trying to push the slower hikers farther than they feel safe traveling. This sort of interpersonal trouble is usually the root cause of a breakdown in a group.

COMPOSED COMMUNICATION AND DOUBLE STANDARDS

Composed communication doesn't mean communication that's robotic and devoid of emotion, including frustration, sadness, and joy, but rather intentional communication tempered to the needs of those who will receive the message. By using composed communication, you meet your participants where they are, so that they can best hear your message. On the Flathead River's rapids, when managing the other paddlers while Caitlin lay in the bottom of the raft, my voice was loud, direct, and intentional. Later, when all were out of harm's way, the adrenaline had passed, and I could be calm but firm with my decision, I communicated the plan to evacuate Caitlin and her family. The one issue, however, with composed communication is that, for women leaders, it can open them to unmerited criticism.

In thinking about leading in the outdoor industry, I have seen and experienced double standards in my leadership. Where a man might be labeled "passionate," I'm called "emotional." And where a man might be called "strategic," I'm seen as "manipulative." It's exhausting to maintain the composure to navigate the ongoing projections of what and how I should communicate, and how I should lead. And it is challenging for me to share "Be your full authentic self," having experienced what I have. But I do it anyway, remembering that composed communication is all about the participants and establishing a bond of trust and clear communication.

AVOIDING OVER-RELIANCE ON TECHNOLOGY

In my experience, technology is not the strongest way to communicate— to let someone know what they need to do, how to do it, and what the outcome should be. I think about my time on the river—trying to share vital information about a flipped raft or whether it's all clear over the rapids—and how challenging it was to rely on hand signaling, although it's the lingua franca of river safety and often the only way to communicate in that setting. Crucial conversations need to be had in person, over the phone, or one-on-one, where everything from distraction to body language can be leveraged or identified, and most importantly, clarified. We lose these nuances when we rely on quick forms of communication like texting or social media.

Thinking "I sent the message [email, text, voicemail]" does not remove your responsibility as the messenger—I don't believe you can have a proper conversation over text or email, though they are useful ways to *recap* a conversation. Instead, I believe it's your responsibility as leader to communicate and over-communicate, and if someone is not communicating back, to let them know what the outcome of their radio silence will be.

TAKEAWAYS
- Be clear and be kind.
- State intentions but remove assumptions.
- Be completely honest, all the time.
- Lead by example (as a leader, you say more with your actions than with words).

- Leadership has a high failure rate. Own it, then lead.
- Communicate confidently. Communicate with commitment. Communicate courageously. Say the hard things and address conflict head-on.

THIRSTY FOR **MORE?**

How do you communicate? What would people say about the way you speak? Where have you been celebrated for being candid, or noted as being guarded?

How do you ensure your message is inclusive and welcoming? What steps do you take to ensure you are transparent and forthright? How do you ensure people understand the opportunity at hand or call to action?

What are ten ways you can improve your communication skills as an outdoor-adventure leader?

ACKNOWLEDGMENTS

Thanks first to my incredible husband and missing piece, Justin. As we roll along together through a lifetime of adventures, your belief and confidence in me, your love, and your gift for helping me to find my footing mean so much to me. It's thanks to you that the endless school and sport emails were actually read and the kids' paperwork was filled out—complete and on time. I appreciate you supporting the "yes," always, taking care of all the details so we can all pursue everything we imagine.

To those kids, Gretel and Thor—my favorite gingers, you will always be my biggest adventure! Writing a book filled with my lived experiences as you were both starting your own was a magical and emotional experience. I love everything about you both with passion beyond compare. I have led you to this point, and I look forward to following your lead.

To my mom and dad. Dad, you have always been my hero; I know that I always felt safe and secure in quiet company when we walked side by side through life. Mom, while you passed unexpectedly shortly before this book was going to print, Justin and I stood on a frozen lake watching the Northern Lights, two hundred miles above the Arctic Circle on a trip meant to celebrate our twentieth anniversary. Our Sámi host described the lights as "a river of spirits." And although you hadn't known of this trip, I am confident you were there with us celebrating our love and also reminding me of the beauty and majesty of patterns of life. We don't get to hold on, forever, to the ones and things we love. We do, however, get to remember the magic of people and the love they shared.

To my brothers, Eric, Steve, and Phillip, I attribute most of my relentlessness and work ethic founded in trying to keep up with you.

To my editors: Mary Metz—I thank you for the postcards to date and look forward to future communications filled with your timeliness, sharp wit, caring and firm guidance, and endless patience as I stumbled through this process. Emily White—I thank you for laughing at my dry humor and for helping me help myself through my doubts in writing and my endless curiosity. I so enjoy your cheerful way and thoughtful commentary. I hope we can all be friends for a long time.

To Mountaineers Books and to Lori Hobkirk, Matt Samet, Callie Stoker-Graham, Janet Kimball, and Laura Shauger. Writing a book was harder than I imagined and when I see the magic you made from my ideas, verbosity, and run-on sentences I am thankful that you made a coherent and relatable best seller. I may be getting ahead of myself, but regardless, I would not be writing these acknowledgments if you had not helped edit and revise the book. Thanks, too, to the illustrator, Latasha Greene, for turning the roughest of concepts into fun and informative graphics. To the Mountaineers team—I really feel like I am on your team, and that is because you have all made me feel cared for, valued, and that we, together, have some good messages to share.

To the leaders who contributed to this book, and who also contribute to my growth as a leader, I thank you for sharing your experiences and demonstrating for me and the world that leadership is indeed about choice, and I am thankful that you choose to lead, and that you chose to work with me.

To the people I have led with who are featured in the book or to those I've led: co-leaders, co-workers, volunteers, and participants. Thank you for the feedback, the successes, and the struggles. Regardless of whether our experience went as we expected, I am confident we laughed, we cried, and we learned.

Thank you to my community. The Tetherball Society, Costa Rica Chicas, Michigan teammates, swimmers, lion chasers, high school rowing parents, and my neighbors who walk and talk and sit by the fire. I thank you for listening, holding space for my tears and fears, checking in, and helping me be at my best when navigating all the changes that life brings.

Finally, I'd like to give a special thank you to five especially strong women who have provided so much support, Erin, Lindsay, Liz, Lisa, and Nicole. Thank you for picking up the phone even when you saw it was me; thank you for helping me grow as a person, as a parent, as a partner. Thank you for sending silly texts and voicemails, listening to my rants, and assuring me that I had something of value to share and be of service when I doubted or when it felt too vulnerable, and thank you for stopping me from offing my offspring.

APPENDIX

PROCEDURES

Use the following to get you started creating procedures for trip leading:

Trip planning procedures:
- How locations and activities are selected, things to research such as permitting, number of people per permit, local ordinances and rules.
- Budgeting for trips including fixed and individual expenses as well as group and individual fees.
- Establishing gear lists for both the group and individuals
- Pre-trip communications and messaging to participants: pre-trip meetings

Equipment: Group and individual gear
- Check-in and -checkout procedures
- Individual gear review

Emergency procedures: Expectations, medical controls, and resources/contacts
- Driving emergency procedures for your program
- Backcountry emergency procedures
- First aid procedures, including medical control for epinephrine or distribution of other medications

Safety briefings: Researched and demonstrated proficiency for various activities.
- Travel (car, trail, boat, bike, etc.)
- Sport specific (climbing, paddling, skiing, etc.)

Camp set-up and take-down (for various environments and group sizes)
- Tent location (trees/hazards) and distribution
- Water source
- Kitchen
- Latrines

CHECKLISTS

The following are helpful reminders for creating some essential checklists for you, your co-leader, and participants.

Training lists:
- Expectations of what participants could expect to do (hiking X miles, carrying Y pounds) and what they will be navigating (paddling, climbing, stairs, etc.)
- Fitness levels and what is required to achieve them
- Highlight for participants not only that they need to be able to manage themselves, but also contribute to the group (carrying gear, portaging boats, etc.)

Documents checklists:
- Permits: camping, boating, launch, etc.
- Passes, including parks or entry fees
- Insurance: general liability, health insurance
- Waiver and release forms
- Maps: driving *and* hiking maps

Food lists:
- Meal planning can vary from people bringing their own to the group cooking together
- Consult books and resources that can help you with planning by meal, by diet, by group size, and budget

Group gear:
- Will vary in type and quantity based the trip's duration based on the activity, number or participants, location, anticipated weather, etc.
- Include communal kitchen items: cook pots, stoves, fuel, etc.

Individual packing lists:
- These include what is needed, how many of the item, any requirements, such as type of sleeping bag and degree requirements, layering systems, footwear, etc.
- Include individual kitchen items: personal cook kit, water bottles for on the trail, mug.

First-aid kit:
- There is no singular "*best*" first aid kit. It needs to be reviewed for each trip and its contents will be determined by where you are going, how many people are going, the activities you may be doing, the medical expertise you have on your trip.

- Categories *may* include: Basic Life Support (CPR mask), gloves, trauma dressings. Wound care, blister care, over the counter and prescription medications, tweezers, bandages, SAM splint.

Van safety kit:
- If you are responsible for transport to the trailhead, you should have a van safety kit that may include an extra source of light, jumper cables, small tool kit (wrench, screwdrivers), etc.

Weather and points of contact:
- Names and contact information for all relevant land management agencies or water (i.e. Coast Guard) authorities for the area you are going as well as current weather reports.

The Ten Essentials

The point of the Ten Essentials, originated by the Mountaineers, has always been to answer two basic questions: Can you prevent emergencies and respond positively should one occur (items 1–5)? And can you safely spend a night—or more—outside (items 6–10)? Use this list as a guide and tailor it to the needs of your outing.

1. **Navigation**: The five fundamentals are a map, altimeter, compass, GPS device, and a personal locator beacon or other device to contact emergency first responders.
2. **Headlamp**: Include spare batteries.
3. **Sun protection**: Wear sunglasses, sun-protective clothes, and broad-spectrum sunscreen rated at least SPF 30.
4. **First aid**: Basics include bandages; skin closures; gauze pads and dressings; roller bandage or wrap; tape; antiseptic; blister prevention and treatment supplies; nitrile gloves; tweezers; needle; nonprescription painkillers; anti-inflammatory, anti-diarrheal, and antihistamine tablets; topical antibiotic; and any important personal prescriptions, including an EpiPen if you are allergic to bee or hornet venom.
5. **Knife**: Also consider a multitool, strong tape, some cordage, and gear repair supplies.
6. **Fire:** Carry at least one butane lighter (or waterproof matches) and firestarter, such as chemical heat tabs, cotton balls soaked in petroleum jelly, or commercially prepared firestarter.
7. **Shelter**: In addition to a rain shell, carry a single-use bivy sack, plastic tube tent, or jumbo plastic trash bag.
8. **Extra food**: For shorter trips a one-day supply is reasonable.
9. **Extra water**: Carry sufficient water and have the skills and tools required to obtain and purify additional water.
10. **Extra clothes**: Pack additional layers needed to survive the night in the worst conditions that your party may realistically encounter.

AFFINITY SPACES

American Alpine Club (americanalpineclub.org)
"We're climbers. Gym climbers and trad climbers. Sport climbers and mountaineers. Boulderers, backcountry skiers, and alpinists. We're the largest community of rock-scaling misfits in the country—and you belong here."

Association of Outdoor Recreation and Education (aore.org)
The Association of Outdoor Recreation and Education (AORE) is the leading organization in the United States dedicated to serving the needs of outdoor recreation professionals and educators from academia to private sector programs.

Brown Girls Climb (browngirlsclimb.com)
Brown Girls Climb envisions an "outdoor" and climbing community that honors our individual relationships to the land, complex histories and truths, centers the experiences and voices of those most impacted by colonization and industrialization of the land, and provides a just redistribution of resources so that everyone can find their relationship to the land around them.

CAMBER (camberoutdoors.org)
Camber is a nonprofit organization founded in 1996 that equips partner organizations across the Outdoor Recreation Economy to implement best practices in Workplace Diversity, Equity, and Inclusion (Workplace DEI).

Green Muslims (greenmuslims.org)
Green Muslims is a volunteer-driven organization working to connect Muslims everywhere to nature and environmental activism. They host educational, service, and outdoor recreational events.

Greening Youth Foundation (gyfoundation.org)
The Greening Youth Foundation's (GYF) mission is to engage under-represented youth and young adults, while connecting them to the outdoors and careers in conservation.

Latino Outdoors (latinooutdoors.org)
An organization that seeks to inspire, connect, and engage Latino communities in the outdoors and embrace cultura y familia as part of the outdoor narrative.

Minority Outdoor Alliance (minorityoutdooralliance.org)
The Minority Outdoor Alliance encourages people from diverse walks of life, ethnic backgrounds, and cultures to make the outdoors an integral part of their lives.

National Park Service (nps.gov)
The National Park Service preserves natural and cultural resources and values for the enjoyment, education, and inspiration of this and future generations. The Park Service cooperates with partners to extend the

benefits of natural and cultural resource conservation and outdoor recreation throughout the US and the world.

Outdoor Afro (outdoorafro.org)
Outdoor Afro celebrates and inspires Black connections and leadership in nature. The network also connects Black people with lands, water, and wildlife through outdoor education, recreation, and conservation.

Outdoor Alliance for Kids (outdoorsallianceforkids.org)
Outdoor Alliance for Kids has the goal of expanding equitable access to nature for children, youth, and families.

Outdoor Asian (outdoorasian.com)
Outdoor Asian works to create a community of Asian & Pacific Islanders in the outdoors.

Outward Bound Adventures (obainc.org/storefront)
Outward Bound Adventures (OBA) is the oldest non-profit in the nation dedicated to outdoor education for BIOPC youth.

Outdoors for All (outdoorsforall.org)
Outdoors for All offers adaptive and therapeutic recreation for children and adults with disabilities, with a goal of enriching the quality of life for children and adults with disabilities through outdoor recreation.

Paradox Sports (paradoxsports.org)
Paradox Sports is dedicated to transforming lives and communities through adaptive climbing opportunities that defy convention.

Pride Outside (prideoutside.net)
Pride Outside is dedicated to connecting the LGBTQ community around the outdoors. It hosts hikes, outdoor skills classes, LGBTQ history working tours, discussions, and more.

SheJumps (shejumps.org)
SheJumps increases the participation of women and girls in outdoor activities.

Society of Outdoor Recreation Professionals (recpro.org)
SORP provides leadership for the outdoor recreation profession through skill development, networking, and technical guidance.

Together Outdoors (togetheroutdoors.com)
Together Outdoors nurtures an environment where all people have access to welcoming outdoor recreation experiences through engagement, partnership, and education across all segments of the outdoor community.

Veteran Outdoor Alliance (veteranoutdooralliance.org)
An organization with the goal of empowering veterans through the outdoors.

SELECTED BIBLIOGRAPHY AND RESOURCES

CHAPTER 3 MANAGEMENT AND SYSTEMS
Books

Anderson, Dave and Molly Absolon. *NOLS Expedition Planning.* Essex, CT: Stackpole Books, 2011.

Association of Outdoor Recreation and Education (AORE), and Geoff Harrison and Mat Erpelding. *Outdoor Program Administration: Principles and Practices.* Ann Arbor, MI: AORE, 2012.

Balerlein, Jeff A. Risk Management for Outdoor Programs: *A Guide to Safety in Outdoor Education, Recreation and Adventure.* Lake Forest Park, WA: Virastar, 2019.

Cole, David and Rich Brame, et al. *NOLS Soft Paths: Enjoying the Wilderness Without Harming It.* Essex, CT: Stackpole Books, 2011.

Curtis, Rick. *The Backpacker's Field Manual, Revised and Updated: A Comprehensive Guide to Mastering Backcountry Skills.* New York: Crown, 2005.

Kosseff, Alex and Sally Manikian. *AMC Guide to Outdoor Leadership.* Boston: AMC Books, 2023.

The Mountaineers. *Mountaineering: The Freedom of the Hills*, 9th Edition. Seattle: Mountaineers Books, 2017.

Smith, Steve, ed. *Beneficial Risks: The Evolution of Risk Management for Outdoor and Experiential Education Programs.* [[Jeannette, provide city/state of publication-mm]]_: Experiential Consulting, 2021.

CHAPTER 4 DIVERSITY, EQUITY, AND INCLUSION
The definition of "privilege" as "the opportunity to act" is Karel Hilversum's definition based on his years of research.
Books

Brown, Adrienne Marie. *Emergent Strategies: Shaping Change, Changing Worlds.* Chico, CA: AK Press, 2017.

Chavez, Deborah J. "Invite, Include, and Involve! Racial Groups, Ethnic Groups, and Leisure" in *Diversity and the Recreation Profession: Organizational Perspectives*, edited by Maria T. Allison and Ingrid E. Schneider (State College, PA: Venture Publishing, 2000) 179–191.

Finney, Carolyn. *Black Faces, White Spaces: Reimagining the Relationship of African Americans to the Great Outdoors.* Chapel Hill, NC: The University of North Carolina Press, 2014.

Garry, Joan. *Joan Garry's Guide to Nonprofit Leadership: Because Nonprofits are Messy.* Hoboken, NJ: John Wiley and Sons, 2017.

Mapp, Rue. *Nature Swagger: Stories and Visions of Black Joy in the Outdoors.* San Francisco: Chronicle Books, 2022.

Mills, James. *The Adventure Gap: Changing the Face of the Outdoors.* Seattle: Mountaineers Books, 2014.

Tecker, Glenn, Paul D. Meyer, Bud Crouch, and Leigh Wintz, CAE. *The Will to Govern Well,* 2nd ed. Washington, DC: ASAE Publications, 2010.

Online articles and videos

"Asian Americans" pbs.org/show/asian-americans.

Bally, Lorena. "3 Plus Ways to be a Better Ally to Diverse Peoples in the Outdoors." diversifyoutdoors.com/blog/2022/8/22/3-plus-ways-to-be-a-better-ally-to-people-in-the-outdoors

Dewan, Shaila. "How Racism and Sexism Intertwine to Torment Asian-American Women." nytimes.com/2021/03/18/us/racism-sexism-atlanta-spa-shooting.html

"Discrimination in America: Experiences and Views of Asian Americans" legacy.npr.org/assets/news/2017/12/discriminationpoll-asian-americans.pdf

Gay, Lauren. "Camping While Black: An Honest Conversation on Race in the Outdoors." outdoorsydiva.com/camping-while-black-honest-converstation-on-race-in-outdoors.

"The Joy Tip Project | Anti-racism in the Outdoors: Resources" joytrip-project.com/joy-trip-project-home-page/anti-racism-resource-guide.

McIntosh, Peggy. "White Privilege: Unpacking the Invisible Knapsack. racialequitytools.org/resourcefiles/mcintosh.pdf.

Robles, David. "Want to Speak Up Against Racism in the Outdoors? Here's How." melaninbasecamp.com/trip-reports/2020/4/25/want-to-speak-up-against-racism-outdoors-heres-how.

Stewart, Emily. "How to Be a Good White Ally, According to Activists." vox.com/2020/6/2/21278123/being-an-ally-racism-george-floyd-protests-white-people.

Williams, Danielle. "The Melanin Base Camp Guide to Outdoor Allyship." melaninbasecamp.com/trip-reports/2019/7/7/mbc-guide-to-outdoor-allyship.

Podcasts
Black in Nature (Diona Reese Williams)
Outside Voices: outsidevoicespodcast.com
Outdoorsy Diva: outdoorsydiva.com/odpodcast

Websites
Diversify Outdoors (diversifyoutdoors.com)
GLAAD Transgender Resources (glaad.org/transgender/resources)
The Joy Trip Project joytripproject.com/about-joy-trip-project.

CHAPTER 12   MAKING MISTAKES
Websites
The Failure Lab (failure-lab.com)

CHAPTER 13   LISTENING
Books

Harley, Shari. *How to Say Anything to Anyone: A Guide to Building Business Relationships that Really Work*. Austin, TX: Greenleaf Book Group Press, 2013.
Stone, Douglas, Bruce Patton and Sheila Heen. (1999) *Difficult Conversation: How to Discuss What Matters Most*. New York: Penguin Random House, 1999.
Voss, Chris. *Never Split the Difference: Negotiating as If Your Life Depended on It.* New York: HarperCollins Publishers, 2016.
Weeks, Holly. *Failure to Communicate: How Conversations Go Wrong and What You Can Do about Them*. Brighton, MA: Harvard Business Review Press: 2010.

Podcasts
Mike Rowe: The Way I Heard It
Malcolm Gladwell: Revisionist History

INDEX

A

ABCDE, 138
Aber, Courtney, 148–49
accidents, 133, 187–89
accountability, 37, 103, 161, 204
achievement, 173–74
acknowledge the differences, 64–65
actions
    consistency in, 100
    words and, for integrity, 96–98
active followership, 200
adaptability, 108
adventure, 120–31
adversity, 108–19
advocating for doing the right thing, 100–03
affinity spaces, 72, 214–15
Allies Academy, 68
anticipated experience, 200
apology, 174–75
asking for help, 175
assessment, 134–36
assimilation, 60, 74, 123
Association of Outdoor Recreation and Education (AORE), 66, 68, 70, 146, 152–54, 163, 170, 183, 204
assumptions
    intentions and, 205
    uncovering of, 70–71
athleticism, 109
authentic self, 148–49, 206
authenticity, 123–24
authoritarian leadership style, 12, 14
autocratic leadership style, 12, 14–15
autonomy, 41

B

Bare, Stacy, 127–28
Barrett, John, 16
BEA. *See* Bureau of Economic Analysis
being present, 161
BHAG, 162–63
biases, uncovering of, 70–71
BLM. *See* Bureau of Land Management
body image, 48
Brown, Brené, 15, 103
Bureau of Economic Analysis, 78
Bureau of Land Management, 197

C

calmness, 162
candor, 175
capacity building, 117

care
    commitment and, 16–18
    continuum of, 12, 87, 156
    in destructive leadership, 18
    levels of, 17–18, 20, 22, 25, 141
    in passive leadership, 20
    in productive leadership, 22
    for self, 12, 17
    in transformative leadership, 25
caving, 130–31
Center for Outdoor Ethics, 96
challenges
    difficult, navigating of, 89–90
    magnitudes of, 87
    "outlasting" of, 85–87
    processing of, 113–15
    responding to, 89
    tolerance for, 108, 115
    working through, 87
change
    commitment to, 75
    intentional, 146–47
    leading, 146–58
    resistance to, 149
change management, 149–50
checking in, 199
checklists, 46, 54, 212–13
choice
    forward momentum through, 89
    leader's responsibility for, 140
    leadership as a, 12, 16–17, 146, 156
    not to choose as, 19–20
clothes, 51–52
coachable, 37–38
COE. *See* Cornell Outdoor Education
co-leading, 24, 39, 97–98, 177
collaboration, 151–52
Collins, Jim, 162
comfortably uncomfortable, 91–93, 161
commitment
    care and, 16–18
    to change, 75
    continuum of, 12, 17, 156
    description of, 12, 17, 87
    in destructive leadership, 18
    levels of, 17–18, 20, 22, 25, 141
    in passive leadership, 20
    in productive leadership, 22
    in transformative leadership, 25
committed communication, 201–02, 204

communication
    committed, 201–02, 204
    composed, 205–06
    confident, 93–94, 201–02
    consistency in, 192
    courageous, 201, 204
    double standards in, 205–06
    of expectations, 103
    failure in, 196
    by leader, 147
    listening during, 180
    nonverbal, 181
    technology for, 206
    two-way nature of, 198
    of vision, 147
compass, 9
competence, 173–74
competitor, 152–53
complacency, 39, 118
compliant leadership, 115
composed communication, 205–06
confidence
    adversity and, 118
    communication used to find, 93–94
    maintaining of, 184
    self-confidence, 83–85, 104
    systems for creating, 54–55
confident communication, 201–02
confidentiality, 184
consistency, 39, 100, 103, 118, 192
consultants, 150–51
continuous improvement, 13
continuum of care for self, 12, 87, 156
continuum of commitment, 12, 17, 156
control, 82, 161
Cornell Outdoor Education (COE), 61
courageous communication, 201, 204
course corrections, 128–29
COVID-19 pandemic, 151–52
culture of listening, 181–82

D

decision-making
    complexity of, 141–42
    consequences of, 140
    difficulty of, 138–40
    failures and, 138, 142–45
    opinions and, 185
    progressive quality of, 132
    right decision vs. best decision, 140–41
    sighting in, 162

"triangle" method, 133–37
as unremarkable and unmemorable, 139–40
wilderness medicine and, 132–33
DEI. *See* diversity, equity, and inclusion
delegative leadership style, 12, 14
democratic leadership style, 12, 14–15
destructive leadership, 18–19
differences, acknowledge the, 64–65
discomfort, 112, 161
diversity, equity, and inclusion
acknowledge the differences principle, 64–65
barriers for, 60–61
co-creation in, 60–61
commit to change principle, 75
connecting with others on similar journey principle, 71–73
expand your knowledge principle, 67–69
explore your identity principle, 65–67
initiatives for, 61–63, 79, 106, 150
invite, include, and involve those who are not present principle, 73–74
outdoor-industry initiatives for, 60–63
"Seven Principles of DEI for the Outdoor Professional," 63–76
strategic plan for, 77
transform your practice principle, 75
uncover assumptions and biases principle, 70–71
Dopp kit, 58
double standards, 205–06
doubt, 144–45, 170–71
Durkee, Lily, 141–42

E
ego, 100–02, 128
emotions, 122
environmental-ethics challenges, 62–63
evacuation, 136–37
expand your knowledge, 67–69
expectations, 57, 90, 103, 198
experiences
first-time, 166
of others, 177
processing of, 113–15
explore your identity, 65–67

F
failure(s)
celebrating, 142–45
in communication, 196
decision-making affected by, 138
embracing, 118
learning from, 171–73
potential for, 81–82
sharing of, 178
Failure Lab, 178
fatigue, 89–90
fear, 112–13
feedback, 37–38, 42, 149, 176–77, 183, 185–86
feelings, 180
Fernandez, Corey, 15–16
first aid, 52, 132–33, 212–13
first-time experiences, 166
fitness, 47–49
followership, 200
food, 157, 212
footwear, 51–52
forgiveness, 71, 174
Four Choices of Leadership matrix
description of, 16–17
destructive leadership, 18–19
passive leadership, 20–22
productive leadership, 22–24
transformative leadership, 25–26

G
gear
buying of, 49–50
checklists for, 212
donating of, 73
simplicity of, 51, 55
tents, 52, 56
2 percent rule for, 50
women's–specific, 51–52
gender, 67–69, 148–49, 155, 157
gloves, 50
Goodwin, Deidra, 123–24
gossip, 104
greater good, leading for, 22, 26–27
group
approval seeking from, 104
collective needs of, 16
dynamics of, 23
interdependence in, 21–24, 173, 182–86
leader's influence on, 17
"pointless" rules in, 103
relationship formation in, 22
growth
feedback for, 37
of leader, 34–35, 37
seeking of, 40–41
self-responsibility for, 67

H
Harkness, Laurel, 35–36
Haroutunian, Kenji, 24
Harrison, Taldi, 151–52
hat, 50
help, asking for, 175

High Impact Leadership Training, 16
HILT. *See* High Impact Leadership Training
Hilversum, Karel, 61–63, 67, 70
honesty, 199–200
Humanergy, 16
hyperawareness, 116–17
hypothermia, 56, 115, 141

I
"I" triad, 73–74
identity, exploring of, 65–67, 110
impostor syndrome, 170–71
including, 73
integrity
admitting of mistakes and, 100–03
advocating for doing the right thing, 100–03
consistent actions and, 100
cumulative currency of, 105–06
definition of, 96
demonstrating of, 96
lapses in, 100, 103
in Leaving No Trace, 101
in outdoors, 106
political landscapes navigated with, 104–05
words and actions aligned for building of, 96–98
intentional change, 146–47
intentions, 205
interdependence, 21–24, 173, 182–86
investing in self, 36–37, 41–42
Invite, Include, and Involve principle, 73–74
involving, 73–74

J
JEDI, 67, 149–51, 153
journey
connecting with others on similar journey, 71–73
leadership as, 10–11
junctions, 199

K
knowledge
expanding of, 67–69
leadership and, 34
what you know and what you don't know, 57

L
laissez-faire leadership style, 12, 14–15
land acknowledgments, 77
lead
capacity to, 10, 12
by example, 201
for greater good, 22, 26–27
intentions in, 205
preparing to, 46

leader
  accountability of, 37
  adaptability of, 108
  adversity of, 108–19
  care and commitment
    levels, 17–18
  as coachable, 37–38
  communication by, 147
  consistency by, 39
  continuous improvement by, 13
  destructive, 19
  emotions of, 122
  feedback for, 37–38
  gear management by, 52
  governance role of, 42–43
  grit of, 81
  growing as, 34–35, 37
  identity of, 110
  influence on others, 17
  learning from other
    leaders, 156
  lifelong learning by, 26, 30,
    34–37
  overextending by, 126
  passive, 20–22
  poor, 13–14
  productive, 22–24
  relevancy of, 147
  resilience of, 81
  self-awareness by, 120, 122,
    124–26
  self-responsibility by, 30–31
  situation assessment by, 134–35
  timing in support of, 24
  traits of, 10, 14, 120, 169
  transformative, 10–11, 25–26,
    156, 166
  transparency of, 108, 118
  vulnerability of, 91, 108, 117
  weather research by, 55
  women as, 15, 109–10, 149, 155,
    157, 171, 184
  world of, 155–56
leadership
  as a choice, 12, 16–17, 146, 156
  actionable ways to further,
    76–77
  change management through,
    149–50
  compliant, 115
  destructive, 18–19
  differences in, 156–57
  interdependence in, 21–24
  knowledge for, 34
  management and, 45
  mistakes in, 31–34
  as ongoing journey, 10–11
  outcomes affected by, 12, 14, 19,
    23, 25
  passive, 20–22
  poor, learning from, 13–14
  practice of, 17

  productive, 22–24
  self-leadership, 30
  servant, 26–27, 152
  sighting in, 162
  styles of, 12–15, 156
  time management and, 46–47
  transferability of skills, 26
  transformative, 10–11, 25–26,
    166
  visionary, 161
leadership matrix
  new, 16–18
  traditional, 14–15
learning
  from each other, 156–57
  from failure, 171–73
  gaps in, 36
  as iterative and imperfect
    process, 169–70
  lifelong, 26, 30, 34–37
  from mistakes, 169–70, 173–76
  opportunities for, 34–35
  from other leaders, 156
  as perspective, 161
  self-initiated, 42
  willingness for, 41
Leave No Trace, 62, 100
Lewin, Kurt, 14
LGBTQIA+ identities, 67, 75–76
lifejackets, 102
lifelong learning, 26, 30, 34–37
listening
  culture of, 181–82
  forums for, 182
  as simple and complicated,
    180–81
  to understand, 186–87
Lopez-Herrera, Victoria, 162–63
M
magnetic north, 9
Malvin, Hannah, 85
management
  characteristics of, 45
  of resources, 52
  time, 46–48
map, 9–10
mental fitness, 49
mental fortitude, 87
mental resilience, 87
mindfulness, 120
mission, 165
mistakes
  accountability for, 204
  admitting of, 100–03
  decision-making affected
    by, 138
  fear of, 169
  in leadership, 31–34
  learning from, 169–70, 173–76
  making of, 169–79
  neglecting to apologize as,
    174–75

  not asking for help as, 175
  sharing of, 178
N
National Outdoor Leadership
  School, 62, 64
NOLS. See National Outdoor
  Leadership School
nongovernmental organiza-
  tions, 61
Nonprofit Enterprise at Work
  Center's Champions for
  Change, 68
nonverbal messages, 181
nylon tarp, 50
O
Obama, Michelle, 15
objective information, 136
Ocasio-Cortez, Alexandria, 15
OF. See Outdoor Foundation
open-water swimming, 121–23,
  161–62
opinions, 184–85
opportunities
  for learning, 34–35
  organizational processes
    for creating, 77
Ostefeld, Jackie, 98–99
outcomes, 12, 14, 19, 23, 25,
  159, 165
Outdoor Foundation, 78–79
outdoor industry
  career opportunities in, 166
  diversity, equity, and inclusion
    initiatives, 60–63, 78–79,
    106
  vision for, 166
outdoorsy, 162
"outlasting," 85–87
overextending, 126
P
packing lists, 57, 212
paraphrasing, 182
participants
  expectations for, 57–58, 90
  sharing by, 76
participative leadership style,
  12, 14
passive leadership, 20–22
personal map, 10
physical fitness, 47–49
Pink, Daniel, 146
plan, 136–37
Porras, Jerry, 162
positive first-time experiences,
  166
prioritizing, 135–36
privilege, 67, 120, 146–47
procedures, 211
processing of experiences, 113–15
productive leadership, 22–24
pronouns, 67–68
purpose, 98–99, 163–65

R

raft guiding, 192–96, 198, 201
rainfly, 52, 56
relationships
 existing, 106
 formation of, 22, 106
 interdependence in, 21
resilience
 of leader, 81
 mental, 87
 toughness versus, 86
resistance to change, 149
resource management, 52
risk assessment, 169
Roosevelt, Franklin Delano, 169
Rowe, Abby, 139–40
Rylander, Elyse, 75–76

S

SCA. See Student Conservation
 Association
scene size-up, 134–35
Schmidt, Rachel, 176–77
self
 accountability to, 161
 as adversary, 90
 authentic, 148–49, 206
 being present, 161
 care for, 12, 17
 investing in, 36–37, 41–42
self-acceptance, 173
self-awareness, 120, 122, 124–26
self-confidence, 83–85, 104
self-determination, 35
self-doubt, 144–45, 170–71
self-esteem, 48
self-identity, 65–67
self-initiated learning, 42
self-leadership, 16, 30
self-responsibility, 30–44
self-understanding, 38
servant leadership, 26–27, 152
"Seven Principles for Leave No
 Trace," 62, 96–97
"Seven Principles of DEI for the
 Outdoor Professional," 63–76
 acknowledge the differences,
  64–65
 commit to change, 75
 connecting with others on
  similar journey, 71–73
 expand your knowledge,
  67–69
 explore your identity, 65–67
 invite, include, and involve
  those who are not present,
  73–74
 transform your practice, 75
 uncover assumptions and
  biases, 70–71
Shackleton, Ernest, 108
shower preparation, 58

Sierra Club Military Outdoors,
 147
sighting, 162
situation assessment, 134–35
skills, 26, 40
Smith, Megan, 53–54
Smith, Nikki, 167–68
SOAP, 133, 136–37
social media, 72
socks, 50
Sotomayor, Sonia, 15
staff training, 36
"stick-to-itiveness," 126, 128–29
Stone, Joe, 88
strength, 85, 87, 117, 124–26
Student Conservation Association, 83
subjective information, 136
supporting of others, 126
systems
 clarity through, 55
 complications resolved
  through, 56
 confidence created through,
  54–55
 establishing of, 54–58
 example of, 46
 importance of, 45–46
 maintaining of, 54–58
 simplicity of, 53
systems thinking, 46

T

talking out loud, 176–77
tarp, 50
team vision, 165
technology, 206
telling, 175
Ten Essentials, 50, 213
tents, 52, 56
"thank you," 71
time management, 46–48
timeliness, 204
Title IX, 109
tolerance
 for adversity, 108–19
 for challenges, 108, 115
"toughing it out," 85–87
toughness, 86
training
 decisions involved in, 47
 mental fitness, 49
 physical fitness, 47–49
transformative leadership, 10–11,
 25–26, 156, 166
transparency, 108, 118
"triangle" method, 133–37
trip expectations, 57
trip planning, 211
true north, 9
trust, 183–84
Turner, Jessica (Wahl), 197–98
2 percent rule, 50

two-way communication, 198

U

uncertainty, 111
uncomfortable, 91–93, 108, 132,
 144, 161
uncovering assumptions and
 biases, 70–71
underrepresented populations,
 152

V

values, 98–99, 159
Velic, Jenn, 171–73
verbal messages, 181
verifying, 183–84
Virtual Inclusive Summit, 66
vision
 championing of, 163–65
 clarity of, 98–99
 communicating of, 147
 definition of, 159, 167
 goals and, 159
 growing of, 167–68
 mission versus, 165
 for outdoor industry, 166
 purpose of, 163–64
 sharing of, 161
 team, 165
 yes and, 159
visionary leadership, 161
vulnerability, 91, 108, 117, 202

W

Watts, Russ, 116–17
weather, 55–56, 213
Wheatley, David, 16
wilderness medicine
 ABCDE in, 138
 description of, 132–33
 prioritizing in, 135–36
 scene size-up in, 134–35
 SOAP, 133, 136–37
Wilderness Medicine Training
 Center, 133
WMTC. See Wilderness Medicine
 Training Center
women
 athleticism of, 109
 double standards, 205–06
 gear specific for, 51–52
 as leaders, 15, 109–10, 149, 155,
  157, 171, 184
 learning opportunities for,
  170–71
 overextending by, 126
wool socks, 50
words
 actions and, for integrity,
  96–98
 honesty with, 100

Y

yes, 159
yourself. See self
youth, 148–49

Mitch Hoffman

ABOUT THE AUTHOR

Jeannette Stawski serves as executive director for the Association of Outdoor Recreation and Education (AORE) and is the chair of the Coalition for Outdoor Access. She was the director of Outdoor Adventures at the University of Michigan for eleven years and has worked as a professional outdoor guide, wilderness medicine instructor, Leave No Trace Master Educator, and NOLS instructor. Leading the charge for change for organizations, Jeannette has a master's in nonprofit administration and a bachelor's degree in resource policy and behavior from the University of Michigan, and she holds a Certified Association Executive [CAE] credentialing that demonstrates knowledge essential to the practice of association management. She lives in Ann Arbor, Michigan, with her husband and their two children.

MOUNTAINEERS BOOKS is a leading publisher of mountaineering literature and guides—including our flagship title, *Mountaineering: The Freedom of the Hills*—as well as adventure narratives, natural history, and general outdoor recreation. Through our two imprints, Skipstone and Braided River, we also publish titles on sustainability and conservation. We are committed to supporting the environmental and educational goals of our organization by providing expert information on human-powered adventure, sustainable practices at home and on the trail, and preservation of wilderness.

The Mountaineers, founded in 1906, is a 501(c)(3) nonprofit outdoor recreation and conservation organization whose mission is to enrich lives and communities by helping people "explore, conserve, learn about, and enjoy the lands and waters of the Pacific Northwest and beyond." One of the largest such organizations in the United States, it sponsors classes and year-round outdoor activities throughout the Pacific Northwest, including climbing, hiking, backcountry skiing, snowshoeing, camping, kayaking, sailing, and more. The Mountaineers also supports its mission through its publishing division, Mountaineers Books, and promotes environmental education and citizen engagement. For more information, visit The Mountaineers Program Center, 7700 Sand Point Way NE, Seattle, WA 98115-3996; phone 206-521-6001; www.mountaineers.org; or email info@mountaineers.org.

Our publications are made possible through the generosity of donors and through sales of 700 titles on outdoor recreation, sustainable lifestyle, and conservation. To donate, purchase books, or learn more, visit us online:

MOUNTAINEERS BOOKS
1001 SW Klickitat Way, Suite 201 • Seattle, WA 98134
800-553-4453 • mbooks@mountaineersbooks.org • www.mountaineersbooks.org

An independent nonprofit publisher since 1960

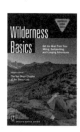
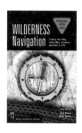